HUMAN ENACTMENT OF INTELLIGENT TECHNOLOGIES

Towards Mètis and Mindfulness

HUMAN ENACTMENT OF INTELLIGENT TECHNOLOGIES

Towards Mètis and Mindfulness

W David Holford

University of Quebec at Montreal (UQAM), Canada

 **World Scientific**

W JERSEY · LONDON · SINGAPORE · BEIJING · SHANGHAI · HONG KONG · TAIPEI · CHENNAI · TOKYO

Published by

World Scientific Publishing Co. Pte. Ltd.

5 Toh Tuck Link, Singapore 596224

USA office: 27 Warren Street, Suite 401-402, Hackensack, NJ 07601

UK office: 57 Shelton Street, Covent Garden, London WC2H 9HE

Library of Congress Cataloging-in-Publication Data
Names: Holford, W. David, author.
Title: Human enactment of intelligent technologies : towards mètis and mindfulness /
    W. David Holford, University of Quebec at Montreal (UQAM), Canada.
Description: Hackensack, New Jersey : World Scientific, [2022] |
    Includes bibliographical references and index.
Identifiers: LCCN 2021012146 | ISBN 9789811237270 (hardcover) |
    ISBN 9789811237287 (ebook for institutions) | ISBN 9789811237294 (ebook for individuals)
Subjects: LCSH: Artificial intelligence--Philosophy. | Automation--Human factors. | Cognition. |
    Reasoning. | Mindfulness (Psychology) | Phenomenology.
Classification: LCC Q335 .H637 2022 | DDC 006.3--dc23
LC record available at https://lccn.loc.gov/2021012146

British Library Cataloguing-in-Publication Data
A catalogue record for this book is available from the British Library.

For any available supplementary material, please visit
https://www.worldscientific.com/worldscibooks/10.1142/12288#t=suppl

Desk Editors: Anthony Alexander/Lai Ann

Typeset by Stallion Press
Email: enquiries@stallionpress.com

Printed in Singapore

The notion of user enactment exists in the design sciences, for example the design of self-driving car software; in short, where the power of artificial intelligence meets the human body and cognition. This notion of user enactment makes it possible, for example, to validate the abilities of the elderly to interact with this type of vehicle.

But the author's intention in this book is not developing design recipes for this or that application in which AI is present. Its avowed aim is to examine the theoretical and philosophical foundations of the human encounter with the achievements and performance of AI. All of this with a practical mind, because W. David Holford is a seasoned engineer and aviation specialist.

How can a large commercial jet pilot land his plane on the Hudson River? This landing raises questions of relevance, knowledge, training, reflexes, and responsibilities.

However, this human enactment of technology is at the same time a new and an old problem; the author does not hesitate to summon the Greek philosophers in his reflection, as well as their successors such as Hegel, Heidegger, Merleau-Ponty, Ellul, or Dreyfus among others, without forgetting specialists in cognitive science or information systems and AI such as Harnad, Damasio, or Newell.

As in many complex activities, solo sailing around the world requires this enactment of technology. A participant, shutdown by his two computers, yet still having his GPS, abandoned the famous Vendée Globe race, in December 2020. Fabrice Amadeo writes:

> *My boat is fine, but since yesterday she's been blind: due to a new computer problem, I can no longer download the weather files, calculate the optimal trajectory, the fastest possible, but also sometimes the wisest possible. /.../ It is possible to continue in the old-fashioned way, without any information and thus cross the Southern Ocean.*

What's that old way of sailing? Undoubtedly the one that Bernard Moitessier (*The Long Way*, 1971) learned at the beginning of the 20th century from the ancient Vietnamese navigators: the Taïcongs. These men with their *Mètis* (adaptive expertise) taught him to listen to the sea and to feel its pulsations and vibrations. Moitessier writes, after hiring his first Taïcong: *"The crew never spoke to him, because the taicong needs all his peace to communicate with the gods and read on their faces."*

And later in his book:

*"I am thinking of the old men of the great sailing navy. For centuries, they have crisscrossed the oceans for discovery or trade. But always for the sea. I think of what they bequeathed to us in nautical documents where the words would mean the sea and the sky, or the arrows would mean the currents and the winds, with the anguish and the joys of these sailors, as if it were possible, **as if the experience of the great laws of the sea could be transmitted, as if the sea could be communicated with words and arrows.**"*

There is non-communicable knowledge — and a manager, engineer, or medical specialist should know when and why it happens. As David Holford writes in his book (p. 71): "/.../cognition depends constitutively on the living body, understood as an autonomous system. The basic idea is that cognition should not be understood as a capacity for deriving world-models, which might then provide a database for thinking, planning and problem-solving. Rather, cognitive processes are viewed as being closely entwined with action, and as such, have the capacity of generating structure, i.e. of 'enacting' a world."

In summary, a paradigmatic book!

Albert Lejeune, PhD
Cognitive Informatics, PhD Business Administration
Director of the Cognitive Science Institute,
Human Sciences Faculty, UQAM

In my opinion, the book proposed by W. David Holford — *Human Enactment of Intelligent Technologies* — will find a captivated audience.

David Holford situates intelligent technologies with the most relevant philosophers on the subject, while at the same time demonstrating his keen knowledge of AI.

I think there is a strong need for this book, first and foremost, across pertinent sociotechnical and psychotechnical approaches discussed in relation to the analysis of AI and its perspectives.

The book starts with an understanding of AI's goals (symbolic AI and connectionist AI) and addresses the questions of representational knowledge. The author then provides a comprehensive inventory of artificial intelligence strategies (and their limitations) in a logical manner.

Different ways of thinking are relevantly presented regarding questions of rationality, causality, and the place of representation. The author explores Knowledge theory in an equally successful manner: namely, the pragmatic view, the modern physical view, the process view (Whitehead).

David Holford clearly demonstrates the difference between signs and symbols, and deduces important considerations in terms of their respective ways of thinking. This becomes the question of meaningful deliberation: how to determine the meaning and relevance of a situation, and its potential prospects for creative acts and development? It is ultimately THE question of adaptive expertise that is asked.

To reach this aim, he discusses the role of *mètis* thought and behaviour, first brought forward by the ancient Greeks. According to Jean-Pierre Vernant, *mètis* cannot be pigeon-holed into one particular category. It is a cunning form of intelligence which eludes explicit formulation, conceptual analysis, or theoretical exposition. *Mètis* is an embodied power which opens the way towards a beneficial solution.

Thus, David Holford highlights situational intelligence, the question of framing and relevance, and finally, addresses in a particularly right way, the question of representation.

In this manner, he manages to inquire into creation and the creation of novelty, as Cornelius Castoriadis did in his time.

I am very happy that such a book could be produced.

Claude Paraponaris
Professor of Innovation Management
Aix Marseille University, CNRS, LEST UMR 7317
35 Av. Jules Ferry, 13626 Aix-en-Provence Cedex 01, France

Former President of the French Speaking Association
in Knowledge Management (AGeCSO)

About the Author

 **W. David Holford (Ph.D., P. Eng.)** is a professional engineer and Professor of Management at the University of Quebec at Montreal, Canada. He has published articles in several prominent journals including *Journal of Business Ethics, Journal of Knowledge Management, Knowledge Management Research and Practice, Futures,* and *Prometheus.* His most recent book publication is in the field of Knowledge Management (KM), entitled *Managing Knowledge in Organizations: A Critical Pragmatic Perspective.* His current research focuses on understanding the nature of tacit, embodied, and embedded expertise within various professions — and how these are affected by intelligent technologies within various digital work environments. His fields of expertise include critical management studies, organizational sensemaking, knowledge theory, phenomenology, and STS (Science, Technology and Society). Prior to his academic career, he worked 20 years in the aerospace industry (Pratt and Whitney, Canada), assuming engineering and management roles of increasing responsibility.

Contents

Introduction

AI and associated "intelligent" technologies are now a socio-material reality within many aspects of our working as well as private lives. "Learning" algorithms have attained impressive levels of performance and can be useful and beneficial tools for society.[1] For example, their superior computational and analytical capabilities allow them to analyze different layers of complex information and masses of data from various sources in order to potentially detect patterns and weak signals.[2] Such technologies can be powerful aids in decision-making within complex digital environments.[3] Conversely, these same technologies can also have deleterious influences (structuring effects) on their environments — an issue raised by numerous researchers and authors, whereby for example, "learning" algorithms within the domain of artificial intelligence (AI) have been argued to be opaquely biased "formalized opinions that have been put into code" within "blackboxed" formats and approaches.[4] Historically, technology's effect on society-at-large has long been a subject of debate.[5-9] With the onset of "learning" algorithms within the digital workplace, attention has been directed, for example, toward their role regarding new forms of control and which future professions are to be valued or maintained.[10]

However, this book is not about these and other "frontal" issues related to AI — many, if not all, of the potentially deleterious as well as beneficial aspects of AI, "learning" algorithms and other "intelligent" technologies in society have been adequately flagged in various excellent papers, volumes, and compendiums.[11-16] Rather, this book takes a different angle on the issue of AI — namely, human mindsets. The book's thesis is relatively simple, but hopefully not simplistic: it is people's mindsets which set technology's enactive effects into motion, whether good or bad. This does not preclude the reciprocal effect of technology's agentive and structuring role within society. However, this book will emphasize people, i.e. their capabilities, epistemologies, assumptions, cognitive processes, psychologies, and most importantly, their enactions. We shall argue, for example, that AI's constraining enactments depend partially (yet, a good deal!) on how we as humans perceive and formalize the relevance of such technologies in the first place. Presently, our overemphasis on both representational knowledge and organizational efficiencies and standardization place "learning" algorithms and standard protocols at the forefront of organizational operations.[17] Breaking out of such mindless enactments requires a mindfulness on our part[18] — a "taking stock" of sorts which can provide the basis for alternative futures involving the active engagement of human actors (and their respective *mètis*) with "intelligent" technologies. More importantly, mindfulness involves an enactive phase of creating relevance — i.e. not just "connecting existing dots in new ways," but creating new and meaningful ones.[19] This is something machines cannot do. Mindfulness, when carried out collectively, requires more time and engagement due to its democratic nature. In this manner, organizations are tempted in avoiding such deviations to its efficient, yet mindless, trajectories.

Mètis, first "re-discovered" by Detienne and Vernant[20] is a form of human adaptive expertise able to discern what is relevant in changing contexts — the latter being a key characteristic required in addressing problems in new or novel situations.[21] Ironically, we shall see how "learning algorithms" (and AI) through the lens of the well-known "frame problem" fail to determine what is relevant within new or unexpected situations.[22] More importantly, "learning" algorithms and AI can be dangerously constraining on human adaptive expertise within various professional domains — with potential consequences on various socio-material practices touching safety, health, creativity, as well as myriads of socio-democratic processes.[23] In both cases (i.e. AI's limitations and its constraining effect on human professional expertise), human mindsets in the form of taken-for-granted epistemologies play a primordial role in why things become "the way things are."[24]

As such, we first (Chapters 1 to 3) demystify what AI is, examine its limitations in comparison to what humans are capable of, and examine the nature of human adaptive expertise by way of the concept of *mètis*.

We then (Chapter 4) examine a particular mindset that we as humans have adopted over the ages, namely a philosophy of knowledge representations. Knowledge representations, in its simplest terms, can be looked upon as a form of "knowledge models" of what we think reality is. We shall show that this mindset has been hardwired into us, and in turn, we have hardwired it into AI — remembering that technology is anything but technological in that it is a kind of thinking — a "certain frame of mind ... of looking at situations."[25] This representational mindset has followed us into numerous fields, including how we perceive and comprehend human cognition (Chapter 5). Mindsets are not bad in themselves, in that they provide us tools to help us wrestle with reality's dynamic complexities. The problem is in sticking to one particular set of tools (or models) in a quasi-obsessive manner to address all of our socio-material issues — leading to Dewey's "with a hammer everything looks like a nail" syndrome.[26] As such, alternative mindsets can be of help, whereby we shall pay particular attention to the embodied "direct reality" perspective as proposed not only by Heidegger and Merleau-Ponty but also by the Sophists themselves in ancient Greece (Chapter 4). We shall present (Chapter 6) this alternative, yet pertinent, viewpoint within the cognitive sciences in the form of radical embodied cognition, and more importantly, how it allows us to better highlight and comprehend human *mètis* and adaptive expertise. We then examine (Chapter 7) why we continue to enact and perpetuate the predominant (or collective) mindset of representations through the phenomena of mindlessness. This is a particularly important core issue at the crux of our behavior to "build our own and ... shared realities and then ... become victims of them — blind to the fact that they are constructs, ideas."[27] Typically, these ideas appear in the form of entrenched metaphors, one of which is the technology-as-tool metaphor.[28] To counter this, we revisit the concept and practice of individual and collective mindfulness (Chapters 8 and 9), which provides a potential "beachhead" in our reappropriation of technology (AI) toward achieving the "best of both worlds" — i.e. allowing human creativity and ingenuity to flourish with AI as a tool to help us do just that. Through the use of "living" or creative metaphors, we propose human-centric, socio-technical design approaches that allow us, as human users and operators, to connect back to our phenomenological senses to reachieve meaningful human control. We then show (Chapter 10) why designing toward meaningful human control is also an ethical approach. We also examine (Chapter 11) current top-of-the-horizon activities and debates regarding quantum physics in relation to the human mind and AI, and how, once again, representational mindsets need not be the "only tool in town". Finally, we conclude (Chapter 12) by highlighting the importance of "getting back to mètis", in that it provides us the possibility to break through entrenched metaphors on efficiency; and thereby reset technology as a supporting, rather than a constraining, tool towards social wellbeing.

Endnotes

[1] See Jarrahi, M.H. (2018). Artificial Intelligence and the future of work: Human-AI symbiosis in organizational decision making. *Business Horizons*. Available at: https://doi.org/10.1016/j.bushor.2018.03.007, regarding AI's outstanding abilities within areas of defined complexity.

[2] See both Marwala, T. (2015). *Causality, Correlation and Artificial Intelligence for Rational Decision Making* (Singapore: World Scientific), as well as Parry, K., Cohen, M. and Bhattacharya, S. (2016). Rise of the machines: A critical consideration of automated leadership decision making in organizations. *Group and Organization Management*, **41**(5), 571–594.

[3] *Ibid.* (note 1).

[4] Citing Dejoux, C. and Léon, E. (2018). *Métamorphose des managers*. First Edition (Paris: Pearson), p. 205; in a similar vein, see Faraj, S., Pachidi, S. and Sayegh, K. (2018). Working and organizing in the age of the learning algorithm. *Information and Organization*, **28**, 62–70; also for blackbox aspect of AI, see Pasquale F. (2015). *The Black Box Society: The Secret Algorithms That Control Money and Information* (Cambridge, MA: Harvard University Press).

[5] Heidegger, M. (1962). *Being and Time* (New York: Harper and Row).

[6] Ellul, J. (1964). *The Technological Society* (New York: Alfred A. Knopf Inc).

[7] Marcuse, H. (1982). Some Social Implications of Modern Technology. In *The Essential Frankfurt School Reader*, A. Arato and E. Gebhart (eds.) (New York: Continuum), pp. 138–162.

[8] Alexander, J.K. (2008). *The Mantra of Efficiency: From Waterwheel to Social Control* (Baltimore: John Hopkins University Press).

[9] Mumford, L. (1970). *Pentagon of Power: The Myth of the Machine*, Volume 2 (New York: Harcourt Brace Jovanovich).

[10] For various forms of control within the workplace, see Moore, P. and Robinson, A. (2015). The quantified self: What counts in the neoliberal workplace. *New Media & Society* [online first]; and on how professions such as radiologists, etc. are now being devalued with the onset of AI and learning algorithms, see Faraj, S., Pachidi, S. and Sayegh, K. (2018). Working and organizing in the age of the learning algorithm. *Information and Organization*, **28**, 62–70.

[11] Bostrom (2014.) *Superintelligence: Paths, Dangers, Strategies* (New York: Barns and Noble).

[12] Boden, M.A. (2016). *AI: Its Nature and Future* (Oxford, UK: Oxford University Press).

[13] Dreyfus, H.L. (2007). Why Heideggerian AI failed and how fixing it would require making it more Heidegerrian. *Artificial Intelligence*, **171**(18), 1137–1160.

[14] Wheeler, M. (2005). *Reconstructing the Cognitive World: The Next Step* (Cambridge, MA: MIT Press).

[15] Pasquale F. (2015). *The Black Box Society: The Secret Algorithms That Control Money and Information* (Cambridge, MA: Harvard University Press).

[16] See Marwala (2015) (note 2).

[17] Dreyfus (2007) (note 8) presents a convincing argument regarding the questionable representational assumptions adopted by AI developers; while organizational standardization in both repetitive and knowledge intensive work environments has gone through a second "digital revival" across Taylorism 2.0, as described by Brown, P., Lauder, H., and Ashton, D. (2011). *The Global Auction: The Broken Promise of Education, Jobs and Incomes* (New York: Oxford University Press, Inc.).

[18] See Langer, E.J. (1989). *Mindfulness* (Cambridge, MA: Perseus Books).

[19] Mindfulness as not simply observing what is pre-existent or already "out there," but as a form of lucidity which visualizes new ways of creating (or enacting) one's reality. See Langer, E. (2009). *Counter Clockwise. Mindful Health and the Power of Possibility* (London, UK: Hodder & Stoughton).

[20] See Detienne, M. and Vernant, J.P. (1978). *Les ruses de l'intélligence. La mètis des Grecs* (Paris: Flammarion).

[21] Various authors have provided rich descriptions and insights regarding *mètis*' adaptive "street smarts," including Raphals, L. (1992). *Knowing Words. Wisdom and Cunning in the Classical Tradition of China and Greece* (Ithaca, NY: Cornell University Press); Scott, J.C. (1998). *Seeing like a State: How Certain Schemes to Improve the Human State have Failed* (Binghamton, NY: Vail-Ballou Press); as well as Baumard, P. (1999). *Tacit Knowledge in Organizations* (London: Sage Publications).

[22] As shall later be presented in this book, Dreyfus (2007) (note 8) explains how humans can determine what is relevant across human embodiment and embeddedness within the context at hand — which is something machines cannot do; while Boden, M.A. (2016). *AI: Its Nature and Future* (Oxford, UK: Oxford University Press) speaks of the relevance of relevance regarding the human capacity to generate creative actions and outcomes, in a manner complementary to Dreyfus' phenomenological arguments, thus explaining why AI cannot be truly creative.

[23] The constraining effects of such algorithmic protocols on airline pilots is shown across an analysis of the automated cockpit environment in the 2009 AirFrance

flight 447 crash off Brazil by Oliver, N., Calvard, T. and Potocnik, K. (2017). Cognition, technology and organizational limits: Lessons from the Air France 447 disaster. *Organization Science*, 28(4), 597–780; also, there are standardized protocols as established across Evidence-Based Medicine, and its effect on medical doctors' ability to properly diagnose contextual cases is presented by Glasziou, P., Moynihan, R., Richards, T. and Godlee, F. (2013). Too much medicine; too little care. *BMJ*, 347, f4247; there is also AI's paradoxical effect on professions, including "deskilling," as presented by Faraj, S., Pachidi, S. and Sayegh, K. (2018). Working and organizing in the age of the learning algorithm. *Information and Organization*, **28**, 62–70; and finally, reaching expert proficiency levels is anything but following rules and procedures according to Dreyfus, H.L. and Dreyfus, S.E. (2005). Peripheral vision expertise in real world contexts. *Organization Studies*, 26(5), 779–792.

[24] Citing Morgan, G. (2006). *Images of Organizations* (Thousand Oaks, CA: Sage Publications), p. 136, regarding how enactment and its effects remains invisible across a cloak of "taken-for-granted" perceptions, which give us the illusion of being "out there" to be "discovered."

[25] Citing Ellul, J. (1980). *The Technological System* (New York: Continuum), pp. 23–33; also Heidegger, M. (1977). *The Question Concerning Technology and Other Essays* (New York: Garland Publishing) in a similar manner refers to the essence of technology as consisting of an enframing human mindset or *Gestell*.

[26] See Dewey, J. (1929). *The Quest for Certainty: A Study of the Relation of Knowledge and Action* (New York: Putnam).

[27] Citing Langer (1989, p. 11) (note 18).

[28] See Nardi, B.A. and O'Day, V.L. (1999). *Information Ecologies: Using Technology with Heart* (Cambridge, MA: MIT Press), p. 25.

Chapter 1

What Do We Mean By Artificial "Intelligence"?

1.1. Introduction

This chapter provides a brief overview of what artificial "intelligence" (AI) consists of. We use the terms "learn," "teach," "train," and "intelligence," yet maintain these in scare quotes in that we adhere to Searle's position — a computer cannot understand the symbols they manipulate.[1] We anthropomorphize artificial systems when speaking of AI concepts.[2] To teach in the human sense implies learning, which entails internalization through self-awareness and consciousness. This is not the case with machines, yet is the domain of endless futuristic speculations amongst the "general" AI communities.[3]

1.2. What is AI?

The term "AI" was first coined in McCarthy *et al.*'s[4] proposal leading toward the first conference on the subject in 1956. Here, AI's definition was in fact a goal (as opposed to an attained reality) consisting of an attempt "to find how to make machines use language, form abstractions and concepts, solve kinds of problems now reserved for humans, and improve themselves … For the present purpose the artificial intelligence problem is taken to be that of making a machine behave in ways that would be called intelligent if a human were so behaving." Yet, the journey to understand if machines could truly think began with Bush's seminal work *As We May Think*, which proposed a system that could accentuate people's own knowledge and comprehensions.[5] Turing then followed with a paper reflecting on the possibility of machines being intelligent.[6] Here, he proposed a method for evaluating whether machines could exhibit intelligent behavior equivalent or indistinguishable from that of a human, through what came to be known as the Turing test. The rationale was that if a computer could imitate the sentience of a human being, would that not imply that the computer itself was sentient? The test itself consists of a human evaluator judging natural language conversations between a human and a machine, and who knows in advance that one of the two partners in conversation is a machine. All participants are hidden from one another with exchanges limited to a text-only channel such as a computer keyboard and screen. If the evaluator cannot reliably distinguish the machine from the human, the machine passes the test. The test results do not depend on the machine's ability to give correct answers to questions, but only on how closely its answers resemble those of a human. Also, the test does not include anything specific — no complex problem solving or requests to create art. To date no machine has passed the Turing test such that a judge can classify a computer as human.[7]

Various applications and techniques based on learning algorithms fall under the term AI.[8] AI is a "surprisingly fuzzy concept," often loosely defined as "intelligent" systems with the ability to "think" and "learn."[9] All current AI involves applications to specific tasks, otherwise known as "narrow" AI.[10] For purpose of scope, this book shall not address other speculative forms of AI that do not currently exist, such as "general" AI and "super" AI, whose objective is to eventually replicate human consciousness and self-awareness.[11]

"Narrow" AI can be divided into symbolic AI (often referred to as "Good Old Fashioned AI" or GOFAI) and connectionist AI.[12] Some scholars, such as Kaplan,[13] have argued that symbolic AI is more suitable for the problems that need abstract reasoning, while connectionist models are better at problems that need interacting with the world or extracting patterns from massive, disordered data. Kaplan[14] takes riding bikes as an example, stating that it is a problem fitting for neural networks through pattern imitation but not symbolic approaches. Indeed, it is very difficult to explicitly represent the expertise a robot needs to ride a bike. Conversely, tasks like formal verification and model checking are viewed as better suited for symbolic AI.

In the following subsections, we examine the differences between symbolic and connectionist AI, keeping in mind that today, most real-world applications are distributed on the spectrum between the two extremes.

1.2.1. *Purely symbolic AI*

AI was first created as symbolic AI, a paradigm that dominated the 1950s–1970s. Pioneers of AI formalized many theories and hypotheses, including The Physical Symbol System Hypothesis (PSSH), first formulated by Newell and Simon, which stated that "a physical symbol system has the necessary and sufficient means for intelligent action," whereby "the symbolic behavior of man arises because he has the characteristics of a physical symbol system."[15] The hypothesis also implies that machines, when provided with proper symbol-processing programs, are capable of intelligent action. Here, we present Simon's description of physical symbols and shall readdress it in Chapters 2, 3, and 5 when presenting counter-arguments as to how the human brain–body functions[16]:

"A physical symbol system holds a set of entities, called symbols. These are physical patterns (e.g., chalk marks on a blackboard) that can occur as components of symbol structures. In the case of computers, a symbol system also possesses a number of simple processes that operate upon symbol structures — processes that create, modify, copy and destroy symbols. A physical symbol system is a machine that, as it moves through time, produces an evolving collection of symbol structures. Symbol structures can, and commonly do, sever as internal representations (e.g., "mental images") of the environment to which the symbol system is seeking to adapt. They allow it to model that environment with greater or less veridicality and in greater or less detail, and consequently to reason about it. Of course, for this capability to be of any use to the symbol system, it must have windows on the world and hands, too. It must have means for acquiring information from the external environment that can be encoded into internal symbols, as well as means for producing symbols that initiate action upon the environment. Thus it must use symbols to designate objects and relations and actions in the world external to the system.

Symbols may also designate processes that the symbol system can interpret and execute. Hence the program that governs the behaviour of a symbol system can be stored, along with other symbol structures, in the system's own memory, and executed when activated.

Symbol systems are called "physical" to remind the reader that they exist in real-world devices, fabricated of glass and metal (computers) or flesh and blood (brains). In the past we have been more accustomed to thinking of symbol systems of mathematics and logic as abstract and disembodied, leaving out of account the paper and pencil and human minds that were required to actually bring them to life. Computers have transported symbols systems from the platonic heaven of ideas to the empirical world of actual processes carried out by machines or brains, or by the two of them working together."

Symbolic AI involves the attempt to explicitly represent human knowledge in a declarative form of statements and rules, and can be summarized by way of three fundamental assumptions or beliefs[17]:

(1) A model representing an intelligent system can be defined in an explicit way;
(2) Knowledge in such a model is represented in a symbolic way (defined in the form of graphs, logic formulas, symbolic rules, etc.); and
(3) Mental/cognitive operations can be described as formal operations over symbolic expressions and structures, which belong to a knowledge model.

The above is based on Minsky's argument that "each type of knowledge needs some form of 'representation' and a body of skills adapted to using that style of representation. Once that investment has been made, it is relatively easy for a specialist to accumulate further knowledge, provided the additional expertise is uniform enough to suit the same style of representation."[18] This, in turn, is anchored on Newell and Simon's hypothesis that symbolic relationships are forms of representations that are exact and complete in defining knowledge. Such symbolic relationships are handled through conventional algorithms or programs containing fixed sequences of instructions executed until a solution is reached.[19] As such, symbolic AI has traditionally been used to deal with well-defined problems, i.e. the system had to systematically process the available information related to the problem(s) at hand. IBM Deep Blue's defeat of world chess champion Garry Kasparov in 1997 was one such example of the symbolic/GOFAI approach. Later examples of predominantly symbolic AI are expert systems that use a network of symbolic relationships to make deductions and determine what questions to ask. Expert system applications excel in domains with well-defined production rules, whereby production rules connect symbols in a relationship similar to an If-Then statement.[20]

In short, predominantly symbolic AI approaches deal best with static problems as opposed to real-time complex-dynamic issues. Such approaches focus on abstract (as opposed to complex-dynamic contextual) reasoning. As we shall see in the next section, dynamic problems can, to a certain extent, be tackled by way of connectionist AI, whereby real-world data are processed to identify and process patterns.

1.2.2. *Predominantly connectionist AI*

Connectionist AI is based on the view that human knowledge representations are distributed through nodes in neural networks.[21] This is in contrast to *purely* symbolic AI, which seeks clear, localized representations in which an idea is assigned to a single representational element or relationship.[22] In symbolic AI, the concept of cat is assumed to be exactly represented by one "cat node." In connectionist AI, however, a cat is represented by a specific pattern of activation through a network of nodes. Such patterns are described in terms of data, whether as a set of numbers, vectors, matrices, or tensors, as opposed to "exact" symbols or symbolic relationships. As such, these patterns are also viewed as approximations of conceptual representations in question (e.g. cat).[23] In connectionist AI, the user does not specify the rules of the domain being modeled. Across the network of nodes, "learning" algorithms statistically infer (across iterations) the rules from data. Here, deep "learning" (DL) across neural networks finds correlations by way of approximations. It approximates an unknown function $f(x) = y$ between any input x and any output y, and in this manner is often referred to as "the universal approximator," whereby it assumes that they are related either by correlation or causation.[24] Connectionist AI includes machine "learning" (ML), consisting of algorithms enabling systems to "learn,"[25] or more precisely, improve their outputs based on previous iterations.[26] ML improves its output by instructing computers to modify (or "teach") their internal algorithms based on previous iterations (i.e. "experience"). In turn, DL is a subset of ML involving artificial neural networks that "learn" from large amounts of data.[27] As mentioned above, such neural networks are designed to identify numerical patterns extracted from mathematical vectors into which all-real world/sensory data (e.g. images, sounds, or text) are translated.[28]

Connectionist AI is inherently hybrid in nature in that it integrates varying degrees of symbolic AI within it. This can be seen, e.g. in regards to the different ways "training" can be carried out within ML — namely supervised learning, reinforcement learning, and unsupervised learning.[29]

Supervised learning involves human intervention in the form of programmers' "training" algorithms across data with labeled inputs and outputs. Fully labeled means that each example in the "training" dataset is tagged with the answer the algorithm should come up with on its own. The algorithm is given a sequence of desired outputs with the goal of learning to produce and adjust the expected output while given a new input.[30] As such, a model is built through this "training" process. Here, the algorithms are required to make predictions. Errors are corrected when the algorithm predictions are wrong. The "training" process continues until reaching a desired level of accuracy on the training data. Reinforcement learning algorithms utilize repeated inter-actions with the environment to improve performance on a specific task.[31] Here, reinforcement cues in the form of "rewards" (or higher numerical scores) are used when an intended outcome is achieved. One particular area of success has been games, where a reinforcement learning algorithm "learns" to play the game by iterating it repeatedly (or "practicing"), and is "rewarded" by numerical scores associated to wins and losses.[32] Finally, unsupervised learning algorithms "learn" without supervision by human programmers. Here, algorithms are handed a dataset without explicit instructions on what to do with it and no correct answer (i.e. unlabeled output data set). As such, a model is prepared by deducing structures present in the input data to extract general rules. It is done either through a mathematical process that systematically reduces redundancy, or through organizing data by similarity.[33]

In all three cases, such algorithmic systems attempt to find structure in the data (e.g. clusters, anomalies, and associations) by extracting useful features, analogous to humans or animals, for whom the structure of the world is understood based on observation. Although each approach is best suited to different tasks, they can be used simultaneously within an AI process.[34] For example, a system may involve semi-supervised learning, in which algorithms use both labeled and unlabeled data to perform an otherwise supervised learning or unsupervised learning task.[35] Here, algorithms must "learn" the structure to organize data as well as to make predictions.

Such "learning" technologies can be used where more tacit type tasks are involved, i.e. where engineers are unable to initially program a machine to simulate the task in question. As such, "learning" machines can eventually master the task through a process of exposure, "training," and reinforcement across the use of sensor and image technologies coupled with information technology.[36] Hence, "machine learning techniques involving image recognition, a process that is difficult to explicitly articulate and explain but that we, as humans, develop through experience, can now discriminate with an accuracy that surpasses our own."[37] This is the case, for example, in the healthcare industry in which "intelligent" heart and lung image recognition algorithms are guiding radiologists toward certain diagnoses that compare favorably with certified doctors.[38] Infervision is one such company that uses supervised DL by way of its InferRead services to help interpret exams, X-rays, and other medical data.[39] Its supervised model is trained with X-ray images of patients diagnosed with the disease in question versus X-ray images of healthy organs. Here, the algorithm learns to recognize when the data are outside an established standard. Its performance is calibrated and validated by radiologists and other human specialists.[40] Such DL technology aims to provide a diagnostic aid toward the detection of lung cancer, pneumonia, tuberculosis, stroke as well as analysis of chest, bone, and mammography imagery.

In ML (and DL), learning algorithms are considerably "opaque because they do not rely on pre-specified instructions [in contrast to traditional algorithms used in symbolic AI], but on evolving weights and networks of connections that get refined with each additional data point."[41] Understanding how such algorithms arrive at their results is often unclear to both users and developers due to the number and complexity of "interactions of the data fed into the algorithm."[42] As such, symbolic AI has increasingly been called upon to be used in combination with connectionist AI, in that connectionist AI components on their own contain the inherent difficulty of human "readability" (or transparency) of representations so as to provide adequate explanations of the systems (or subsystem components) put in place.[43]

1.2.3. *"Hybrid" systems*

As mentioned in the previous section, all connectionist models are hybrid systems, having symbolic components to some extent. In recent years, there has been an intentional push to combine the symbolic AI approach with connectionist AI (DL) with the aim of providing AI systems a way to identify logical concepts, rather than just feeding it data and waiting for it to understand patterns.[44] This approach is also being used to help address AI's transparency problem. The connectionist component is used to solve low-level tasks such as pattern matching and generalizing from data. The symbolic component is used for "inherently symbolic" tasks. While connectionist dimensions are often used for sensory and motor "learning," symbolic aspects are typically used to address formal as well as language-like tasks, the two can overlap. For example, Miikkulainen[45] developed the DISCERN network that uses distributed neural network to model symbolic information of story understanding.

One well-known contemporary example of hybrid AI is IBM's Watson, a "natural language" algorithm which uses, on the one hand, symbolic AI in its construction of grammar rules, but is structured in parallel, and in combination with, specific forms of machine "learning" search approaches which "assign multiple meanings to terms and concepts" by way of statistical approximations and probabilities."[46] Across such technologies, Watson was able to beat human world champions at the game of Jeopardy.

Another notable example of hybrid AI is Google's DeepMind (AlphaGo), which is a predominantly (but not totally) connectionist (DL) system, based on Monte Carlo Tree Searching (MCTS) and neural networks, which was able to beat 18 time Go world champion Le Sedol 4 games out of 5 in early 2017. More precisely, AlphaGo uses, on the one hand, deep neural networks that "...were trained by supervised learning from human expert moves, and by reinforcement learning from self-play."[47] The supervised "learning" aspect in itself, as discussed in the previous section, in itself contains symbolic AI components. Furthermore, the MCTS aspect originated directly from the symbolic paradigm. At the same time, symbolic models are never purely symbolic AI structured, but are typically combined through networks (e.g. semantic networks). Finally, the training process of AlphaGo included certain "handcrafted local features which encoded 'common-sense Go rules.'"[48]

Through both Chapter 2's "frame problem" and Chapter 3's examination of human creativity and adaptive expertise across various human endeavors and spheres (including linguistics as well as various professional domains), we shall argue that mixed-mode AI applications such as IBM's Watson and Google's AlphaGo do not display any form of general intelligence or understanding, in that Watson, for example, astutely exploits statistical "hooks" and so-called "smart" rules which soon hit their limits in terms of determining what is relevant or meaningful[49]; while for applications such as AlphaGo, they involve very narrow problem-solving tasks with very simple rules.[50]

In the next chapter...

In the next chapter, we shall present and argue why AI is unable to determine relevancy in changing situations through an examination of what is known as the "frame problem." Determining what is relevant is critical toward being able to creatively adapt to one's changing situation[51,52] — keeping in mind situations in themselves are always (more or less) changing.[53]

Endnotes

[1] See Searle, J.R. (1980). Minds, brains, and programs. *Behavioral and Brain Sciences*, **3**(3): 417–457.

[2] See Proudfoot, D. (2011). Anthropomorphism and AI: Turing's much misunderstood imitation game. *Artificial Intelligence*, **175**(5–6), 950–957.

[3] For example, see Kaplan, A. and Haenlein, M. (2019). Siri, Siri, in my hand: Who's the fairest in the land? On the interpretations, illustrations, and implications of artificial intelligence. *Business Horizons*, **62**(1), 15–25. https://doi.org/10.1016/j.bushor.2018.08.004.

[4] McCarthy, J., Minsky, M.L., Rochester, N. and Shannon, C. (1955). A Proposal for the Dartmouth Summer Research Project on Artificial Intelligence. Available at: http://www-formal.stanford.edu/jmc/history/dartmouth/dartmouth.html.

[5] See Bush, V. (1945). As we may think. *The Atlantic Monthly*, July.

[6] See Turing, A. (1950). Computing machinery and intelligence. *Mind*, **49**: 433–460.

[7] See Proudfoot (2011). Note 2; as well as Russell, S. and Norvig, P. (2010). *Artificial Intelligence: A Modern Approach*, 3rd Edition (Upper Saddle River, NJ: Prentice Hall).

[8] For example, see Jarrahi, M.H. (2018). Artificial Intelligence and the future of work: Human-AI symbiosis in organizational decision making. *Business Horizons.* https://doi.org/10.1016/j.bushor.2018.03.007.

[9] Citing Kaplan and Haenlein (2019) note 3, p. 15; also see Russell and Norvig (2010), note 7.

[10] Here, one can refer to the following report: OECD (2018). OECD Science, Technology and Innovation Outlook 2018: Adapting to Technological and Societal Disruption. Paris: OECD Publishing. https://www.oecd-ilibrary.org/science-and-technology/oecd-science-technology-and-innovation-outlook-2018_sti_in_outlook-2018-en

[11] See Kaplan and Haenlein (2019). Note 3.

[12] For example, see Garnelo, M. and Shanahan, M. (2019). Reconciling deep learning with symbolic artificial intelligence: representing objects and relations. *Current Opinion in Behavioral Sciences*, **29**, 17–23.

[13] Kaplan, J. (2016). *Artificial Intelligence. What Everyone Needs to Know* (New York, NY: Oxford University Press).

[14] *Ibid.*

[15] See Newell, A. and Simon, H.A. (1976). Computer science as empirical inquiry: Symbols and search. *Communications of the ACM*, **19**(3), pp. 113–126.

[16] Citing Simon, H. (1996), *The Sciences of the Artificial, 3rd Edition* (Cambridge, MA: MIT Press), pp. 22–23.

[17] See Flasinski, M. (2016). *Introduction to Artificial Intelligence* (Springer), Heidelberg, Germany, p. 15.

[18] Citing Minsky, M. (1988). *Society of Mind* (New York, NY: Simon & Schuster), p. 72.

[19] For example, see Hopcroft, J.E. and Ullman, J.D. (1983). *Data Structures and Algorithms* (Boston, MA: Addison-Wesley).

[20] Here, "digestible" explanations are provided by: Sun, R. (2000). Artificial intelligence: Connectionist and symbolic approaches. *International Encyclopedia of the Social & Behavioral Sciences.* https://doi.org/10.1016/B0-08-043076-7/00553-2.

[21] For example, see Clark, A. (2003). *Associative Engines*. A Bradford Book (Cambridge, MA: MIT Press).

[22] Minsky, M. (1988). Society of Mind. Simon & Schuster, New York, NY.

[23] The example of a cat being represented across numerous representational nodes is provided by Palit, A.K. and Popovic, D. (2005). *Computational Intelligence in Time Series Forecasting: Theory and Engineering Applications* (New York: Springer).

[24] *Ibid.*

[25] Authors such as Jarrahi (2018) (see note 8) use anthropomorphic terms such as "learn," "teach" and "experience".

[26] Terms such as "teach" and "learn" are avoided by authors and researchers such as Mitchell, T.M. (2006). The Discipline of Machine Learning (No. CMU-ML-06-108). Available at: http://reports-archive.adm.cs.cmu.edu/anon/ml/CMU-ML-06-108.pdf), as well as Buchanan, B. and Miller, T. (2017). Machine Learning

for Policymakers. Paper, Cyber Security Project, Belfer Center for Science and International Affairs. Available at: https://www.belfercenter.org/sites/default/files/files/publication/MachineLearningforPolicymakers.pdf, who prefer the more exact computational terms such as "iterations", "modify" and "improve".

[27] For example, see LeCun, Y., Bengio, Y. and Hinton, G. (2015). Deep learning. *Nature*, **521**(7553): 436–444. https://doi.org/10.1038/nature14539.

[28] For more on this, see Hagan, M.T., Demuth, H.B., Beale M.H. and Jesús O.D. (2014). *Neural Network Design*, 2nd Edition (Martin Hagan Publisher), Stillwater, Oklahoma.

[29] See Arulkumaran, Deisenroth, M.P., Brundage, M. and Bharath, A.A. (2017). Deep reinforcement learning: A brief survey. *IEEE Signal Processing Magazine*, **34**(6): 26–38. doi: 10.1109/MSP.2017.2743240.

[30] For more on this, see both Ghahramani, Z. (2004). Unsupervised Learning. In *Advanced Lectures on Machine Learning*, Bousquet *et al.*, (eds.) (Springer Verlag), as well as Kotsiantis, S. B. (2007). Supervised machine learning: A review of classification techniques. *Informatica*, (31), 249–268.

[31] For more details on reinforcement learning, see Arulkumaran *et al.*, note 29.

[32] For example, reinforcement learning has been used in the successful development of AlphaGo's algorithm which "learned" to play and eventually win against world champion Le Sedol at the game of Go, as reported by Silver, D., Schrittwieser, J., Simonyan, K., Antonoglou, I., Huang, A., Guez, A. and Hassabis, D. (2017). Mastering the game of Go without human knowledge. *Nature*, **550**(7676), 354–359. https://doi.org/10.1038/nature24270.

[33] See Ghahramani (2004) (note 30).

[34] See Silver *et al.* (2017) (note 32).

[35] See Zhu., X. (2005). Semi-supervised learning literature survey. Computer Sciences Technical Report 1530, University of Wisconsin-Madison.

[36] Autor, D.H. (2015). Why are there still so many jobs? The history and future of workplace automation, *Journal of Economic Perspectives*, **29**(3): 3–30.

[37] Citing Faraj, S., Pachidi, S. and Sayegh, K. (2018). Working and organizing in the age of the learning algorithm. *Information and Organization*, **28**: 62–70.

[38] See Mukherjee, S. (2017). AI v. MD. April 3, *New Yorker*. Available at: https://www.newyorker.com/magazine/2017/04/03/ai-versus-md

[39] As reported by Liao, R. (2018). China's Infervision is helping 280 hospitals worldwide detect cancers from images. Available at: https://techcrunch.com/2018/11/30/infervision-medical-imaging-280-hospitals/

[40] See Marr, B. and Ward, M. (2019). *Artificial Intelligence in Practice: How 50 Successful Companies Used AI and Machine Learning to Solve Problems* (Hoboken, NJ: Wiley).

[41] Citing Faraj *et al.* (2018, p. 63) (note 37), who in turn refers to Burrell, J. (2016). How the machine "thinks": Understanding opacity in machine learning algorithms. *Big Data & Society*, **3**(1), 1–12, as well as Michalski, R.S., Carbonell, J.G. and Mitchell, T.M. (2013). *Machine Learning: An Artificial Intelligence Approach* (Springer Science & Business Media), Berlin, Germany.

[42] See Faraj *et al.* (2018) (note 37).

[43] Much has been written on issues of transparency related to connectionist AI by Markus, G. and Davis, E. (2019). *Rebooting AI: Building Artificial Intelligence We Can Trust* (Pantheon), New York, NY.

[44] See Garnelo and Shanahan (2019) (note 12).

[45] Miikkulainen, R. (1993). *Subsymbolic Natural Language Processing: An Integrated Model of Scripts, Lexicon, and Memory* (Cambridge, MA: MIT Press).

[46] Citing Jarrahi (2018, p. 578) (note 8); also see Ferrucci, D.A. (2012). Introduction to 'This is Watson.' *IBM Journal of Research and Development*, **56**(3–4): May–June.

[47] Citing Silver *et al.* (2017, p. 354) (note 32).

[48] See Fu, M.C. (2016). AlphaGo and Monte Carlo Tree Search: The Simulation Optimization Perspective. In *2016 Winter Simulation Conference (WSC)*, pp. 659–670. Available at: https://doi.org/10.1109/WSC.2016.7822130.

[49] See both Ferrucci (2012) (note 46) as well as Elish, M. and Boyd, D. (2018). Situating methods in the magic of Big Data and AI. *Communication Monographs*, **85**(1): 57–80.

[50] See Elish and Boyd (2018) (note 49).

[51] Dreyfus, H.L. and Dreyfus, S.E. (2005). Peripheral vision expertise in real world contexts. *Organization Studies* **26**(5), 779–792.

[52] Boden, M.A. (2010). *Creativity and Art: Three Roads to Surprise* (Oxford, UK: Oxford University Press); Boden, M.A. (2016). *AI: Its Nature and Future* (Oxford, UK: Oxford University Press).

[53] Such dynamic/changing environments as acknowledged by McCarthy, J. and Hayes, P.J. (1969). Some philosophical problems from the standpoint of artificial intelligence. In *Machine Intelligence*. Vol. 4, Meltzer, B. and Michie, D., (eds.) (Edinburgh: Edinburgh University Press), pp. 463–502.

Chapter 2

The Issue of Relevance
in Artificial Intelligence

2.1. Introduction

In this chapter, we shall examine what is often referred to as the "frame problem" in AI, and as such, argue that "intelligent" algorithms are (as yet) unable to determine what is relevant and meaningful within new or unexpected situations.[1] As we shall further see in Chapter 3, determining what is relevant is a fundamental aspect of human adaptive expertise as well as creativity.

The frame problem was first presented during the "era" of symbolic AI and, to some extent, is still seen as an issue *strictly* related to the limitations of symbolic manipulations.[2] Yet, Dreyfus' Heideggerian analysis identified a more taken-for-granted issue — namely the problem of *representation*.[3] Some researchers, such as Stevan Harnad, have argued the "frame problem" as being a symptom of symbolic AI's "ungrounded symbols", and thereby proposed connectionist AI networks to "ground" or "situate" symbols.[4] More recent hybrid AI attempts to address the "frame problem" have been further inspired by authors such as Kahneman, who argues that humans have two cognitive systems, one which is fast, automatic, and subconscious, and the other being slow, rule-governed, and conscious, yet both involving distributed representation.[5] However, herein lies two basic assumptions first exposed by Searle and Dreyfus in the first place — i.e. on whether or not the human brain's first reflex consists of[6]:

(1) Symbolic manipulation, and
(2) Knowledge representations.

While both are often interrelated, the second assumption on its own reminds us that connectionist AI, like symbolic AI, also consists of (albeit, distributed) knowledge representations. Furthermore, as discussed in the previous chapter, connectionist AI inherently integrates various degrees of symbolic AI. As such, we shall argue that *both* purely symbolic, as well as connectionist AI are equally affected by the frame problem — or what Dreyfus refers to as the problem of *relevance*.[7]

2.2. The Frame Problem First Exposed

The frame problem was first *formally* introduced by McCarthy and Hayes.[8] A symbolic AI model was proposed that would decide which actions to take by deductively inferring that a certain sequence of actions or events would lead to a desired goal. The model, however, would not only require rules specifying what changes occur during or after an event but also have rules determining what remained the same — otherwise, the model would not be able to define the new situation in question. However, according to the authors, this would require an overwhelming number of rules specifying non-changes with the consequence that the system would lose itself in performing endless and irrelevant deductions. Interestingly, four years earlier, Dreyfus had informally brought up certain aspects of the frame problem by arguing that robots could not carry out tasks in a human way unless they could take into account the specific situation in which these actions occurred.[9] Proponents of symbolic AI subsequently countered this could easily be addressed by establishing a complete set of "smart" rules or "frame".[10] In the same spirit, McDermott proposed the "sleeping dog" strategy — i.e. not every part of the data representing an ongoing situation need be examined, but only those parts that represent aspects of the world that have changed.[11]

Yet, Dreyfus, in his earlier philosophical critique of symbolic AI, had pertinently argued that humans do not create (in their brains) internal representations of objects in the world.[12] Drawing from the works of Heidegger and Merleau-Ponty, Dreyfus argued that the brain's reflex is to simply learn how to see the world directly, something that Heidegger referred to as "readiness-to-hand". Here, humans are always interconnected or embedded within a context-at-hand in which human agency occurs within what Heidegger referred to as "thrownness", i.e. the individual finds himself "already in" a context "which delimits both the range of actions which it makes sense to perform, and of those which it is valuable to perform."[13] Human readiness-to-hand is also what Dreyfus and Dreyfus referred to as "knowing-how", and is the way individuals deal with things normally.[14] In this mode, individuals take actions without the use of symbolic reasoning, whether in recognizing a face, saying the right thing in a conversation, or driving to work. Moreover, such adaptive behavior occurs without having to conduct a methodical analysis of alternatives.[15] Such "common sense" is also the essence of adaptive expertise, whereby our intuitions have been trained such that we forget rules and simply size up the situation and adaptively react.[16] Key to such adaptive capability is the individual's background sense of the context at hand — i.e. of knowing what is pertinent given the situation, rather than searching through combinations of possibilities and alternatives. This "background" knowing is a form of knowledge embodied within us, rather than symbolically stored in our brains.[17]

As such, Dreyfus argued the frame problem to be a consequence of the fallacious assumption that intelligent behavior is based on representation-guided behavior.[18] Furthermore, in response to McDermott's attempt, among others, to address the frame problem issue in regards to symbolic AI by way of so-called "smart rules", Dreyfus pointed out the issue of infinite regress — i.e. "if each context can be recognized only in terms of features selected as relevant and interpreted in a broader context, the AI worker is faced with a regress of contexts," and a resultant impoverishment (or loss) of relevant contextual knowledge.[19] Still, researchers in symbolic AI continued their efforts in trying to formalize common sense, across various strategies, such as the use of mathematical "default statements".[20] These approaches, however, other than within contexts of well-defined rules (e.g. chess), failed to show any significant progress in real-world applications requiring human common sense and adaptive expertise.[21]

2.3. Beyond Symbolic AI

Many in the field of AI development acknowledged that symbolic AI had failed as an approach to determine relevant features within real-life contexts, because "cognition is both embedded and embodied".[22] Harnad had, in a similar way, foreshadowed the death knell of symbolic AI by arguing that it lacked situational grounding and proposed grounding mechanisms by way of a connectionist perspective.[23] However, Dreyfus had also aimed the same criticism towards connectionist AI, in which he argued that the frame problem could not be avoided simply by side-stepping the formal use of symbolic representations.[24] Simply put, deep learning through neural networks is in certain ways a reduction of GOFAI, in that rules are created implicitly through pattern detections and the use of labelled or pre-categorized data in the form, "if A then B, where A is a pattern and B a label or symbol representing a category."[25] Furthermore, distributed representations through networks of nodes are *still* representations.[26] Adding to this, are the more recent calls toward increasing symbolic AI within connectionist AI, in that connectionist AI on its own contains the inherent difficulty of human "readability" (or transparency) of representations in providing adequate explanations of the systems put in place.[27]

Yet, for certain AI researchers such as Wheeler,[28] Dreyfus' Heideggerian analysis suggested that the frame problem could well disappear if certain "fallacious concepts of representationalism" about intelligence were abandoned. Based on both Heidegger's concept of "thrownness", in which the body is immersed as well as tied into an inter-related and holistic environment, and the complementary view from Haugeland[29] that cognition is embedded and embodied, Wheeler adhered to, and in a way reinforced, Winograd's earlier initiative of integrating a Heideggerian approach within AI which took into account embodiment and embeddedness.[30] However, Wheeler's understanding of what he considers "fallacious representationalism" seems to limit itself to what he describes as non-dynamic framing, i.e. where "computing is digital, deterministic, discrete … and temporally austere (in that time is reduced to mere sequence)."[31] For Wheeler, situated coping as described by both Heidegger and Merleau-Ponty can be reproduced in AI by way of a dynamical systems model, i.e. where action-oriented representations or frames are used to reproduce Heidegger's ready-to-hand coping.[32] Here, Wheeler adopts the mechanistic approach of "adaptive coupling" of the body (as internal representations) with the context (as external representations), in which relevance is achieved when frames from the contextual environment are recognized and matched with frames from the body itself. Yet, the holistic and phenomenological tenet of Heidegger and Merleau-Ponty in regards to embedded embodied coping is that "as absorbed skillful copers, we are not minds at all but one with the world"; and that any recognition of reaching an equilibrium with one's immediate environment is completely non-representational in nature in that we simply feel a relief in tension with the environment as we (momentarily) attain equilibirum.[33] Conversely, Wheeler's dynamic frame approach has merely reduced itself to finer grade, discrete, and interrelated frames with all the (frame) problems which come with these.[34] As such, the Heideggerian AI proposed by Wheeler, which is essentially a mixture of connectionism and GOFAI,[35] comes back to being a matter of "finesse rather than" of solving "the frame problem".[36] A system of frames "isn't in a situation" and "embodied beings like us take as input energy from the physical universe, and respond in such a way as to open themselves to a world organized in terms of their needs, interests, and bodily capacities without their minds needing to impose meanings on a meaningless given."[37] To this Dreyfus adds[38]:

> Heidegger's important insight is not that, when we solve problems, we sometimes make use of representational equipment outside our bodies [which is what Heidegger calls being within a present-at-hand mode in which we conduct representative reflections when facing a situation which baffles us completely], but that being-in-the-world is more basic than thinking and solving problems; that it is not representational at all. That is, when we are coping at our best, we are drawn in by solicitations and respond directly to them, so that the distinction between us and our equipment — between inner and outer — vanishes.

In this manner, Dreyfus sees Wheeler's proposal as merely a piecemeal approach to Heidegger (i.e. "pseudo-Heideggerian"). For Heidegger, representational accounts constitute a problem, no matter how fine-grained it is made in regards to both time and situation, as adopted by Wheeler's action-oriented representations, and more specifically, does not solve the frame problem but rather "has so far proven to be a dead end."[39] The reason is that, through embodied coping in a particular context, we learn to ignore in a non-representational, or "whole-body" manner, all that is not relevant to us. In turn, our sense of what is relevant comes with our experience of past significant encounters through the same "whole-body" approach.[40] By "whole-body," we mean the brain is not in a separate "observer" state to the body, but rather is in intra-action with the body's senses and motor activities. This "whole-body" learning phenomenon helps us refine our background know-how abilities, which identifies within a given changing situation what is significant and needs to be verified versus what has not changed. Dreyfus draws upon Merleau-Ponty's "intentional arc" and Freeman's physiology of perception to defend and further explain this point.[41] The intentional arc is an individual's "unitary" ability, which consists essentially of inseparable motion, vision, and comprehension.[42] As such, body movement is not merely physiological, nor is it the "handmaid" of consciousness.[43] Freeman provides a holistic neuro-dynamic summary of the body-brain when an individual perceives a familiar event as "information [which] spreads like a flash fire through the nerve cell assembly."[44] Furthermore, learning and building one's repertoire of what is significant or relevant involves "brain activity patterns [which] are constantly dissolving, reforming and changing, particularly in relation to one another," whereby learning to respond to a new event involves "a shift in all other patterns, even if they are not directly involved with the learning. There are no fixed representations, as there are in computers; there are only significances."[45] Such brain-body activity is "not an isolate brain state" and is contrary to the classical (or non-embodied) cognitivist stance "of representations" in which "a representation exists apart from what it represents."[46] As such, Freeman provides an approach which is not associative, whereby "as one learns, one adds more and more fixed connection," but rather "instantiates the basis of a genuine intentional arc in which there are no linear casual connections between world and brain nor a fixed library of representations, but where, each time a new significance is encountered, the whole perceptual world … changes so that the significance that is directly displayed in the world is continually enriched."[47] In this manner, Dreyfus criticizes Wheeler's Heideggerian AI as not being sufficiently Heideggerian to address the ongoing problem of frames and significance. Wheeler subsequently defended himself on the basis that his use of frames and representations was based on Heidegger's reference to present-at-hand coping, i.e. where one applies reflective and abstractive thinking when facing an event that goes beyond one's actual know-how.[48] Dreyfus, however, had earlier criticized Wheeler on this point in that he argued that ready-to-hand (i.e. non-representational) coping was by far the mode individuals used in the majority of their day-to-day activities, including (and most especially in regards to) the skillful application of high-level expertise.[49] Others, such as Ratcliffe, have gone further in their criticism of Wheeler by arguing that the position that science gives access to completely deworlded objects is fallacious in that "presence-at-hand does not escape readiness-to-hand but is a kind of abstraction from it."[50] In attempting to separate readiness-to-hand from the context (or world) in which it is rendered relevant and to then apply a "scientific" present-at-hand framing, along with environmental "interpretations" as "nudges, to finally call it 'Heideggerian'"[51] becomes a Heideggerian cognitive science undertaking, which Ratcliffe argues as "the project of seeking to understand our being-in-the-world in cognitive science is nonsensical."[52]

2.4. Some Preliminary Words in Regards to "Today"

More recently, AI researchers such as Margaret Boden have judged the various combinations of connectionist and symbolic approaches attempted by AI developers as being unsuccessful in identifying suitable knowledge representations which would avoid the frame problem, and as such are "as yet" unable to determine what is relevant within new or changing situations.[53] The difficulty, according to Boden, has been that being able to achieve something significant and relevant requires knowledge of social beliefs, values, and practices that are highly tacit by way of their embodied and embedded nature — and to which many others have argued cannot be reduced to explicit representations.[54]

As we shall see in further in the next chapter, determining what is relevant is an important aspect of creativity.[55] Today, machine learning algorithms consist of "glorified data-fitting procedures" — very much like curve-fitting to a set of datapoints but involving much more elaborate ways of fitting multi-dimensional curves (or more precisely, patterns) to huge numbers of datasets.[56] In this manner, for example, art-generating algorithms have been seen at best, as being pseudo-creative, rather than truly creative in nature.[57] For example, recent technologies such as Neural Style Transfer involves the transfer of neural network correlation statistics from a painting of a given style to a photograph, thus producing a new painting of the input photograph within a similar artistic style.[58] Project Magenta at Google is more ambitious in that it generates "new" artistic genres from a combination of already defined datasets or representations.[59] Yet, as Douglas Eck of the Google Magenta Project states, "I think it's unlikely to me that a machine learning algorithm is going to come along and generate some transformative new way of doing art. I think a person working with this technology might be able to do that."[60] We shall return to Eck's latter point in Chapters 8 and 9. Suffice to say, such technologies are for Boden, a form of combinatorial or pseudo-creativity that cannot be creative beyond the bounds of defined representations (in this case, distributed representations across the neural networks of machine learning) and as such, "we cannot expect real breakthroughs from them ... no fundamental novelties or truly shocking surprises are possible."[61]

Closely related to creativity is adaptive expertise, i.e. "the ability to respond to cues not previously encountered and to develop new solutions ... applicable to novel situations."[62] Like creativity, adaptive expertise requires the ability to determine what is relevant or meaningful in a changing or new situation. In both Chapters 3 and 7, we shall look at how "intelligent" or "learning" algorithms can erode or remove human adaptive expertise when viewed and adopted within organizational contexts in a *mindless* manner.

In the next chapter...

In the next chapter, we shall examine the relevance of relevance. As mentioned in this chapter, being able to determine what is relevant in a changing or new situation is key to both adaptive expertise and transformative creativity, i.e. a creativity that breaks established paradigms. As such, we shall examine in more detail what adaptive expertise (by way of the inconspicuous perspective of mètis) and creativity entails. In turn, we shall argue that both involve non-representational phenomena, and thus, are anathema to the very essences of both AI and classical cognitive approaches (Dreyfus, 2007; Chemero, 2009).[63]

Endnotes

[1] As is later discussed in the chapter, Dreyfus (2007) explains how humans can determine what is relevant across human embodiment and embeddedness within the context at hand, which is something machines cannot do; while Boden (2016) speaks of the relevance of relevance in regards to generating creative actions and outcomes, thereby providing the reason why AI cannot be truly creative.

[2] See Bayne, T., Cleeremans, A. and Wilken, P. (2009). *The Oxford Companion to Consciousness* (Oxford University Press, Oxford, UK).

[3] See Dreyfus, H.L. (1992). *What Computers Still Can't Do: A Critique of Artificial Reason* (MIT Press, London, UK).

[4] See Harnad, S. (1990). The symbol grounding problem. *Physica D*, **42**, 335–346, as well as Harnad, S. (1993). Problems, Problems: The frame problem as a symptom of the symbol grounding problem. *Psycoloquy*, **4**(34), frame-problem.11.harnad.

[5] See Kahneman, D. (2011). *Thinking, Fast and Slow*, 1st edn (New York: Farrar, Straus and Giroux).

[6] See Searle, J.R. (1980). Minds, brains, and programs. *Behavioral and Brain Sciences*, **3**(3): 417–457, as well as Dreyfus (1965). *Alchemy and Artificial Intelligence* (Santa Monica, CA: Rand Corporation), Dreyfus, H.L. (1972). *What Computers Can't Do* (New York, NY: MIT Press), Dreyfus, H.L. (1992). *What Computers Still Can't Do: A Critique of Artificial Reason* (London, UK: MIT Press), and Dreyfus, H.L. (2007). Why Heideggerian AI failed and how fixing it would require making it more Heidegerrian. *Artificial Intelligence*, **171**(18), 1137–1160.

[7] See Dreyfus (2007) (note 6).

[8] See McCarthy, J. and Hayes, P.J. (1969). Some Philosophical Problems from the Standpoint of Artificial Intelligence. In: Meltzer, B. and Michie, D. (eds.) *Machine Intelligence*. Vol. 4 (Edinburgh: Edinburgh University Press), pp. 463–502.

[9] See Dreyfus (1965) (note 6).

[10] See principally McDermott, D. (1987). We've Been Framed: Or Why AI is Innocent of the Frame Problem. In: Pylyshyn, Z.W. (ed.) *The Robot's Dilemma: The Frame Problem in Artificial Intelligence* (Norwood, NJ: Ablex), pp. 113–122, or in a more implicit manner, Minsky, M. (1988). *Society of Mind* (New York, NY: Simon & Schuster).

[11] See McDermott (1987) (note 10).

[12] See Dreyfus (1965 and 1972) (note 6).

[13] Citing Young, J. (2000).What is Dwelling? The Homelessness of Modernity and the Worlding of the World. In: Wrathall, M. and Mapas, J (eds.) *Heidegger, Authenticity and Modernity: Essays in Honor of H.L. Dreyfus*. Vol. 1 (MIT Press, London UK), pp. 187–188.

[14] See Dreyfus, H.L. and Dreyfus, S.E. (1986). *Mind Over Machine* (New York, NY: The Free Press).

[15] See Dreyfus (1972 and 1992) (note 6).

[16] See Dreyfus (1972, 1992 and 2005) (note 6).

[17] *Ibid.*, note 16.

[18] *Ibid.*, note 15.

[19] Citing Dreyfus (1992, p. 289) (note 6) in response to McDermott (1987), note 10.

[20] As argued by Shanahan, M. (1997). *Solving the Frame Problem: A Mathematical Investigation of the Common Sense Law of Inertia* (Cambridge, MA: MIT Press).

[21] As argued by Dreyfus (2005) in note 6, as well as acknowledged by Wheeler, M. (2005). *Reconstructing the Cognitive World: The Next Step* (Cambridge, MA: MIT Press).

[22] The embodied and embedded aspects of the human "mind" as posited by Haugeland, J. (1998). Mind Embodied and Embedded. In *Having Thought: Essays in the Metaphysics of Mind* (Cambridge, MA: Cambridge University Press), along with many of Dreyfus' (1992) phenomenological descriptions of human behavior, were subsequently incorporated into "Heideggerian AI by Wheeler" (2005) in Wheeler, M. (2005). *Reconstructing the Cognitive World: The Next Step* (Cambridge, MA: MIT Press).

[23] See Harnad, S. (1990) (note 4).

[24] See Dreyfus (1992) (note 6).

[25] *Ibid.*, note 24; also see Palit, A.K. and Popovic, D. (2005). *Computational Intelligence in Time Series Forecasting: Theory and Engineering Applications* (New York: Springer).

[26] See Dreyfus (2007) (note 6).

[27] See Markus, G. and Davis, E. (2019). *Rebooting AI: Building Artificial Intelligence We Can Trust* (New York, NY: Pantheon).

[28] See Wheeler (2005) (note 22).

[29] See Haugeland (1998) (note 22).

[30] On this earlier initiative, see Winograd, T. (1976). Artificial intelligence and language comprehension (pp. 1–26). Washington, DC: National Institute of Education).

[31] Citing Wheeler, M. (2002, pp. 344–345). Change in the Rules: Computers, Dynamical Systems, and Searle. In J. Preston & M. Bishop (eds.), *Views into the Chinese Room: New Essays on Searle and Artificial Intelligence* (Oxford, England: Clarendon Press), pp. 338–359.

[32] See Wheeler (2005) (note 22).

[33] Citing Dreyfus (2007, pp. 1146–1147) (note 6).

[34] Refer to Dreyfus' (2007, p. 1147) argument (note 6).

[35] See Masis, J. (2014). Naturalizing Dasein. Aporias of the neo-Heideggerian approach in cognitive science. *Cosmos and History: The Journal of Natural and Social Philosophy*, 10(2), 158–181.

[36] Citing Dreyfus, H.L. (2008), Why Heideggerian AI Failed and How Fixing It Would Require Making It More Heideggerian. In P. Husbands, O. Holland & M. Wheeler (eds.) *The Mechanical Mind in History* (Cambridge, MA: MIT Press), p. 335, pp. 331–371.

[37] Citing Dreyfus (2007, p. 1138) (note 6).

[38] Citing Dreyfus (2007, p. 1146) (note 6).

[39] Citing Dreyfus (2007, p. 1158) (note 6).

[40] See Dreyfus (2007) (note 6).

[41] See Freeman, W.J. (1991). The physiology of perception. *Scientific American*, **264**, 78–85.

[42] See Reuter, M. (1999). Merleau-Ponty's notion of pre-reflective intentionality. *Synthese*, **118**(1), 69–88.

[43] Citing Reuter (1999, p. 73) (note 42).

[44] Citing Freeman (1991, p. 83) (note 41).

[45] Citing Freeman (1991, p. 22) (note 41).

[46] Citing Dreyfus (2007, p. 1154) (note 6).

[47] *Ibid.* Note 46.

[48] Citing Wheeler, M. (2008). God's machines: descartes on the mechanization of mind. In: P. Husbands, O. Holland and M. Wheeler (eds.) *The Mechanical Mind in History* (Cambridge, MA; London: The MIT Press), pp. 307–330.

[49] See Dreyfus (2007) (note 6).

[50] Citing Ratcliffe, M. (2012). There Can Be No Cognitive Science of Dasein. In: J. Kiverstein and M. Wheeler (eds.) *Heidegger and Cognitive Science* (Basingstoke; New York: Palgrave Macmillan), p. 141, pp. 135–156.

[51] Citing Masis (2014, p. 176) (note 35).

[52] Citing Ratcliffe (2012, p. 138) (note 50).

[53] See both Boden, M.A. (2010). *Creativity and Art: Three Roads to Surprise* (Oxford University Press, Oxford, UK) and Boden, M.A. (2016). *AI: Its Nature and Future* (Oxford, UK: Oxford University Press).

[54] For example, both Dreyfus (2007), note 6, and Gallagher, S. (2009). The philosophical antecedents of situated cognition. In: Robbins, P. and Aydede, M. (eds.) *The Cambridge Handbook of Situated Cognition* (Cambridge University Press, Cambridge, UK) have argued the non-reducibility of phenomenological whole-bodied aspects of human actions and practices, while Collins, H. (2010). *Tacit and Explicit Knowledge* (Chicago, IL: University of Chicago Press) has provided similar arguments from a knowledge theory perspective, namely in the form of tacit knowledge.

[55] See Boden (2010) (note 53).

[56] For more on this, see Brooks, R. (2017). The seven deadly sins of AI predictions. *MIT Technology Review*, October 6.

[57] For more on this see both Boden, M.A. (1998). Creativity and artificial intelligence. *Artificial Intelligence*, **103**, 347–356 and Boden (2010), note 53, as well as McCormack, J. and D'Inverno, M. (2012). *Computers and Creativity* (New York, NY: Springer).

[58] See Gatys, L.A., Ecker, A.S., Bethge, M. Hertzmann, A. and Shechtman, E. (2016). Controlling perceptual factors in neural style transfer. *Proceedings of the IEEE Conference on Computer Vision and Pattern Recognition*, 2016, pp. 2414–2423.

[59] See Metz, C. (2017). How A.I. is creating building blocks to reshape music and art. *The New York Times*.

[60] Cited in Metz (2017) (note 59).

[61] Citing Boden (1998, p. 353) (note 67), also see Boden (2010) (note 53).

[62] Citing Adams, R.J. and Ericsson, A.E. (2000). Introduction to cognitive processes of expert pilots. *Journal of Human Performance in Extreme Environments*, 5(1), 44–62, 53. doi: 10.7771/2327-2937.1006

[63] See Dreyfus (2007) (note 6) as well as Chemero, A. (2009). *Radical Embodied Cognitive Science* (Cambridge, MA: The MIT Press).

Chapter 3

The Relevance of Relevance:
From *Mètis* to Creativity

3.1. Introduction

Determining what is relevant is a key aspect of adaptive expertise and creativity. In the previous chapter, we presented Dreyfus' argument that both symbolic and connectionist AI are not able to determine relevance in new circumstances that go beyond what their inherent frames of reference (or representations) can define, because frames in themselves cannot capture all features that may or may not be relevant in the first place.[1] Algorithms manipulate predefined signs and/or existing data (whether structured or unstructured). Humans on the other hand, as we shall see in the following chapter, can creatively improvise "something from nothing" — i.e. "creatively respond to novel situations" to develop relevant responses in the face of "untrainable" situations.[2] We call this *mètis*, or adaptive expertise. Here, we shall see that determining relevance is a mindful and creative act (or enactment). Finally, we describe how such creativity involves symbolic transformations (i.e. creative outcomes enacted from open-ended ambiguity), as opposed to being mere algorithmic combinations of defined signs and existing data.

3.2. *Mètis* — Adaptive Expertise Through Mindful Enactments of Context and Relevance

On January 15, 2009, US Airways flight 1549 made an emergency landing on New York City's Hudson River. While five passengers were seriously injured, and many more treated for hypothermia, there were no fatalities.

The aircraft, an Airbus 320 with 150 passengers and 5 crew members, had taken off from La Guardia's International Airport, when two minutes into take-off, flew into a flock of geese. Both engines were affected, losing all of their thrust. After unsuccessfully trying to restart the engines, the pilot (Captain Sullenberger) notified air traffic control that he was returning to La Guardia. Upon further descent, Sullenberger believed the plane could not reach the airport, and renotified air traffic control that he was going to attempt a very rare and risky water landing, for which he and his co-pilot (Jeffrey Skiles) had never been trained for. Exactly 208 seconds after having lost engine power, Captain Sullenberger, with the calming aid of first officer Skiles, successfully glided the plane onto the Hudson River.[3]

Wickens and Dehais evaluated the events surrounding the 2009 emergency water landing of US Airways Flight 1549 by Capt. Chesley B. Sullenberger III, and his first officer, Jeffrey Skiles, as well as other airline events which involved pilots saving lives, including the landing of crippled United Airlines Flight 232 (July 19, 1989) with no steering capability onto a runway at Sioux Falls Iowa — and refers to these as piloting which calls upon "incredible skill" involving a great deal of adaptive expertise.[4] Similarly, Adams and Ericsson's evaluation of expert pilot decision-making (in which six commercial aviation events occurring between 1972 and 1989 were reviewed) highlights the importance of adaptive expertise, i.e. "the ability to creatively respond to novel situations and develop an appropriate response with some reasonable chance for a successful outcome."[5] Each involved experienced pilots in the face of "untrainable" emergency situations. These were all cases (e.g. United Airlines Flight 232 (DC-10) engine explosion and landing at Sioux City, Iowa; cargo door failure leaving a gaping hole in United Airlines Flight 811 (B-747) during climb-out; Aloha Airlines Flight 243 (B737) fuselage failure; Air Canada Flight 143 (B-767) fuel starvation incident) in which there were "no specified procedures, no previous simulator training and certainly no past experience" in regards to the emergency situations at hand.[6] Adams and Ericsson describe such expert pilot performance as "adaptive" — i.e.

"the ability to respond to cues not previously encountered and to develop new solutions ... applicable to novel situations"; involving a mix of "knowing-how," "knowing when," and "knowing-what".[7] We return to this "ambiguous mix" in the following paragraphs. Pilot adaptive expertise is fast, whereby relevant or meaningful relationships are quickly perceived, decisions made, and actions taken rapidly, based on insight and intuition.[8] This latter point concurs with recent literature, in which expert pilots were found to have greater skills at extracting relevant information in shorter amounts of time and able to adapt to rapidly changing circumstances.[9] Importantly, experience was found to play a positive role in both their diagnostic abilities and mindfulness in seeking out relevant perceptual cues following inflight failures which, in turn, contributed toward more accurate and faster decision-making.[10] Finally, Meshkati and Kashe's analysis of Captain Sullenberger and Jeffrey Skiles' handling of US Airways Flight 1549 highlights adaptive expertise through "successful improvisation in the face of ambiguous information."[11]

Correlating with the literature on expert pilots' adaptive expertise is Detienne and Vernant's description of an obscure form of "intelligence" the early Greek Sophists referred to as *mètis*, i.e.[12]:

"... a type of intelligence and of thought, a way of knowing ... [which] combines flair, wisdom, forethought, subtlety of mind, resourcefulness, vigilance, opportunism, various skills and experience acquired over years. It is applied to situations which are transient, shifting, disconcerting and ambiguous."

Raphals refers to such metic intelligence as a "general knack for handling, whatever comes along."[13] In emphasizing its ability to deal with ambiguous situations, Baumard refers to *mètis* as "multiple and polymorphous."[14] While *mètis* "spurns idealizations and established representations it also embraces the knowledge of rules and procedures, that is "knowing-what," as long as they are not considered in isolation or as "stand-alone" — i.e. stripped of all contextual relevance and meaning.[15] Such "know-what" is also integrated with "know-how" and "know-when," whereby conceptual and practical knowledge co-emerge as non-idealized relationships applicable to contextualized or situational events, that is to say, as prudent rules-of thumb.[16] "Knowing how and when to apply the rules of thumb in a concrete situation is the essence of *mètis*."[17]

Mètis' "know-when" involves speed or swiftness when required, yet always mixed with a sufficient depth of both know-how and know-what acquired through experience, as explained by Detienne and Vernant[18]:

> "Mètis is impulsive, swift, but in no way does it act lightly. With all the weight of acquired experience that it carries, it involves thought that is dense, rich and compressed … it anchors the wind securely in the project which it has devised in advance thanks to its ability to look beyond the immediate present and foresee a more or less wide slice of the future."

The above quickness and depth of *mètis* rejoins the classic combination of "street smarts" and "deep smarts" — the former being the ability to quickly detect and react (i.e. adapt) to anomalies, and the latter as both a deep conceptual and practical/situational understanding of associated patterns, phenomena, and anomalies of a given domain.[19]

Mètis involves "vigilance" or "keen attention,"[20] or more precisely, a "mindful experience" by way of "mindful observation" that is called upon to achieve the required responsive anticipation and skill.[21] By mindfulness, we mean being "open to novelty, alertness to distinction, context sensitivity, multiple perspectives, and present orientation."[22] Mindfulness involves the deliberate attention toward unfolding experience of the present moment while withholding judgement.[23] In this manner, it allows for the perception of dynamic complexity within the practice-at-hand without falling into premature conceptualizations or interpretations that may be irrelevant in nature.[24] Mindfulness is both an act of learning and creativity[25]; it induces a meta-awareness of "nowness," or more precisely, an "agency of the present" — in which the "pasts and the futures" are both "experienced" and "reshaped," bringing forth a past solution creatively adapted for the future.[26] As such, we can relate this to Sullenberger's following words[27]:

> "I served in Vietnam [on military jet fighters] … and many years of manual commercial jet experience … I had to summon up from me somewhere this professional calm … and intuitively understand … the approach I needed to take. It was partly a result of my military flight training, from being a fighter pilot…even though we had never trained for this, because I had such a well-defined paradigm in my mind about how to solve any aviation emergency, I was able to impose that paradigm on this situation and turn it into a problem that I could solve."

Of particular importance is that "from a mindful perspective, one's response to a particular situation is not an attempt to make the best choice from among available options but to create options"[28]; or more simply put, "if we are mindful, we can create the context."[29] This, in a sense, also rejoins Adams and Ericsson's[30] description of expert pilot's adaptive expertise, for example, which depend on the ability to not only perceive cues (situational awareness) but also rapidly create meaningful relationships within the new situation at hand. Such adaptive expertise involves the mindful "boldness" to intervene and "create the context" to address the ambiguities of the emergency at hand[31]; or as Capt. Sullenberger explains[32]:

> "There are rare occasions ... you need to pull harder than the flight control system might otherwise allow ... to confidently ... and effectively intervene ... when the automation isn't doing what they expect."

3.3. The Relevance of Adaptive Expertise

Aristotle singled out navigation and medicine as two activities in which the adaptive expertise of *mètis* acquired through long experience, was indispensable to expert performance. "These were seen as *mètis*-laden activities in which responsiveness, improvisation, and skillful, successive approximations were required ... The problem, as Aristotle recognized, is that certain practical choices cannot, even in principle, be adequately and completely captured in a system of universal rules."[33] Adaptive expertise has been recognized as a key characteristic in expert performance within various domains such as aircraft piloting, medical care, and engineering.[34] For example, Adams and Ericsson[35] speak of expert pilots' "adaptive" expertise in regards to developing successful solutions in the face of "untrainable emergency situations"; Pusic et al.[36] refers to the criticality of adaptive expertise of expert medical practitioners in the face of "complex patients with complex needs requiring bespoke solutions"; and Pierrakos et al.[37] speak of how future engineers will require the ability to adapt quickly and engage in novel problem-solving.

Adams and Ericsson's[38] description of expert pilot adaptive expertise rejoins *mètis*' "multiple, polymorphous,"[39] "variegated and multicolored"[40] qualities, as they relate its mixture of "knowing-how," "knowing when," and "knowing-what" by way of the following performance characteristics:

(1) Rapid cognitive access to a well-organized body of conceptual and procedural knowledge.
(2) Keen, quick decisions as well as a direct perception of the proper course of action to take in a rapid and effective manner.

As already mentioned in Section 3.2, pilot adaptive expertise, such as *mètis*, is rapid, whereby relevant or meaningful relationships are quickly perceived, decisions made, and actions taken rapidly based on insight and intuition.[41] This also concurs with recent literature, in which expert pilots were found to have greater skills at extracting relevant information in shorter amounts of time and able to adapt to rapidly changing circumstances.[42] Yet, as we saw with *mètis* in Section 3.2, combined with this quickness is sufficient depth, as seen through Meshkati and Kashe's[43] analysis of Captain Sullenberger and Jeffrey Skiles' handling of US Airways Flight 1549's successful landing on the Hudson River. Here, the authors speak of "successful improvisation in the face of ambiguous information," whereby improvisation is defined as a reluctance to simplify, the ability to interpret signals in different ways and be sensitive to different variety of inputs in order to come out with new solutions addressing the ambiguous situation at hand.[44] In this sense, we also rejoin *mètis*' mindfulness, in regards to expert pilots' ability to seek out relevant perceptual cues following inflight failures which, in turn, contributed toward more accurate and faster decision-making.[45] In fact, such mindful ability an the part of expert pilots to perceive cues (situational awareness) leads to the "rapid" and "bold" "creation of meaningful relationships" within the new situation at hand.[46]

The importance of such adaptive expertise has been recognized in many other domains, including medicine and engineering.[47] For example, Croskerry[48] highlights the fact that:

"... medical error is now ranked as the third leading cause of death in the US (citing Makary and Daniel 2016) and that diagnosis failure is the major issue (citing Tehrani *et al.*, 2013) suggests that they do not. To function effectively within the constraints imposed by the complexity described here suggests that attaining the level of classic expertise will not always be enough. In fact, adaptive expertise may be what is missing in the cases where the diagnosis is missed, delayed, or wrong. The importance of adaptive expertise has been recognized in many other domains ... where one might expect less uncertainty than that found in many medical milieus."

Of particular interest is the difference between what Croskerry refers to as classic expertise and adaptive expertise — the former more commonly referred to as "routine expertise" and involving high proficiencies toward performing routine tasks at hand within a given domain, yet limited in dealing with novel or new problems.[49] On this point, Bereiter and Scardamalia[50] go further by arguing that routine experts are not "true experts" if they fail to engage in "progressive problem solving" that goes beyond routine problems of professional practice — rejoining Dreyfus and Dreyfus'[51] description of the "expert professional level" (and what they also refer to as "level 5" being the highest level of expertise) involving the ability to creatively respond to novel situations and develop appropriate responses.

3.4. Achieving Relevance Through the Creative Ambiguity (and Symbolic Transformations) of *Mètis*

As mentioned previously, the ability to determine what is relevant within new situations is a fundamental aspect of human adaptive expertise,[52] to which we have subsequently argued and developed is inherent to *mètis*.[53]

Relevance is often achieved through the use of analogies and metaphors, which involves transferring a cognitive structure from one context where it is well established to a new context where it has never been used, often providing leaps in insight.[54] This rejoins the semantic aspect of creativity through the use of metaphors, in which linguistic relevance is made beyond the literal rules and elements of syntax and semantics, and yet can still produce a comprehensible utterance.[55] Of interest is Searle's attempt to understand metaphors from a linguistic viewpoint in which he concluded that they could not be analyzed in a representational manner[56]:

"There are ... whole classes of metaphors that function without any underlying principles of similarity. It just seems to be a fact about our mental capacities that we are able to interpret certain sorts of metaphors without the application of any underlying "rules" or "principles" other than the sheer ability to make certain associations. I don't know any better way of describing these abilities than to say that they are nonrepresentational mental capacities."

A crucial factor of semantic complexity as emergent creativity is the endless diversity of interpretive perspectives or ambiguity,[57] in which "even if a common syntax is present, interpretations are often different."[58] As such, meaning and relevance between interpreting subjects transcends mere syntactic units, yet for AI, as Lorino *et al.* explain[59]:

> "The very notion of 'data' (= 'given' in Latin) assumes that the semantic problem has been solved: elementary units of meaning are presumed to exist, thanks to the syntactic structure of the representation. [Yet,] The 'elements' of an organizational system are interpreting subjects, who can permanently transform the meaning of signs and the spatial and temporal framework of their action. At any moment, the list of the system's so-called 'variables', and the semantic and pragmatic content of each one, can be modified. The first question for the inquirer is thus not the relational complexity of descriptions, but whether the system altogether is describable in a meaningful [relevant] way."

Utterances are personal and reconstructed all the time.[60] Furthermore, no utterance or no speech can be attributed to the speaker alone; it is the product of interaction between interlocutors. Or as Tsoukas, as inspired by Bakhtin, states, "an utterance has a potential to mean, but...its potential is realized through another's response."[61] As such, conversation cannot be reduced to mere "'data' processing" — it is a "dialogical meaning-making process" transcending representational syntactics inherently involving both uncertainty and ambiguity.[62]

Natural language and conversation's inherent "fog" or indeterminancy (as uncertainty and ambiguity) requires the adaptive nature of *mètis*.[63] *Mètis* is the "knowledge of ambiguity," involving both collective and individual tacit know-how as well as explicit know-what.[64] *Mètis* is "multiple and diverse" able to deal with the conversational aspects "of movement, of multiplicity, and of ambiguity."[65] To make sense and find relevance in complex and fluid situations, thinking must become more adaptive, i.e. more "supple, even more shifting, even more polymorphic" than these situations.[66] In this manner, we rejoin both Weick and

Baumard's arguments that dynamically ambiguous environments can only be dealt with a "requisite" and intentional ambiguity.[67] *Mètis'* inherent ambiguity allows it to adaptively couple to conversational ambiguity by drawing upon individual and social symbolic dimensions.[68] Needleman and Baker provide a descriptive comparison between so-called "objective," or more precisely, unequivocal concepts vs the ambiguous and emergent characteristic of artistic symbols[69]:

> "A scientific notion has an unequivocal meaning and, in the exact sciences, a mathematical form, in the sense of course, of quantitative mathematics. On the other hand, a symbol can never be taken in a final and definite meaning … a symbol itself possesses an endless number of aspects from which it can be examined and it demands from a man approaching it the ability to see it simultaneously from different points of views … A symbol can never be fully interpreted. It can only be experienced."

Symbols are a means of complex communication that can have multiple levels of meaning (multivocal and polysemic), some of which are ineffable and non-representational in a manner similar to metaphors — which is different from signs (or data), as signs have only one meaning.[70] According to Tillich, there has been a great deal of confusion between signs and symbols. More specifically[71]:

> "The mathematician has usurped the term 'symbol' for mathematical 'sign', and this makes a disentanglement of the confusion almost impossible. The only thing we can do is to distinguish different groups, signs which are called symbols, and genuine symbols. The mathematical signs are signs which are wrongly called symbols."

Words or sentences in languages can be both signs (which are purely representational) and symbols (which can be both representational and non-representational in nature), whereby they can either point to one explicit meaning or to multiple levels of explicit and ineffable meanings.[72] "Peter hit Paul" or "Paul was hit by Peter" say approximately the same thing whereby the identity of meaning is attributable to the grammatical transformation rule from active to passive verb form.[73] Yet, to recognize that "every rose has thorns" and "there are no unmixed blessings" goes beyond formal grammar and semantic rules — it involves symbolic transformations, "a jungle, whose depth psychologists have been valiantly attempting to chart."[74] Symbols in narratives, with their multi-meaning and ambiguous sense, allow readers to activate personal, prior, and oftentimes tacit knowledge as well as engage in active transformation and processing.[75] More importantly, narratives, by way of symbols, allow humans to "make meaning and to forge connections between seemingly disparate bits of knowledge and experience" — or in other words, creatively achieve relevance across open-ended ambiguity.[76]

Of particular interest is on how symbols (as opposed to mathematical or algorithmic signs) can suscitate creativity by way of hard to explicate (i.e. tacit) emotions and imaginations.[77] In this manner, Kuuva speaks specifically of "experiencing" symbols, thus depicting its embodied non-representational aspect.[78]

3.5. A Few Words on Creativity

Creativity has often been defined as the ability and process of creating something new (in the sense of novelty) and useful.[79] Boden defines creativity as the ability to generate ideas or artefacts that are new, surprising, and valuable.[80] Seyidov has argued that human creativity is inherently paradoxical — in trying to isolate and model creativity, we impose rules and generalities to it, keeping in mind that creativity abhors rules in the first place.[81] The end result, according to Seyidov, is that when we try to capture creativity by both choosing and setting variables associated to it, creativity dissipates within our hands. Researchers have acknowledged its complex and interdisciplinary character.[82] In cognitive psychology, for example, creativity has been examined from different angles, such as the role of traditional intelligence as well as emotions in relations to creativity.[83] More specifically, a minimal level of traditional intelligence (IQ) was found to be a necessary, yet insufficient condition for creative potential[84]; while there can be emotional variations involved in creative processes, the converse can also be true, in that creative processes can, in turn, generate emotions.[85]

Of particular interest is on how symbols (as opposed to signs) can generate (or more precisely, enact) creativity.[86] For example, Kuuva speaks specifically of "experiencing" symbols.[87] Here, Kuuva shows specifically how visual symbols evoke artistic creativity by way of hard-to-explicate emotions and imaginations. Furthermore, creativity is viewed as having both a conscious, intentional, and controlled aspect as well as an unconscious, random, and unpredictable dimension.[88] Symbols invoke not only explicit associations, but also emotional concepts related to bodily or embodied experiences in the form of sensations and motor activities,[89] keeping in mind that we are constantly attempting to correspond formal representations or explicit knowledge (concepts, models, etc.) with actual experiences of our senses (i.e. tacit embodied non-representational knowledge).[90] However, creativity has to do with generating new or novel ideas and outputs. It is insufficient to just say that we become creative by having an experienced symbol invoke existing tacit and explicit knowledge that resides within us — otherwise, we are simply speaking of "creativity" in the sense of combinations of existing entities and processes. Boden, on the other hand, argues that individuals create new knowledge when there is already a fundamental base of tacit knowledge upon which to draw upon.[91] Along these lines, Alony and Jones show, by way of a qualitative ethnographic study, how, in the Australian film business, tacit knowledge residing within various film workers and specialists is transformed into new ideas which in themselves carry both an explicit and tacit (i.e. ineffable non-representational) dimension.[92] This synthesis of both the tacit and explicit realms is further highlighted across researchers who have looked at what is known as "embodied cognition" involving a synthesis of both mind and body and its importance on how it helps us address mathematical concepts through both visual and sensory-motor memories.[93] Here, we posture, gesture, point, and use tools when expressing mathematical ideas as evidence of our holding mathematical ideas in the motor and perceptual areas of the brain — whereby, when explaining ideas, even when we do not have the words we need, we tend to draw shapes in the air.[94] Hence, the body, which contains a great deal of tacit knowledge,[95] is an intrinsic part of cognition (which we shall return to in Chapter 6 across a more detailed examination of embodied cognition).

When we return to Boden's definition of creative ideas and artefacts needing to be new, surprising, and valuable, we begin to appreciate the complexity and challenges involved. Coming out with something new is not enough.[96] The manipulation of explicit signs (which is what AI algorithms do) may well give us a new combination never thought of before, yet is not considered truly creative.[97] This is the case, for example, with IBM's Chef Watson, in which through machine learning processes data (to the equivalent of approx. 10,000 cooking recipes) and combines these to achieve new recipes satisfying predefined cooking styles (whether Mediterranean, Asian, Italian, etc.).[98] It is at best, only pseudo-creative in achieving combinatorial creativity, yet is not transformationally creative by going into "uncharted" territories.[99] One must achieve an idea/artefact which produces a surprise in regards to existing social practices and beliefs, as well as value in regards to these same social beliefs and values. This is exactly what Boden refers to as being able to achieve an idea or artefact that is relevant.[100] Being able to achieve something significant and relevant requires knowledge of such social beliefs, values, and practices that are highly tacit (and often distributed) in nature, which Collins refers to as collective (or strong) tacit knowledge.[101] This is also why, according to Boden, who has worked on machine creativity, AI cannot be as creative as humans since machines cannot determine what is relevant within realms that have not yet been defined. This is because AI algorithms cannot conduct symbolic transformations (i.e. the creative enactment of relevance starting from an open-open ended ambiguity), but only manipulate explicit representational signs.[102]

In the next chapter...

In the next chapter, we shall examine some of the historic as well as psychological underpinnings involving our strong and sometimes "mindless" adherence to, as well as quest for, knowledge as representations.[103]

References

Makary, M.A. and Daniel, M. (2016). Medical error-the third leading cause of death in the US. *BMJ*, **353**, i2139.

Tehrani, A.S.S., Lee, H.W., Mathews, S.C., Shore, A., Makary, M.A., Pronovost, P.J. and Newman-Toker, D.E. (2013). 25-year summary of US malpractice claims for diagnostic errors 1986–2010: An analysis from the National Practitioner Data Bank. *BMJ Quality & Safety*, **22**, 672–680.

Endnotes

[1] See Dreyfus, H.L. (2007). Why Heideggerian AI failed and how fixing it would require making it more Heidegerrian. *Artificial Intelligence*, **171**(18), 1137–1160.

[2] Citing Adams, R.J. and Ericsson, A.E. (2000), Introduction to cognitive processes of expert pilots. *Journal of Human Performance in Extreme Environments*, **5**(1), 44–62. DOI: 10.7771/2327-2937.1006.

³ See Wachter, B. (2015). My interview with Capt. Sully Sullenberger: On aviation, medicine and technology. *The Hospital Leader*, February 23. Available at: https://thehospitalleader.org/my-interview-with-capt-sully-sullenberger-on-aviation-medicine-and-technology/.
⁴ Wickens, C.D. and Dehais, F. (2019). Expertise in Aviation. In *The Oxford Handbook of Expertise* in Ward, P, Schraagen, J.M., Gore, J. and Roth, E.M. (Eds), pp. 662–689 (Oxford, UK: Oxford University Press).
⁵ Citing Adams, R.J. and Ericsson, A.E. (2000, p. 53) (note 2).
⁶ Citing Adams and Ericsson (2000, p. 48) (note 2).
⁷ Citing Adams and Ericsson (2000, p. 58) (note 2); the authors also refer to Dreyfus, H.L. and Dreyfus, S.E. (1986). *Mind Over Machine* (New York, NY: The Free Press) regarding "knowing how," "knowing what," and "knowing when."
⁸ See Adams and Ericsson (2000, p. 60) (note 2).
⁹ See Li, W.-C., Chiu, F.-C., Kuo, Y. and Wu, K.-J. (2013). The investigation of visual attention and workload by experts and novices in the cockpit. In: *International Conference on Engineering Psychology and Cognitive Ergonomics*, Springer, pp. 167–176.
¹⁰ See Wickens and Dehais (2019, note 4) as well as Schriver, A.T., Morrow, D.G., Wickens, C.D. and Talleur, D.A. (2008). Expertise differences in attentional strategies related to pilot decision making. *Human Factors*, **50**(6), 864–878.
¹¹ Citing Meshkati, N. and Khashe, Y. (2015). Operators' improvisation in complex technological systems: Successfully tackling ambiguity, enhancing resiliency and the last resort to averting disaster. *Journal of Contingencies and Crisis Management*, **23**(2), 90–96.
¹² Citing Detienne, M. and Vernant, J.P. (1978). Les ruses de l'intélligence. La mètis des Grecs. Flammarion, Paris, p. 4.
¹³ Citing Raphals, L. (1992). *Knowing Words. Wisdom and Cunning in the Classical Tradition of China and Greece*, p. xi (Ithaca, NY: Cornell University Press).
¹⁴ Baumard, P. (1999). *Tacit Knowledge in Organizations* (London: Sage Publications), p. 65.
¹⁵ Citing Baumard (1999, p. 54) (note 14).
¹⁶ See both Baumard (1999) (note 14) and Scott, J.C. (1998). *Seeing Like a State: How Certain Schemes to Improve the Human State have Failed* (Binghamton, NY: Vail-Ballou Press).
¹⁷ Citing Scott (1998, p. 317) (note 16).
¹⁸ Citing Detienne and Vernant (1978, p. 8) (note 12).
¹⁹ For informal nature of situational "street smarts," see Hatt, B. (2016). Street smarts vs. book smarts: The figured world of smartness in the lives of marginalized urban youth. *Urban Review*, **39**(2), 145–166; for internalized nature of "deep

smarts" consisting of in-depth situational knowledge such as personal "rules of thumb" and intuitions emerging from experience, see Leonard, D. and Swap W. (2004). Deep smarts. *Harvard Business Review*, **30**(2), 157–169; the development and subsequent mobilization of "street smarts" and "deep smarts" by proficient professionals is well described by Dreyfus, H.L. and Dreyfus, S.E. (2005). Peripheral vision expertise in real world contexts. *Organization Studies*, **26**(5), 779–792.

[20] See Detienne and Vernant (1978, p. 4) (note 12).

[21] *Mètis* as mindful experience and mindful observation is described by both Raphals (1992, p. xi) (note 13) and Aftel, M. (2014). *Fragrant: The Secret Life of Scent* (New York: Penguin Books), while Baumard (1999) (note 14) refers to this as responsive anticipation (and skill).

[22] See Siegel, D.J. (2007). *The Mindful Brain. Reflection and Attunement in the Cultivation of Well-being* (New York, NY: Norton).

[23] Guiette, A. and Vandenbempt, K. (2016). Learning in times of dynamic complexity through balancing phenomenal qualities of sensemaking. *Management Learning*, **47**(1), 83–99.

[24] *Ibid.*

[25] See Langer, E.J. (2000). Mindful learning. *Current Directions in Psychological Science*, **9**(2), 220–223.

[26] See Hernes, T. (2014). *A Process Theory of Organization* (Oxford, UK: Oxford University Press).

[27] See Wachter (2015) (note 3).

[28] Citing Langer, E. (1997). *The Power of Mindful Learning* (Cambridge, MA: Da Capo Press), p. 133.

[29] Citing Langer, E. (2009). *Counter Clockwise. Mindful Health and the Power of Possibility* (London, UK: Hodder & Stoughton).

[30] See Adams and Ericsson (2000, pp. 54–55) (note 2).

[31] As per both Meshkati and Khashe (2015, p. 95) (note 11) and Langer (2009, p. 182) (note 29).

[32] See Wachter (2015) (note 3).

[33] Citing Scott (1998, p. 322) (note 16).

[34] For aircraft pilots, see Adams and Ericsson (2000) (note 2); for medical physicians, see Pusic, M.V. *et al.* (2018). Learning to balance efficiency and innovation for optimal adaptive expertise, *Medical Teacher*, **40**(8), 820–827, https://doi.org/10.1080/0142159X.2018.1485887; and for engineers, see Pierrakosa, O., Welch, C.A. and Anderson, R.D. (2016). Measuring adaptive expertise in engineering education. In *2016 ASEE Southeast Section Conference*, Paper ID. 17095.

[35] Citing Adams and Ericsson (2000, p. 48) (note 2).

[36] Citing Pusic *et al.* (2018, p. 820) (note 33).

[37] See Pierrakos *et al.* (2016) (note 34).

[38] See Adams and Ericsson (2000, p. 58, 60) (note 2), who also cites Dreyfus and Dreyfus (1986) in relation to "knowing how," "knowing what" and "knowing when."

[39] See Baumard (1999, p. 65) (note 14).

[40] See Raphals (1992, p. 6) (note 13).

[41] See Adams and Ericsson (2000, p. 60) (note 5).

[42] See Li, W.-C., Chiu, F.-C., Kuo, Y. and Wu, K.-J. (2013). The investigation of visual attention and workload by experts and novices in the cockpit. In: *International Conference on Engineering Psychology and Cognitive Ergonomics*, Springer, pp. 167–176.

[43] See Meshkati and Khashe (2015) (note 11).

[44] Citing Meshkati and Khashe (2015, p. 91) (note 11).

[45] See both Wickens and Dehaie (2019) (note 4) and Schriver, A.T., Morrow, D.G., Wickens, C.D. and Talleur, D.A. (2008). Expertise differences in attentional strategies related to pilot decision making. *Human Factors*, **50**(6), 864–878.

[46] Citing both Adams and Ericsson (2000, pp. 58–59) (note 2) and Meshkati and Khashe (2015, p. 95) (note 11).

[47] Adaptive expertise in engineering is described by Hicks, N.M., Bumbaco, A.E., Douglas, E.P. (2014). Critical thinking, reflective practice, and adaptive expertise in engineering. *121st ASEE Annual Conference and Exposition*, (Indianapolis, IN: USA); In medicine, see Croskerry, P. (2018). Adaptive expertise in medical decision making, *Medical Teacher*, **40**(8), 803–808. https://doi.org/10.1080/0142159X.2018.1484898; and for professions in general, see Hatano, G. and Inagaki, K. (1986). Two courses of expertise. In *Child Development and Education in Japan*, Stevenson. H., Azuma, H. and Hakuta, K. (eds.) (New York, NY: Freeman), pp. 262–272.

[48] Citing Croskerry (2018, p. 806) (note 47).

[49] See both Adams and Ericsson (2000) (note 2) and Hatano and Inagaki (1986) (note 47).

[50] See Bereiter C. and Scardamalia M. (1993). *Surpassing Ourselves* (Chicago, IL: Open Court Press).

[51] See Dreyfus and Dreyfus (2005) (note 19).

[52] As per Adams and Ericsson (2000) (note 2), Wickens and Dehais (2019) (note 4) and Li *et al.* (2013) (note 42).

[53] As per Scott (1998) (note 16) and Baumard (1999) (note 14).

[54] See Dunbar, K. (1995). How scientists really reason: Scientific reasoning in real-world laboratories. In *The Nature of Insights*, Sternberg, R.J. and Davidson, J.E. (eds.) (Cambridge, MA: The MIT Press), pp. 365–395.

[55] For the use of metaphors in language and conversation, see Ortony, A. (1979). *Metaphor and Thought* (Cambridge, UK: Cambridge University Press); Mooij, J.J.A. (1976). *A Study of Metaphor* (Amsterdam: North Holland); Ricoeur, P. (1978). *The Rule of Metaphor* (London, UK: Kegan Paul) as well as Pedriali, W.B. (2017). Speaking images: Chomsky and Ricoeur on linguistic creativity. *Ricoeur Studies*, **8**(1), 83–110.

[56] Citing Searle, J.R. (1983). *Intentionality: An Essay in the Philosophy of Mind* (Cambridge, UK: Cambridge University Press).

[57] See Cussins, A. (1992). Content, embodiment and objectivity. The theory of cognitive trails. *Mind*, 101(404), 651–688.

[58] Citing Carlile, P.R. (2002). A pragmatic view of knowledge and boundaries: Boundary objects in new product development. *Organization Science*, 13(4), 442–455.

[59] Citing Lorino, P., Tricard, B. and Clot, Y. (2011). Research methods for non-representational approaches to organizational complexity: The dialogical mediated inquiry. *Organization Studies*, 32(6), 769–801.

[60] See Tsoukas, H. (2009). A dialogical approach to the creation of new knowledge in organizations. *Organization Science*, 20(6), 941–953.

[61] *Opt cit.*, p. 944.

[62] Citing Lorino *et al.* (2011, p. 793) (note 59).

[63] See Baumard (1999) (note 14).

[64] *Ibid.*

[65] Citing Detienne and Vernant (1978, p. 18, 20) (note 12).

[66] *Opt cit.*, p. 20

[67] See Baumard (1999) (note 14) and Weick, K.E. (2015). Ambiguity as grasp: The reworking of sense. *Journal of Contingencies and Crisis Management*, 23(2), 117–123.

[68] See Needleman, J. and Baker, G. (2004). *Gurdjieff: Essays and Reflections on the Man and His Teachings* (New York, NY: Continuum).

[69] *Opt cit.*, p. 55.

[70] See Womack, M. (2005). *Symbols and Meaning* (New York: Altamira Press).

[71] Citing Tillich, P. (1987). *The Essential Tillich* (Chicago, IL: The University of Chicago Press), p. 46.

[72] See *Ibid.* as well as Clancey, W.J. (1997). *Situated Cognition: On Human Knowledge and Computer Representations* (Cambridge UK: Cambridge University Press).

[73] See Rapoport, A. (1969). The impact of cybernetic ideas on psychology. *Kybernetica*, 5(5), 363–377.

[74] *Opt cit.*, p. 373

[75] See Graesser, A.C. and McMahen, C.L. (1993). Anomalous information triggers questions when adults solve quantitative problems and comprehend stories. *Journal of Educational Psychology*, 85(1), 136–151.

[76] Citing Blyler, N. and Perkins, J. (1999). Culture and the power of narrative. *Journal of Business and Technical Communication*, 13(3), 245–248.

[77] See Kuuva, S. (2010). Symbol, Munch and Creativity. Metabolism of Visual Symbols. Academic Dissertation, University of Jyvaskyla, Jyvaskyla Studies in Humanities.

[78] *Opt cit.*, p. 178.

79 See Amabile, T.M. (1996). *Creativity in Context* (Boulder, CO: Westview Press).

80 See Boden, M.A. (2004). *The Creative Mind: Myths and Mechanisms*. 2nd Edition, expanded/revised (London: Routledge).

81 See Seyidov, S. (2013). *Phenomenology of Creativity* (London: Author-House UK).

82 See Pearson, A.W. and Ingleton, C.C.P. (1994). Measuring and improving creativity and innovation. In *Total Quality Measurement in the Oil Industry*, Symonds J.D. (ed.) (Dordrecht: Springer), pp. 120–142.

83 See Runco, M.A. (2007). *Creativity. Theories and Themes: Research, Development and Practice* (London: Elsevier Academic Press).

84 As per both Runco (2007) (note 83) and Jauk, E., Benedek, M., Dunst, B. and Neubauer, A.C. (2013). The relationship between intelligence and creativity: New support for the threshold hypothesis by means of empirical breakpoint detection. *Intelligence*, 41(4), 212–221.

85 See Runco (2007, p. 121) (note 83).

86 See Kuuva (2010) (note 77).

87 *Ibid.*, p. 178.

88 See Runco (2007) (note 83).

89 See both Womack (2005) (note 70) and Kupers, W. (2008). Embodied "inter-learning" — an integral phenomenology of learning in and by organizations. *The Learning Organization*, 15(5), 388–408.

90 See Tsoukas, H. (2003). Do we really understand tacit knowledge. In *The Blackwell Handbook of Organizational Learning and Knowledge Management*, Easterby-Smith, M. and Lyles, M. (eds.) (New York: Blackwell), pp. 410–427.

91 Citing Boden (2004, p. 12) (note 80).

92 See Alony, I. and Jones, M. (2007). Tacit knowledge, explicability and creativity — A study of the Australian film industry, University of Wollongong (Australia), Working Paper. Available at: http://sitem.hertz.ac.uk/artdes_research/papers/wpdesign/index.html.

93 See Nemirovski, R., Rasmussen, C., Sweeney, G. and Wawro, M. (2012). When the classroom floor becomes the complex plane: Addition and multiplications as ways of bodily navigation. *Journal of the Learning Sciences*, 21(2), 287–323.

94 See both Nemirovski *et al.* (2012) (note 93) and Alibaba, M.W. and Nathan, M.J. (2012). Embodiment in the mathematics teaching and learning: Evidence from learners' and teachers' gestures. *Journal of the Learning Sciences*, 21(2), 247–286.

95 See Tsoukas (2003) (note 90).

96 See Boden (2004) (note 90).

97 See both Boden (2004) (note 90) and Boden, M.A. (1998). Creativity and artificial intelligence. *Artificial Intelligence*, 103, 347–356.

[98] See Pinel, F. (2015). What's cooking with Chef Watson? An interview with Lav Varshney and James Briscione. *IEEE Pervasive Computing*, **14**(4), 58–62.

[99] See Boden (1998) (note 97).

[100] See Boden, M.A. (2010). *Creativity and Art: Three Roads to Surprise* (Oxford: Oxford University Press).

[101] See Collins, H. (2010). *Tacit and Explicit Knowledge* (Chicago, IL: University of Chicago Press).

[102] See both Boden (2010) (note 100) and Boden, M.A. (2015). *Artificial Intelligence* (Boston: MIT Technology Review).

[103] See Langer, E.J. (1989). *Mindfulness* (Cambridge, MA: Perseus Books).

Chapter 4

Historic Underpinnings to Our Quest for Knowledge Representations

4.1. Introduction

In this chapter, we review certain historic underpinnings to "our" continued quest for knowledge representations. While certain Far Eastern traditions viewed the tacit and embodied aspects of human expertise as a holistic whole that could not be "captured" (abstracted), "isolated" (categorized), and "converted" into an explicit form,[1] "our," in contemporary terms, is more or less global in connotation. As we shall first see, Socrates, Plato, and Aristotle played important roles toward Western rational and empirical abstractionism by way of both the idea of the universal (as positivistic generalizations) and categories.[2] As a result, establishing explicit rules and representations on the nature of "things" and processes has become our predominant priority by materializing itself into Artificial Intelligence (AI) as well as Information Technology/Information Systems (IT/IS) expert system approaches.[3] In parallel, alternative holistic, relativistic, and hard-to-categorize "direct" (i.e. non-representational) perspectives, as inspired by the Sophists' view on *mètis* have, to a large extent, been repressed in Western thought. Interestingly, such hard-to-classify expertise has re-entered contemporary debates through various interpretations of Aristotle's *phronesis,* including but not limited to, both phenomenology and AI philosophy.[4]

4.2. Socrates, Plato, and Aristotle's Contribution to Western Rational and Empirical Abstractionism

It is often said that ancient Greek philosophers greatly influenced Western intellectual tradition.[5] While mention is made of the different philosophies and thinking which rivalled and competed with one another, starting from Thales to the Stoics and the Skeptics, many agree that it is Socrates, Plato, and Aristotle's thinking which left an "everlasting mark" on Western society.[6] According to Whitehead, "the safest general characterization of the European philosophical tradition is that it consists of a series of footnotes to Plato."[7] In a similar spirit, Dreyfus argues that Socrates and Plato greatly influenced "mainstream" cognitive sciences in which Socrates assumed that "intelligence is based on principles and ... Plato ... [added] the requirement that these principles must be strict rules, not based on taken-for-granted background understanding."[8] In turn, science's interpretation of Aristotle's *Categories* played a fundamental role in its quest for classifications and certainty.[9]

Both Socrates and Plato had explicit preferences for the life of reason and rational thought, and more specifically, the search for knowledge associated with the search for universal Truth. Plato saw knowledge-as-truth across the concept of universal objects of knowledge known as *Forms* (*The Republic VII*). *Forms*, being a-spatial and a-temporal, became the "objective blueprints," i.e. the purest *representations* for perfection of all things. In turn, true knowledge, or *intelligence*, became the mind's ability to grasp and justify the world of *Forms* as being true by way of the rational thought (and rules) of dialectics (*noesis*).[10]

For Plato, particular "things" and "beings" change in the material world, while *Forms* remain separate, unchanging, and universal. Let us take the example of *Perfect Universal Dog* as a *Form*. Through sensory observations, we know that "Lassie is a dog" — which we then *rationally* compare to knowledge of the perfect concept (or *Form*) of a *Perfect Universal Dog*. Lassie is not a *Perfect Universal Dog*, yet contains universal "dogness," which is not just in Lassie, but in other things. The *Perfect Universal Dog represents* the "commensurate universal," which all the particulars have in common to various degrees. Hence, the *Perfect Universal Dog* becomes *the perfect* model, as an abstract representation of perfection.[11] This, of course, is in contrast to the holistic pragmatic view of reality which considers models as *approximations* (i.e. approximate abstractions), and not perfect versions, of the material.[12]

Aristotle also viewed knowledge as being what is true and justified through the rational logic of dialectics (*noesis*) — yet differed with Plato as to where truth resided. Aristotle's argument was that truth is *within* the material world, and *not* in an otherworldly or "ideal" place. This differentiated Aristotle's empiricism with Plato's extreme rationalism. Yet, Aristotle's inauguration of *Categories*, which would eventually have a deep influence on Western philosophical thought, became another form of abstractionism, this time by way of classifications.[13]

4.3. The Rise of Absolute Rules and Representations

Plato's theory of forms led to the knowledge of forms, i.e. of the what, the why, and the where absolute truths resided, which he and Socrates referred to as *episteme*. Plato was also fascinated by the idea of a kind of *techne* that is informed by *episteme* — i.e. a knowledge in the form of rules associated with knowing how to do certain activities, in which *episteme* would indicate its theoretical aspects.[14] Both *episteme* and *techne's* legacy in the form of linguistically coded mental representation-as-rules was later reinforced by Descartes, who believed that knowledge could be gained independently of the body's senses through reason, the latter being superior to the body's sense experience as a source of knowledge.[15]

Socrates' and Plato's quest for universal rules and tenets to describe knowledge which experts and professionals in their respective domains "possessed" eventually served as inspiration for symbolic AI's "knowledge engineers" such as Feigenbaum and McCorduck, who argued that "almost all the thinking that professionals do is by [heuristic rules of] reasoning."[16] Dreyfus and Dreyfus later criticized such "expert system" perspectives by arguing that they failed to capture situational complexities and ambiguities of an expert in action — "the expert is simply not following any [hard and fast] rules! He or she is doing just what Socrates and Feigenbaum feared — discriminating thousands of special cases."[17]

Platonic abstractionism residing within an ideal realm had also found renewed traction through Roy Bhaskar's critical realism (along with a number of British social theorists, including Margaret Archer, Mervyn Hartwig, Tony Lawson, Alan Norrie, and Andrew Saye), i.e. a neo-platonic and essentialist belief that there exists an absolute and immanent reality that is "mind-independent" in nature and provides the fundamental "condition of possibility" for natural science in the form of an ultimate *episteme*.[18] While this book does not provide any opinion for or against Bhaskar's position of a possible accessibility to "ultimate truths" as an ideal, it is the misinterpretations of his views and approach in numerous domains and spheres of IS and IT which we question. However, before addressing this directly, we return to the Aristotelian thought of classifications, which influenced Western science by way of an "order of nature and an order of things."[19] Here, Dewey specifically objected to the positivistic and essentialist tone (albeit, empirical) applied to classifications.[20] As such, two issues converge — namely, positivism and categorizations — into contemporary interpretations of critical realism as applied within the domains of IS/IT.

While Bhaskar believed an absolute truth existed, he emphasized there was no guarantee that one (or society) could attain it easily, or attain it at all, despite the conceptual and methodological roadmap he proposed.[21] One of the first steps to be carried out within his dialectical approach is to analyze the world into discrete structures, such as "human persons" or "social networks" — hence, analogous to Hegel's thesis.[22] Here, many IS practitioners of critical realism erroneously assume that once structures have been "identified," they become "more or less" permanently stabilized.[23] Yet, Bhaskar was quite clear as to the next step: "we proceed by thinking through how interactions between these structures lead to changes in their properties or relationships or even to the emergence of new structures."[24] Hence, categories are not just "more or less" modified, but can be completely restructured into new entities as a result of interactions — hence, analogous to Hegel's antithesis. This particular aspect of his approach is not far off from Barad's agential realist dynamic process of material-discursive enactment into new agential cuts, as we shall later see in Chapter 8. In a similar spirit, Bhaskar also recognized science to be "a human activity that is inevitably mediated (if not determined) by human language and social power."[25] From an operational point of view, the back and forth between thesis and antithesis was meant to be carried out in almost endless fashion, yet in practice, has been often halted after the establishment of a "first thesis."[26]

4.4. Repression of the Sophistic Perspective

Contrary to both Plato and Aristotle, the Sophists did not believe in the notion of knowledge as truth by way of either an absolute ideal separate to the material world (Plato) or of an absolute category within the material world.[27] Across both Gorgias and Protagoras, the Sophists adopted both a subjective and constructivist posture. According to Gorgias, "nothing exists ... if something does exist, we cannot know it" — humans cannot transcend their languages and cultural systems, and as such, cannot obtain any absolute viewpoint.[28] Furthermore, "if we come to know it, we cannot teach it to others." Rejoining this latter point, is Protagoras' "man is the measure of all things," leading to the relativistic argument of two different viewpoints being simultaneously valid — e.g. air can be hot for one and cold for the other.[29]

Sophists were especially skilled in the practical application of rhetoric toward civic and political life.[30] More specifically, the Sophists were often able of rendering the weaker argument stronger, through a keen awareness of change, and a capacity to respond adaptively to it, which Détienne and Vernant refer to as *mètis*.[31] Yet, nowhere in Greece do we find any written theory relating to the cunning intelligence and ambiguous nature of *mètis*[32]:

> "Although *mètis* operates within so vast a domain, although it holds such an important position within the Greek system of values, it is never made manifest for what it is, it is never clearly revealed in a theoretical work that aims to define it ... There is no doubt that *mètis* is a type of intelligence and of thought, a way of knowing; it implies a complex but very coherent body of mental attitudes and intellectual behaviour which combine flair, wisdom, forethought, subtlety of mind, deception, resourcefulness, vigilance, opportunism, various skills and experience acquired over the years."

According to Julien, the only way Detienne and Vernant could identify *mètis* was through their hermeneutical study of myths, "where it is detectable but always more or less below the surface, immersed in practical operations that, even when they use it, show no concern to make its nature explicit or to justify its procedures."[33] Although the Sophists attempted to philosophize on its nature, *mètis* was soon suppressed, whereby the very term itself disappeared from the Greek language.[34] Plato intentionally ignored *mètis*, keeping it aside in his Gnoseological Theory.[35] Rather, he embraced *episteme*, considering it as the highest form of knowledge — and resisted all "intuitive" shades that could somehow "blemish" its rational light.[36] As such, Plato viewed unarticulated/uncodified practical knowledge as inferior in that it did not make use of Dialectical Reason (*noesis*), while also being linked to the body and senses — the so-called "Dionysiac" forms which Plato considered as inferior and non-virtuous.

Plato saw reality as a world of pre-existent *Being*, in which invention was brought about solely by discovery of what already existed.[37] The Sophists, on the other hand, considered the importance of practice in its own right in which construction and creation could lead to distinct novelty. This involved an emergent world of *Becoming* in which *mètis* played a central role.[38] In an informal (unwritten) manner, *mètis* remained central to the Greek system of values, despite it being officially suppressed by subsequent Platonic traditions, which emphasized a world of *Being* "both in the philosophy of the Greeks themselves and in their successors."[39] As of the fifth century AD, *mètis* was relegated to the shadows,[40] while Western rationalism and empiricism continued to build upon Plato and Aristotle's legacy of both universal and categorical abstractions.[41] As Scott explains[42]:

> "... universalist claims seem inherent in the way in which rationalist knowledge is pursued. ... there seems to be no door in this epistemic edifice through which *mètis* or practical knowledge could enter on its own terms. It is this imperialism that is troubling ... the great failure of rationalism is not its recognition of technical knowledge, but its failure to recognize any other. By contrast, *mètis* does not put all its eggs in one basket; it makes no claim to universality and in this sense is pluralistic."

Although formally cast out as knowledge in its own right, *mètis* remained present in everyday work life throughout the ages through the emergence and evolution of various arts and crafts and their associated guilds.[43]

4.5. The Interesting Case of Aristotle's Phronesis — Representational or Non-Representational?

Aristotle, like Plato, emphasized the superiority of *episteme* and *techne* as the foundation of "proper knowledge,"[44] in which he presented a coherent rationality or *reasoning* in the form of true logical statements about what exists in regards to both *episteme*, as linguistically articulated generalizations using propositional forms, and *techne,* as precise, measurable, codifiable instructions.[45] Aristotle eventually referred to *techne* as also being *episteme* in that he viewed it as a practice grounded in an account — i.e. practice articulated in terms of theoretical knowledge.[46]

For Aristotle, it was not so much being "practically competent or 'hands-on' that made one knowledgeable, but possession of a detached universal understanding of the underlying causes of phenomena. Despite the differences in their emphasis, both Plato and Aristotle assumed that knowledge could only be called so if it was logically and rigorously arrived at — and presupposed the possession of mental representations mirroring an external reality."[47]

Interestingly, Aristotle also spoke of *phronesis,* or "practical wisdom" in a somewhat ambiguous manner. For example, Chia states "Aristotle also posited (though less emphatically) the existence of *phronesis* (practical wisdom) as a form of personal knowing which differs qualitatively from *episteme* and *techne* but which nevertheless shapes and disposes an individual and 'expresses the kind of person that one is.'"[48] Furthermore, one can argue that an important connection can be made between sophistic *mètis* and *phronesis* — yet, Aristotle "displaced and devalued" *mètis.*[49] In the Nicomachean Ethics, *phronesis* is roughly translated as prudence, which is shared with *mètis,*[50] and when it is defined, it shares additional adjectives (such as "acuity" and "acumen") in common.[51] On the other hand, Dolmage[52] argues that Aristotle's

> "... *phronesis* is linked more closely to *episteme* (or scientific knowledge) and is regulated by habits of character with the goal of 'truth' and wisdom, while *mètis* has the freedom to be less moral and seeks an isolated result. In this way, *phronesis* 'rises above *mètis*' (citing Halverson, 2004: 47) ... we have generally accepted the idea that mètis is 'bad' *phronesis,* that cunning intelligence must be made more systematic and epistemic to be acceptable. This also requires a certain disembodiment of this form of intelligence, at least to the degree that its bodily entailments must also be made standard."

Aristotle refers to a person with *phronesis* as "able to deliberate nobly about what is good and beneficial."[53] Practical wisdom is achieved through a process of pedagogical thinking and reasoning — a cognitive process of reflecting on practice, such as "what am I doing?" and "can I do this better?"[54] It has a praxeological reasoning in regards to how one should act (Hacking, 2002: 3). In other words, an ethical virtue (*eudaimonia*) in regards to "the capacity to act based on reasoning with regard to things that are good or bad for humanity."[55]

Interestingly, John McDowell,[56] a notable proponent of direct realism, also refers to *phronesis* in the same light

> "... the right sort of thing to serve as a model for the understanding, the faculty that enables us to recognize and create the kind of intelligibility that is a matter of placement in the space of reasons."

Interestingly, direct realism views the world as being qualitatively identical with our perceptions, senses, and conceptions. Furthermore, as Esfeld points out, direct realism has become "fashionable" in that it appears to "avoid the gap between thought and world that is a major issue in modern philosophy."[57] However, according to McDowell, rational conceptions is second-natured[58]:

> "We need to recognize the Aristotelian idea that the normal mature human being is a rational animal, but without losing the Kantian idea that rationality operates freely in its own sphere. The Kantian idea is reflected in the contrast between the organization of the space of reasons and the structure of the realm of law. Modern naturalism is forgetful of second nature; if we try to preserve the Kantian thought that reason is autonomous within the framework of that kind of naturalism, we disconnect our rationality from our animal being, which is what gives us our foothold in nature ... *we need to see ourselves as animals whose natural being is permeated with rationality, even though rationality is appropriately conceived in Kantian terms.*"

Such "rational" direct realism, however, would come under criticism when viewed through the radical constructivist argument of individuals, who in a cognitive mode of learning or "assimilation," construct subjective representations — i.e. abstractions of details.[59] We shall later examine radical constructivism in Chapter 6 in regards to its complementary role within the alternative perspective of *radical embodied cognition*. Suffice to say that McDowell now faces a potential incompatibility. On the one hand, he seeks to avoid the "gap" between thought and world.

However, closing such a gap presupposes that cognition is direct and non-representational, i.e. suffers no "distortions" by way of epistemic mediation.[60] Interestingly, such an objectivist account has served as inspiration to AI philosophy's resolve toward addressing the frame problem. The logic here would be that if one could somehow "model," as McDowell terms it, second-hand reasoning into AI representations (whether symbolic or connectionist), AI would then be able to capture or mimic the equivalent "direct cognitive reality" of humans."[61] Needless to say, this approach has not yet proven successful within AI's quest to overcome the frame and relevance problem previously discussed in Chapter 2.[62]

A second, complementary argument can be made against McDowell's second-natured "rationality," which Dreyfus launches through Heidegger's interpretation of Aristotle's *phronesis*, which renders it possible for an individual to provide an immediate response to a "full concrete situation"[63]:

> "[The phronimos] ... is determined by his situation in the largest sense ... The circumstances, the givens, the times and the people vary. The meaning of the action ... varies as well ... It is precisely the achievement of *phronesis* to disclose the [individual] as acting now in the full situation within which he acts' (citing Heidegger, 1997: 101). Of course, there will be problematic cases of conflicting goods where the phronimos does not see immediately what must be done. Thus, Aristotle says the phronimos must be able to deliberate well (citing Aristotle, 1955: 180). But, according to Heidegger, most of our ethical life consists in simply seeing the appropriate thing to do and responding without deliberation, as when we help a blind person cross the street or when, after years of experience, we unreflectively balance, case by case, the demands of our professional and personal lives. As Aristotle says: *"Phronesis* ... involves knowledge of the ultimate particular thing, which cannot be attained by systematic knowledge but only by 'perception' (citing Aristotle, 1955: 182)."

According to Heidegger's interpretation, the individual is in a predominantly non-rational, embodied, and direct (or non-representational) mode with reality. Only in situations going beyond an individual's abilities does he/she stop to reflect. Furthermore, all other reflections in regards to second-natured actions are "retroactive rationalizations."[64]

"For Heidegger, it is only through the physical experience of actual living in and coping with the exigencies of a multitude of situations — of being-in-the-world — that we subsequently develop the capacity for distancing, reflection, linguistic articulation, cognitive representation and conscious thought. The capacity to build involves intellectual distancing and forethought but this is only possible because we have always already experienced dwelling in the variety of circumstances we found ourselves in the past. The latter mode of engagement with the world precedes the former."[65] Hence, such a direct realism through the phenomenological senses or perceptions becomes viable and coherent without having to deal with the distorting "epistemic mediations" of so-called "second-natured rationalisations."[66]

Aristotle's words in regards to knowledge of "ultimate particulars things" through "perception" once again rejoins *mètis*[67] — i.e. *mètis* as a type of "conjectural" or oblique knowledge which refuses to be categorized.[68] In remaining true to his *Categories* (or represent), one should not be surprised that while "Aristotle also strongly defended oblique forms of knowledge," there was an overwhelming drive "to convert mètis into a more logical, prudent, systematic, and understandable form."[69] In this manner, we have remain conditioned (and oftentimes convinced) that rational thought and cognition precedes direct sensual experiences.[70] Yet, as we shall see in Chapter 6, research (and arguments) in radical embodied cognition disputes this long-standing premise.

In the next chapter...

In the next chapter, we shall critically examine the traditional perspective on cognition that consists of precise internal representations which, in turn, derives solely from discreet causal (and local) mechanisms located within the brain. We shall also see that this traditional view is driven by the computational theory of mind and decision-making.

References

Aristotle (1955). *The Ethics of Aristotle*, trans. J. A. K. Thomson (Harmondsworth: Penguin).

Hacking, I. (2002). Inaugural lecture: Chair of Philosophy and history of scientific concepts at the College de France, 16 January 2001, *Economics Society*, **31**(1), 1–14.

Halverson, R. (2004). Accessing, documenting, and communicating practical wisdom: The phronesis of school leadership practice. *American Journal of Education*, **111**, 90–121.

Heidegger, M. (1997). *Plato's Sophist*, trans. R. Rojcewicz and A. Schuwer (Bloomington, IN: Indiana University Press).

Endnotes

[1] See Scharmer, C.O. (2001). Self-transcending knowledge: Sensing and organizing around emerging opportunities. *Journal of Knowledge Management*, **5**(2), 137–151.

[2] See Dewey, J. (1929). *The Quest for Certainty: A Study of the Relation of Knowledge and Action* (New York: Putnam); Whitehead, A.N. (1929). *Process and Reality, An Essay in Cosmology* (New York: Macmillan); as well as Baumard, P. (1999). *Tacit Knowledge in Organizations* (London: Sage Publications).

[3] See both Dreyfus, H.L. and Dreyfus, S.E. (2005). Peripheral vision expertise in real world contexts. *Organization Studies*, **26**(5), 779–792, as well as Gorski, P.S. (2013). What is critical realism? And why should you care? *Contemporary Sociology: A Journal of Reviews*, **42**(5), 658–670.

[4] This is highlighted, e.g. by Chia, R. (2009). The Nature of Knowledge and Knowing in the Context of Management Learning, Education and Development. In *The SAGE Handbook of Management Learning, Education and Development*, S.J. Armstrong & C.V. Fukami (eds.) (London: SAGE Publications Ltd), pp. 25–41. doi: 10.4135/9780857021038.n2; also see debate on interpretation of Aristotle's work concerning *Phroenesis* between Dreyfus, H.L. (2014). *Skillful Coping: Essays on the Phenomenology of Everyday Perception and Action* (Oxford, UK: Oxford University Press) and McDowell, J. (1996). *Mind and World* (Cambridge, MA: Harvard University Press).

[5] See Griffin, J., Boardman, J. and Murray, O. (2001). *The Oxford History of Greece and the Hellenistic World* (Oxford [Oxfordshire]: Oxford University Press), p. 140.

[6] See Dewey (1929) (note 2); Whitehead (1929) (note 2); Baumard (1999) (note 2); Dreyfus, H.L. (1988). The Socratic and Platonic basis of cognitivism. *AI & Society*, **2**, 99–112. https://doi.org/10.1007/BF01891374; and Detel, W. (2005). *Foucault and Classical Antiquity: Power, Ethics and Knowledge*, trans. D. Wigg-Wolf (Cambridge, UK: Cambridge University Press), ISBN 0521833817. Translated by David Wigg-Wolf).

[7] Citing Whitehead (1929, part 2, Chapter 1) (note 2).

[8] Citing Dreyfus (1988, p. 99) (note 6).

[9] See both Dewey (1929) (note 2) as well as Kuntz, M.L. and Kuntz, P.G. (1988). Naming the categories: Back to Aristotle by way of Whitehead. *The Journal of Speculative Philosophy, New Series*, **2**(1), 30–47.

[10] See Dreyfus (1988) (note 6).

[11] See Ross, W.D. (1951). *Plato's Theory of Ideas* (Oxford, UK: Clarendon Press).

[12] See Winther, R.G. (2014). James and Dewey on abstractions. *The Pluralist*, 9(2), 1–28.

[13] See both Dewey (1929) (note 2) as well as James, W. (1950). *The Principles of Psychology* (New York, NY: Dover).

[14] See Parry, R.D. (1996). *Plato's Craft of Justice* (Albany, NY: State University of New York Press).

[15] See Chia, R. (2009). The Nature of Knowledge and Knowing in the Context of Management Learning, Education and Development. In *The SAGE Handbook of Management Learning, Education and Development* S. J. Armstrong and C. V. Fukami (eds.) (London: SAGE Publications Ltd), pp. 25–41. doi: 10.4135/9780857021038.n2

[16] Citing Feigenbaum, E. and McCorduck, P. (1983). *The Fifth Generation: Artificial Intelligence and Japan's Computer Challenge to the World* (Reading, MA: Addison-Wesley), p. 18.

[17] Citing Dreyfus, H.L. and Dreyfus, S.E. (2005).Peripheral vision expertise in real world contexts. *Organization Studies*, 26(5), 779–792.

[18] See both Bhaskar, R. (1994). *Plato, etc.: Problems of Philosophy and their Resolution* (London: Verso) as well as Bhaskar, R. (1997). A Realist Theory of Science, 2nd edition (London: Verso); also see Gorski (2013) (note 3).

[19] See Whitehead, A.N. (1926). *Science and the Modern World* (Cambridge, MA: Cambridge University Press).

[20] See analysis of Dewey's (1929) (note 2) thoughts across Fischer, C. (2014). *Gendered Readings of Change: A Feminist-Pragmatist Approach* (New York, NY: Palgrave-MacMillan).

[21] See Bhaskar, R. (1998). Critical Realism and Dialectic, Dialectic. In *Critical Realism: Essential Readings*, M. Archer, R. Bhaskar, A. Collier, C. Lawon and A. Norrie (eds.) (London: Routledge), pp. 589–640.

[22] See Gorski (2013) (note 3).

[23] We see this assumption, e.g. in both Cuellar, M.J. (2016). Critical realism as a sociomaterial stream of research. *The DATA BASE for Advances in Information Systems*, 47(4), 60–66 and Mutch, A. (2013). Sociomateriality — taking the wrong turning? *Information and Organization*, 23(1), 28–40.

[24] Citing Bhaskar (1998) (note 21) in Gorski (2013, p. 667) (note 3).

[25] Citing Bhaskar (1997) (note 18) in Gorski (2013, p. 62) (note 2).

[26] See Gorski (2013) (note 3).

[27] See both Aristotle (2004). *Nicomachean Ethics* (R. Crisp, Trans.). Cambridge, UK: Cambridge University Press) and Aristotle. (1955 — *The Ethics of Aristotle*, tr. J. A. K. Thomson, Harmondsworth: Penguin)

[28] See Hirschheim, R.A. (1992 — Information Systems Epistemology: An Historical Perspective'. In R. Galliers (Ed.), *Information Systems Research: Issues,*

Methods and Practical Guidelines (pp. 28–60). London: Blackweel Scientific Publications).

[29] See Schiappa, E. (1991). *Protagoras and Logos. A Study in Greek Philosophy and Rhetoric* (Columbia: University of South Carolina Press).

[30] See both Detienne, M. and Vernant, J.P. (1978). *Les ruses de l'intélligence. La mètis des Grecs* (Paris: Flammarion) and Kerferd, G.B. (1981). *The Sophistic Movement* (Cambridge University Press: Cambridge, UK).

[31] See Detienne and Vernant (1978) (note 30).

[32] Citing Detienne and Vernant (1978, p. 14) (note 30).

[33] Citing Jullien, F. (2004). *A Treatise on Efficacy Between Western and Chinese Thinking* (Honolulu, HI: University of Hawaii Press), p. 9.

[34] *Ibid.*

[35] See Vernant, J.P. (1985). *Mythe et pensée chez les Grecs. Études de psychologie historique* (Paris : Éditions de la Découverte).

[36] See both Vernant (1985) (note 35) and Scott, J.C. (1998). *Seeing like a State: How Certain Schemes to Improve the Human State have Failed* (Binghamton, NY: Vail-Ballou Press).

[37] See Miller, C.R. (2008). The Aristotelian Topos: Hunting for Novelty. In *Rereading Aristotle's Rhetoric*, Gross A.G. and Walzer, A.E. (eds.) (Carbondale, IL: Southern Illinois University Press), pp, 130–148.

[38] See both Detienne and Vernant (1978) (note 30) and *Ibid.*

[39] Citing Miller (2008, p. 138) (note 37).

[40] As per Baumard (1999) (note 2).

[41] See Winther (2014) (note 12).

[42] Citing Scott (1998, p. 340) (note 36).

[43] See both Scott (1998) (note 36) and De Certeau, M. (1984). *Practice of Everyday Life* (Berkeley: University of California Press).

[44] See Chia (2009) (note 4).

[45] See Dunne, J. (1993). *Back to the Rough Ground: Phronesis and Techné in Modern Philosophy and in Aristotle* (London: University of Notre Dame Press).

[46] See Parry, W.T. and Hacker, E.A. (1991). *Aristotelian Logic* (State University of New York Press: Albany, NY).

[47] Citing Chia (2009, p. 28) (note 4).

[48] Citing Chia (2009, p. 26) (note 4) who in turn cites Dunne, J. (1993) (note 45).

[49] Citing Detienne and Vernant (1978, p. 5) (note 30).

[50] See Detienne and Vernant (1978) (note 30).

[51] Citing Knudsen, F. (2005). Seamanship and anthropoship: Reflecting on practice. Arbejds: og Maritimmedicinsk Publikationsserie, rapport nr. 11.

[52] Citing Dolmage, J. (2009). Metis, Mêtis, Mestiza, Medusa: Rhetorical bodies across rhetorical traditions. *Rhetoric Review*, **28**(1), pp. 1–2.

[53] Citing Aristotle (2004, p. 107) (note 27).

[54] Citing Ellett Jr, F.S. (2012). *Practical Rationality and a Recovery of Aristotle's 'Phronesis' for the Professions*, Ch. 2. In *Phronesis as Professional Knowledge: Practical Wisdom in the Professions* (Rotterdam: Sense Publishers), pp. 13–34.
[55] Citing Thompson, M. (2017). How Managers Understand Wisdom in Decision Making: A Phronetic Research Approach, Ch. 9. In *Wisdom Learning: Perspectives on Wising Up Business and Management Education*, Kupers, W. and Gunnlaugson, O. (eds.) (Routledge, London and New York: Taylor & Francis), pp. 211–228.
[56] Citing McDowell, J. (1996). *Mind and World* (Cambridge, MA: Harvard University Press), p. 79.
[57] Citing Esfeld, M. (2000). Aristotle's direct realism in "De Anima." *The Review of Metaphysics*, **54**(2), 321–336.
[58] Citing McDowell (1996, p. 85) (note 56).
[59] Citing von Glasersfeld, E. (2001).The radical constructivist view of science. *Foundations of Science*, **6**, 31–43. https://doi.org/10.1023/A:1011345023932.
[60] See Esfeld (2000) (note 57).
[61] See McDowell (1996) (note 56).
[62] See Boden, M.A. (2016). *AI: Its Nature and Future* (Oxford, UK: Oxford University Press).
[63] Citing Dreyfus (2014, pp. 109–110) (note 4).
[64] Citing Dreyfus (2014, p. 110) (note 4).
[65] Citing Chia (2009, p. 30) (note 4).
[66] See Esfeld (2000) (note 57).
[67] See Detienne and Vernant (1978) (note 30).
[68] See both Detienne and Vernant (1978) (note 30) and Baumard (1999) (note 2).
[69] Citing Dolmage (2009, pp. 11–12) (note 52).
[70] See Chia (2009) (note 4) and Dreyfus (2014) (note 4).

Chapter 5

Human Cognition and Behavior: A Computational and Representational Decision-Making Perspective

5.1. Introduction

In this chapter, we first show that the central hypothesis of classical cognitive science consists of thinking that can best be understood in terms of representational structures in the mind, and computational procedures that operate on those structures. While there is much disagreement about the nature of the representations and computations that constitutes thinking, the central hypothesis is general enough to encompass the current range of thinking in cognitive science, including connectionist theories that model thinking using artificial neural networks. However, we shall revisit some of the criticisms that have been voiced, arguing that the classical view may be strongly biased, if not misleading in nature. More specifically, some philosophical critics to the computational-representational approach to cognitive science have argued that this approach is fundamentally mistaken. Critics have offered arguments such as:

The emotion argument: Cognitive science neglects the important role of emotions in human thinking.[1]

The world argument: Cognitive science disregards the significant role of physical environments in human thinking, which is embedded in and extended into the world.[2]

The body argument: Cognitive science neglects the contribution of embodiment to human thought and action.[3]

The social and enactive argument: Human thought is inherently social and enactive in ways that cognitive science ignores.[4]

The mathematics argument: Mathematical results show that human thinking cannot be computational in the standard sense, so the brain must operate differently.[5]

A cognitivist account of decision-making views choice behavior as a serial process of deliberation and commitment, which is separate from perception and action. By contrast, recent work in embodied and enactive decision-making has argued that this account is incompatible with emerging neurophysiological data. Today, much of cognitive science claims to be embodied, but embodied is often meant in a very weak sense, and one that differs from radical embodied cognitive science, which we will examine in the next chapter.[6] Typically, those writing about embodied cognitive science start with the early work of Rodney Brooks — as a form of cognitivism that is still based on a computational theory of mind.[7] Often, there is reference to "the extended mind" or "extended cognition,"[8] implying that "machinery of the mind" can extend beyond the biological body, but always within a perspective of computationalism. Some refer to this as computationalism in which cognition is explained in terms of representations in computational systems that span brain, body, and environment. As such, as we shall further show in this chapter, embodied cognitive science, while being highly influenced by the Jamesian transactional and embodied worldview, is still a form of the computational-representational theory of mind.[9]

5.2. Cognitive Science and the Classical (Symbolic) Computer Theory of the Mind

Historically, the cognitive sciences have drawn their basic theoretical assumptions from the Classical Computer Theory of the Mind (CCTM).[10] While CCTM's formal articulation is often credited to Hilary Putnam,[11] one can go back to McCulloch and Pitts[12] as being the first to have made use of computation to address (what the then-already established community of biophysicist researchers in neural networks referred to as) the "mind–body problem" — and thereby, provide the basis for the first modern computational theory of mind and brain.[13] CCTM views that the mind is a computational system similar in many respects to a Turing machine.[14] As such, most work in representational (or classical) cognitive science assumes that the mind has mental representations analogous to computer data structures, and computational procedures similar to computational algorithms. Such cognitive theorists have proposed that the mind contains mental representations such as logical propositions, rules, concepts, images, and analogies, and that it uses mental procedures such as deduction, search, matching, rotating, and retrieval. In a similar vein, most twentieth-century AI researchers in classical (symbolic) AI followed Descartes and other rationalist philosophers such as Leibniz in arguing that all knowledge "consists in forming and using appropriate symbolic representations," thus drawing heavily on such representationalism for their underlying assumptions.[15]

In turn, the Classical Computational Theory of Reasoning (CCTR) is a subset of CCTM, which posits that reasoning depends on symbol manipulation, or more specifically, "human reasoning processes depend on algorithmically specifiable processes that are ... defined over the syntactic properties of compositionally structured mental representations."[16] Here, reasoning is viewed as being computable in the same way classical computational devises can imitate the input and output relationships which human reasoning processes are assumed to exhibit. Furthermore, such a computational account of reasoning should take neither more time nor more computational resources than human beings. Finally, CCTR assumes there is a "psychologically plausible classical computational account of human reasoning,"[17] thus rejoining Newell and Simon's account[18]:

"The symbol-system hypothesis implies that the symbolic behaviour of man arises because he has the characteristics of a physical-symbol system. Hence, the results of efforts to model human behaviour with symbol systems become an important part of the evidence for the hypothesis, and research in artificial intelligence goes in close collaboration with research in information processing psychology, as it is usually called."

As previously discussed in Chapter 2, the issue of relevance and the closely associated frame problem became a critical objection and roadblock to such a classical computational account of reasoning, leading to a regress of contexts.[19] Furthermore, implicit to the issue of relevance as argued by Dreyfus is a re-questioning of CCTR's assumption that there is "psychologically plausible classical computational account of human reasoning" — namely by way of the alternative view of an embodied and embedded cognition.[20] More specifically, both Searle's and Dreyfus' conceptions of *intentionality* and *background* challenge the CCTR assumption that mental states and processes can be reduced to mere syntactic representations, and thus, can be processed in an algorithmic fashion.[21]

First, Searle's well-known Chinese room thought experiment can be summarized as follows: the formal syntactic use of Chinese ideograms by a Turing machine does not involve the understanding of their semantic content (i.e. meaning).[22] Such understanding would involve the process of interpretative inference and assignment of meaning to symbols — which is impossible by way of the computer's purely formal syntactic sequencing. More importantly[23]:

> "What goes for Chinese goes for other forms of cognition as well. Just manipulating the symbols is not by itself enough to guarantee cognition, perception, understanding, thinking and so forth. And since computers, qua computers, are symbol — manipulating devices, merely running the computer program is not enough to guarantee cognition"

In turn, Searle argued that the semantic content of the human mind is affected or governed by intentionality, which is an intentional state that "either causes or is caused by its conditions of satisfaction."[24] Hence, meaning making, which depends on establishing such a psychological state of satisfaction, is both a subjective and ambiguous enterprise — and thus cannot be met by way of the formal and predefined syntactic approach of a computer program without falling into circularity and regress.[25] Yet, Searle's argument was still considered representational in nature, i.e. according to Dreyfus, an intentionality that is limited to the mind's eye.[26] Dreyfus taps into both Heidegger and Merleau-Ponty to show that our intentional interaction with the world is not driven by representation — rather, it involves a direct contact through embodied skillful coping.[27] First:

> "According to Heidegger intentional content isn't in the mind, nor in some 3rd realm (as it is for Husserl), nor in the world; it isn't anywhere. It's an embodied way of being towards."

Reaching a mastery of skills requires a direct embeddedness or "thrownness" into the context at hand in which there are no rules or guidelines to follow (i.e. being "authentic"). And it is here that Merleau-Ponty builds upon Heidegger's account by stressing the body: "when you're skillfully coping ... without thinking, without rules, your body and its skills are drawing you to get this optimal grip on the situation."[28] "Therefore, cognition and intentionality are explained from the perspective of an embodied being that, due to his body skills, is ontologically and dynamically coupled to the world."[29] Second, coping takes place on the background of a basic non-representational, holistic, absorbed, kind of intentionality.[30] This background is not a "mindless," "mechanical," or "zombielike behavior", but is nonetheless "non-mental," "non-cognitive," "unthinking activity".[31] It involves an individual's background sense of the context, and in turn, allows us to adapt to a given situation — i.e. of knowing what is pertinent given the situation, rather than searching through combinations of possibilities and alternatives. This "background knowing" is a knowledge embodied within us, rather than symbolically stored in our brains.[32] Here, Dreyfus draws upon Merleau-Ponty's[33] "intentional arc" and Freeman's[34] physiology of perception to further defend and explain this point.[35] The intentional arc is an individual's ability, which consists essentially of inseparable motion, vision, and comprehension.[36] As such, body movement is not merely physiological, nor is it the "handmaid" of consciousness,[37] while Freeman provides a holistic neuro-dynamic summary of the body–brain when an individual perceives a familiar event as "information [which] spreads like a flash fire through the nerve cell assembly."[38] Learning and building one's repertoire of what is significant or relevant involves "brain activity patterns [which] are constantly dissolving, reforming and changing, particularly in relation to one another," whereby learning to respond to a new event involves "a shift in all other patterns, even if they are not directly involved with the learning. There are no fixed representations, as there are in computers; there are only significances."[39] Such brain–body activity is "not an isolate brain state" and it is not associative whereby "as one learns, one adds more and more fixed connection," but rather "instantiates the basis of a genuine intentional arc in which there are no linear casual connections between world and brain nor a fixed library of representations, but where, each time a new significance is encountered, the whole perceptual world ... changes so that the significance that is directly displayed in the world is continually enriched."[40] This phenomenological coupling (through bodily senses) with one's environment (embeddedness) also brings forth (i.e. shapes) a world. Such a coupling bridges the embedded character of

Hedeigger's "throwness" of one's self into a given context, or Merleau-Ponty's "inseperateness with one's environment," with the enactive aspect of embodiment as proposed by Varela *et al.* — i.e. "the enactment or bringing forth of meaning from a background of understanding."[41] As we enact a world, we are also embodied in it, i.e. it involves the necessity of a physical body whose sensory–motor experiences result in cognition. This non-representational intelligence not only adaptively detects but also creates what is significant within one's perceptual world.

Freeman's[42] physiology of perception as described above brings up two other interrelated issues regarding CCTR, namely the problems of holism[43] and the globality problem.[44] The problem of holism is well summarized as follows by Samuels[45]:

"Given that (almost) any belief can be relevant, under the appropriate conditions, to the assessment of (almost) any other, how do we determine (with reasonable levels of success) which of our beliefs are in fact relevant to a specific instance of belief revision?"

As such, Dietrich and Fields[46] argue that a holistic system would need to consider all the information available in the Universe, thus rendering it unfeasible in a representational/computational system. In a similar fashion, globality amplifies the problem of relevance[47]:

"Holism, you may recall, appears to imply that the beliefs relevant to a given inferential task can, in principle, come from anywhere in one's belief system. The globality problem goes one step further ... Fodor takes the problem to show is that for almost any instance of belief revision, the set of beliefs that a classical computational device would need to consider will be very large indeed: whole theories or even the totality of one's epistemic commitments (referring to Fodor, 2000). In other words, it's not merely that relevant beliefs might come from anywhere, it's that they routinely come from (almost) everywhere. The relevance problem with a vengeance."

In a similar vein, in attempting to model Tononi's theory of consciousness as integrated information, non-computable functions arise; more specifically, "if integration is necessary for consciousness, then somewhere between the stimulus entering the brain and the decision leaving the brain, there is a point where the information cannot be fully disentangled from the rest of cognition ... this integrated processing cannot be localised to any part of the brain or any specific point in time ... the contents of cognition are effectively unified."[48] As such, global cognition involves a complex *irreversible* tangle that is core consciousness.[49] According to Tononi, consciousness exhibits key phenomenological properties, which can differentiate a large number of experiences, yet also integrate these experiences in a unity, rejoining Freeman's physiology of perception.[50] Conscious states, which are informationally rich and are highly integrated, lead to a gestalt unity that is non-computable.[51]

5.3. The Connectionist Approach to Cognition and its Attempt to Emulate Human Abduction

The dominant mind–computer analogy in cognitive science has taken on another analog, the brain and its neural networks, through the use of connectionist approaches. Connectionists have proposed ideas about representation and computation that use neurons and their connections as inspirations for data structures, and neuron firing and spreading activation as inspirations for algorithms. Cognitive science then works with a complex three-way analogy among the mind, the brain, and computers. Mind, brain, and computation can each be used to suggest new ideas about the others. There is no single computational model of mind, since different kinds of computers and programming approaches suggest different ways in which the mind might work. In its "pure" form, rather than using rules, "connectionist information processing is defined by quantitative connections between microfeatures (which are simply components of distributed representation and are usually individually uninterpretable) and takes place at subsymbolic levels" — and in this manner, cognition is viewed as "an emergent effect of these interactions."[52] It has been argued that connectionist models are able to "learn a set of real-valued weights on connections among neuron-like processing units that support the generation of appropriate, context-sensitive, conditional expectations. Discrepancies between predicted and observed outcomes provide feedback for learning, in the form of gradual weight adjustment."[53] Yet, one of the questions that neither classical nor connectionist computationalists have answered satisfactorily is the question of how a human brain built from relatively slow neurons (compared to silicon-based components in digital computers) execute certain operations that in a model require quick and sophisticated computations to achieve.[54] Furthermore, and as previously mentioned in Chapter 1, connectionism is not mutually exclusive of classical computational approaches, in that one may be nested into the other.[55] More recently, general Computational Theory of Mind (CTM), which involve a range of computational approaches, has attracted numerous objections, the most pertinent being in regards to how human creativity and abductive reasoning eludes computational modeling.[56]

Work in AI has been especially interested in reproducing human abduction, which arguably has been linked to the ability to generate new scientific discoveries. Abduction combines logical reasoning, aesthetic judgment (the hypothesis must be "elegant") and pre-reflexive moves (Peirce speaks of "flashes") — in other words, it mixes intuition and reasoning,[57] and it involves the process of linking single events are to the tacit knowing of "family resemblance" between those events.[58] Abduction involves direct perceptual judgements in which "the abductive suggestion comes to us as a flash. It is an act of insight,"[59] as well as the general process of invention: "It [abduction] is the only logical operation which introduces any new ideas."[60] Abduction is both an act of insight and an inference.[61] Pierce proposed it as both "the process of forming an explanatory process" (as invention/construction) and the "the process of choosing a hypothesis" (selection).[62] Peirce gave the often-quoted formula[63]:

"The surprising fact, C, is observed

But if A were true, C would be a matter of course

Hence, there is reason to suspect that A is true."

As can be seen, the first step of perceived surprise can be directly related to the previous discussion in relation to one of the tacit, complex aspects of creativity, namely the question of relevance. Structured probabilistic approaches to AI have attempted to dissect out the human abductive process through a series of statistically derived algorithmic steps that, according to Patokorpi, is different from the more holistic character of human abduction, which involves a good deal of perception-based reasoning that retains a connection to meaning "because percepts make sense to us."[64] In contrast, probabilistic approaches take the stand that it is crucial to specify the goal of cognitive processes at an abstract and computational level of analysis. As such, it has been criticized as being a logical homologous representation which "entails interfering with the phenomenon through complicated data massaging," which becomes a form of truncation of the phenomena in question.[65] It involves algorithmic inferences using statistical methods that attempt to reproduce human intuitive inferences.[66]

Such an approach has been viewed as highly reductionist in that assigning "correct" probabilities to events ignores its inherent subjectivity.[67] Furthermore, human abduction, starting with Pierce's[68] description, involves both intuitive inferences as well as more holistic Gestalt intuition ("flashes"), as depicted in experiments on visual interpretations by Moriarty, as well as subsequent research conducted by Pretz on the use of intuition in problem-solving strategies conducted by both novices and experts.[69] As such, the overall intuitive aspect of abduction renders it highly ubiquitous. More recent connectionist AI approaches have adopted a more holomorphic approach through mimesis to try and address the "Gestalt shortfall."[70] Here, the idea is that images are more apt at representing natural processes in all their complexity. However, a phenomenological cross-argument is that, while a picture can represent "a thousand words," it is still a matter of feeling, interpretation, meaning, and significance.[71] Connectionist systems, on the other hand,[72]

"... being enabled to adapt to environmental conditions by sensor data, attain their functionality solely through conveniently designed algorithms from outside, based on propositional knowledge about their field of application. They, therefore, are lacking own intentionality and self-determined activity as indispensable material basis for perception, sense-making, and experience. With respect to sign processes, they solely operate signals which are, as quasi-signs, lacking the references to experienced objects of the world and, hence, cannot "know" for what the signals stand or what they are about. And with respect to abductive reasoning, they are lacking the human capability to create an appropriate hypothesis for transcending the bonds of an existing formal symbol system."

As such, one can argue that connectionist approaches exhibit the same or similar issues classical symbolic approaches suffered from, as they are still formal (albeit, distributive) attempts to representatively capture the complexities, ambiguities and uncertainties of what dynamic realities entail. In the next section, we look at how more recent efforts by computational cognitivists have strived to readjust their approaches in factoring in the "embodied and embedded realities" of cognition.

5.4. Representational "Embodied and Embedded" Cognition and Heideggerian AI

In recent years, hybrid symbolic-connectionist approaches have attempted to model embodiment and embeddedness.[73] This includes the use of dynamic frames as proposed by Wheeler, where action-oriented representations or frames are used to reproduce Heidegger's ready-to-hand coping.[74] Here, Wheeler adopts the approach of "adaptive coupling" of the body (as internal representations) with the context (as external representations), in which relevance is achieved when frames from the contextual environment are recognized and matched with frames from the body itself. Dynamic approaches also involve the use of "dynamic fields," being formalizations "of how neural populations represent the continuous dimensions that characterize perceptual features, movements and cognitive decisions."[75] Furthermore, sensor-provided data grounds representations in a bottom-up manner somewhat analogous to Harnad's[76] symbol/representation grounding, albeit by way of a neuronal-distributed approach, as an attempt to address embeddedness.[77]

However, as Ziemke aptly points out, it is important to first go back and ask ourselves: what conception(s) of embodiment do AI researchers refer to?[78] The answer is more or less provided through Brooks' conception of systems being *physically* grounded, whereby "everything is grounded in primitive sensor motor patterns of activation," which in turn provides the "here and now of the world directly influencing the behavior of the system."[79] According to Ziemke however, Searle would reject this by arguing that such systems still lacks the intentionality that characterizes human cognition.[80]

Furthermore, AI researchers have tended to ignore the biological,[81] autopoietical (i.e. enactive), and "layered/nested network of bodily self-regulation mechanism"[82] arguments of embodiment.[83] In contrast, AI systems until very recently were "typically viewed as some kind of input and output device that provides physical grounding to the internal computational mechanisms."[84] This, on the other hand, seems to be changing and as seen through Ziemke's[85] citation regarding Johnson's[86] own work on embodiment:

> "In retrospect I now see that the structural aspects of our bodily interactions with our environments upon which I was focusing were themselves dependent on even more submerged dimensions of bodily understanding. It was an important step to probe below concepts, propositions, and sentences into the sensori-motor processes by which we understand our world, but what is now needed is a far deeper exploration into the qualities, feelings, emotions, and bodily processes that make meaning possible."

That being said, such research into embodiment is still pursued by way of a representational perspective. Wilson[87] refers to this as "wide computationalism" in "which we explain cognition in terms of representations in computational systems that span brain, body, and environment."[88] This seemingly tautological observation on our part brings us to a basic confrontation with the non-representationalist perspective of direct realism as advocated by Dreyfus, Gibson, and Chemero.[89] One can argue that current "embodied" AI's "mainly mechanical or electrical devices enabling sensor-controlled" approach provides a "reductionist view of 'embodiment,'" which fails to discern and determine relevant and meaningful cues and actions in changing situations — in that it attempts to attain an "optimal grip" on a situation through the inadequacy of representations as opposed to that provided by the direct contact of the phenomenological body.[90]

5.5. Preliminary Thoughts on "So What?"

The full implications of representational "intelligent" technologies within organizations are far and profound. While we hold off from discussing these in sufficient depth until Chapter 7, in that additional important ideas and concepts regarding the phenomena of *mindlessness* need to be unpacked beforehand, in this section we briefly examine issues which immediately come to mind.

Historically, robots and computers were used to eliminate cognitively monotonous, physically demanding, repetitive, and/or dangerous jobs. For example, the automotive industry used robots as far back as the early to mid-1960s (GM) to carry out spot-welding, and later more complex arc-welding as well as general materials handling tasks in the 1970s.[91] In the late 1970s and early 1980s, development in robotics was mainly concentrated on assembly with the objective of higher repeatability, acceleration, and velocity in order to shorten manufacturing cycle times.[92] In the 1980s, the metal industry was also another important user of robots with their heavy, hot, and inhospitable working environment. By that time, material transfer, painting, and welding were all economically viable for robotization.[93] However, machines are now making inroads into areas that were previously thought reserved only to human capabilities. On the one hand, high-level reasoning can now be adequately codified via algorithms, resulting in computers outdoing humans both in terms of speed and performance in a variety of tasks. In this sense, "learning" algorithms have attained impressive levels of performance and can be useful and beneficial tools for society.[94] Their superior computational and analytical capabilities allow them to analyze different layers of complex information and masses of data coming from various sources in order to *potentially* detect patterns and weak signals.[95] Such technologies, for example, can be powerful aids in decision-making within complex digital environments.[96] Furthermore, where more tacit-type tasks or movements are involved, and thereby where engineers are unable to initially program a machine to simulate the task/movement in question, machines can eventually master the task through a process of exposure, training, and reinforcement (or "deep learning").[97] Here, sensor and image technologies, coupled with information technologies, play key roles. Hence, "machine learning techniques involving image recognition, a process that is difficult to explicitly articulate and explain but that we, as humans, develop through experience, can now discriminate with an accuracy that surpasses our own."[98]

Yet, because of the frame regress issues arising as a result of the limitations of representational computational technologies, such algorithmic "learning" technologies can also be dangerous in promising too much, because of "fallacious context-stripping" and reductionist abstractionisms.[99] Contemporary manifestations of such abstractionism are now being seen through the digital Taylorization of certain professions as mere executants and "extensions" of algorithmic configurations.[100] This is certainly one issue that we as human actors working with such technologies, must become meta-mindful toward (which we shall further develop and revisit through both Chapters 7 and 8).

Several studies, for example, have confirmed that cockpit automation involving "operator hands-off" software protocols and technologies lead to pilots' erosion of expertise, such that when emergencies do occur, they no longer have the required hands-on adaptive expertise to deal with them.[101] This was the case of the crash of Air France Flight 447 into the Atlantic Ocean in which, after the Airbus A330 pitot tubes iced over in a thunderstorm, the flight computers transitioned from protected mode to "direct law" — making the fly-by-wire aircraft behave very much like a conventional plane — yet, the crew were unable to cope with the emergency due to inexperience in manual flying.[102] More precisely, the cockpit automation technology imposed organizational limits onto the pilots.[103] This was in the form of automated procedures, checks, and controls the pilots followed and worked with such that they became cognitively conditioned toward continuous operation within safe operational limits.[104] The consequential side effect was to reduce the pilots' "cognitive experience of the system and jumble...when approaching boundaries"[105] — thus, never stimulating challenge and enquiry, which in turn, undermined situational awareness and mindfulness.[106] Hence, when unfamiliar or unexpected circumstances occurred, such erosion led to limited coping abilities on the part of the pilots.[107]

Along similar lines, certain critiques have been raised regarding Evidence-Based Medicine (EBM).[108] EBM was first introduced with the intent to apply the conscientious, explicit, and judicious use of current best evidence in making decisions about the care of individual patients.[109] However, the pertinence of "average results" has been called in question relative to real patients who do not fit "textbook" descriptions and differ from those in research trials. Second, such evidence is being increasingly transformed into algorithmic rules in computerized decision support systems, structured templates, and point-of-care prompts, which can "crowd out" situational expertise and individualized aspects of clinical consultations.[110] Glasziou *et al.*[111] have argued that, in such circumstances, inexperienced clinicians may (partly through fear of litigation) engage mechanically and defensively with decision support technologies, stifling the development of a more nuanced clinical expertise embracing accumulated practical experience, tolerance of uncertainty, and the ability to apply practical judgements in unique situations.

While it is true that the superior computational and analytical capabilities of learning algorithms has far surpassed humans in complex tasks in which the rules are known and agreed to, they remain highly dependent on the available data and their pertinence to the situation-at-hand.[112] Furthermore, learning algorithms, even in situations of purely defined complexity, are also biased in that they "are formalized opinion that have been put into code" such that critical thinking is paramount.[113] Most importantly though, is the inability of such algorithms to determine what is relevant during changing circumstances (as discussed in previous sections regarding AI and computational algorithm's "frame problem"), thus being unable to compensate for human adaptive expertise or *mètis*. And all of these issues equally apply to what is known as transfer "learning" in ML, which focuses on storing knowledge gained while solving one problem and applying it to a different but related problem (e.g. knowledge gained in recognizing cats transferred and applied to recognizing tigers). Paradoxically, such unaddressed issues, which have the potential of generating disturbances and other unknown and unexpected outcomes,[114] become catastrophic as professions progressively lose their adaptive capabilities (*mètis*) due to the constraining effects such learning algorithms enact upon the organization of work. This rejoins a more general point raised by Faraj *et al.*,[115] in that "for skilled professions whose expertise and training are dependent upon tasks suitable for learning algorithms, the reliance on such technologies by incumbents for routine tasks may threaten the development of the profession's future experts" in that "as incumbent experts retire, the replenishment of the occupational expertise that understands the tasks taken over by the algorithm is in question." Along similar lines, learning algorithms are guiding radiologists, for example, toward certain diagnoses that compare favorably with certified doctors, thereby initiating calls within the IT community to cease training radiologists.[116] Yet, deep expert understanding of these tasks is of utmost importance in that expert radiologists are still in better positions to make correct interpretations when looking at complex situations involving weak, contradictory, and/or disparate signals.[117] Unfortunately, such lack of organizational awareness or mindfulness towards such *mètis*, risks reinforcing "learning" algorithms' enactive effect within the digital workplace, resulting in erroneous perceptions as to which future professions are to be valued or maintained.[118]

In the next chapter…

In the following chapter, we examine radical embodied cognition — a perspective that rejects representationalism. Radical embodied cognitive science considers a theory of the relationship between mind and world as general as provided by both Gibson[119] and phenomenologists (see previous discussions involving Dreyfus' arguments in Chapters 2 and 4). Radical embodiment proposals are based on the "enactive" view that cognition depends constitutively on the living body, understood as an autonomous system. The basic idea is that cognition should not be understood as a capacity for deriving world-models, which might then provide a database for thinking, planning, and problem-solving. Rather, cognitive processes are viewed as being closely entwined with action, and as such, have the capacity of generating structure, i.e. of "enacting" a world.

Endnotes

[1] See Damasio, A. (2003). Feelings of emotion and the self. *Annals of the New York Academy of Sciences*, **1001**, 253–261.

[2] See both Gibson, J. J. (1979). *The Ecological Approach to Visual Perception* (Boston, MA: Houghton Mifflin) as well as Dreyfus, H.L. (2007). Why Heideggerian AI failed and how fixing it would require making it more Heidegerrian. *Artificial Intelligence*, **171**(18), 1137–1160.

[3] See Dreyfus (2007) (note 2).

[4] See Varela, F.J., Thompson, E. and Rosch, E. (2017). *The Embodied Mind: Cognitive Science and Human Experience* (New York, NY: MIT Press).

[5] See both Maguire, P., Moser, P., Maguire, R. and Griffith, V. (2014). Is Consciousness Computable? Quantifying Integrated Information Using Algorithmic Information Theory? In *Proceedings of the 36th Annual Conference of the Cognitive Science Society*, P. Bello, M. Guarini, M. McShane, & B. Scassellati (eds.) (Austin, TX, Cognitive Science Society), pp. 2615–2620 as well as Tononi, G. (2008). Consciousness as integrated information: a provisional manifesto. *The Biological Bulletin*, **215**(3), 216–242.

[6] See Chemero, A. (2009). *Radical Embodied Cognitive Science* (Cambridge, MA: The MIT Press).

[7] See Brooks, R.A. (1991). Intelligence without representation. *Artificial Intelligence*, **47**, 139–160.

[8] See Clark, A. (1997). Being there: Putting brain, body, and world together again. Cambridge, MA: MIT Press.

[9] For example, see Wheeler, M. (2005). *Reconstructing the Cognitive World: The Next Step* (Cambridge, MA: MIT Press).

[10] See Horst, S. (1999). Symbols and computation: A critique of the computational theory of mind. *Minds and Machines*, **9**, 343–381; also see Piccinini, G. (2004). The first computational theory of mind and brain: A close look at McCulloch and Pitt's "Logical calculus of ideas immanent in nervous activity."

Synthese, **141**, 175–215; and finally, see Kiverstein, J.D. and Rietveld, E. (2018). Reconceiving representation-hungry cognition: An ecological-enactive proposal. *Adaptive Behavior*, **26**(4), 147–163.

[11] See both Putnam, H. (1960). Minds and Machines. In *Dimensions of Mind*, S. Hook (ed.) (New York: New York University Press) as well as Putnam, S. (1961). Brains and Behavior. Originally read as part of the program of the American Association for the Advancement of Science, Section L, December. N. Block (ed.) (1980). *Readings in the Philosophy of Psychology* (Cambridge, MA: Harvard University Press).

[12] McCulloch, W.S. and Pitts, W. (1943). A logical calculus of the ideas immanent in nervous activity. *Bulletin of Mathematical Biophysics*, **5**, 115–133.

[13] See Horst (1999) and Piccinini (2004) (note 10).

[14] See McCulloch and Pitts (1943) (note 12).

[15] Citing Kenaw, S. (2008). Hubert L. Dreyfus's critique of classical AI and its rationalist assumptions. *Minds and Machines*, **18**, 228–238, who in turn cites Dreyfus, H.L. (1992). What computers still can't do: A critique of artificial reason (Cambridge, MA: MIT Press).

[16] Citing Samuels, R. (2010). Classical computationalism and the many problems of cognitive relevance. *Studies in History and Philosophy of Science*, **41**, 280–293.

[17] Citing Samuels (2010, p. 282) (note 16).

[18] Citing Newell, A. and Simon, H.A. (1990). Computer Science as Empirical Enquiry. In *The Philosophy of Artificial Intelligence*, M. A. Boden (ed.) (Oxford: Oxford University Press).

[19] See Horst (1999) (note 10) and Dreyfus (2007) (note 2).

[20] See Dreyfus (2007) (note 2).

[21] As argued by Negru, T. (2013). Intentionality and background: Searle and Dreyfus against classical AI theory. *Filosofia Unisinos*, **14**(1), 18–34, who makes reference to both Searle, J. (1983). *Intentionality: An Essay in the Philosophy of Mind* (London: Cambridge University Press) as well as Dreyfus, H.L. (2009). How Representational Cognitivism Failed and is being replaced by Body/World Coupling. In *After Cognitivism: A Reassessment of Cognitive Science and Philosophy*, K. Leidlmair (ed.) (Dordrecht, Springer), pp. 39–75.

[22] See Searle, J. (1984). *Minds, Brains and Science: The 1984 Reith Lectures (Can Computers Think?)* (London: British Broadcasting Corporation).

[23] Citing Negru (2013, p. 20) (note 21) who in turn cites Searle, J. (1990). Is the brain's mind a computer program? *Scientific American*, **262**(1), 26–31. http://dx.doi.org/10.1038/scientifi camerican0190-26.

[24] Citing Searle (1983, p. 123) (note 21).

[25] See Horst (1999) (note 10).

[26] See Dreyfus (2009) (note 21).

[27] See Dreyfus (2009, p. 53) (note 21).

[28] Citing conversation between Dreyfus, H.L. and Kreisler, H. (2005). Meaning, relevance and the limits of technology — conversation with H.L. Dreyfus.

Conversations with History, Institute of International Studies, UC Berkeley; also see Dreyfus, H.L. (2014). *Skillful Coping: Essays on the Phenomenology of Everyday Perception and Action* (Oxford, UK: Oxford University Press).

[29] Citing Negru (2013, p. 18) (note 21).

[30] See Dreyfus (2009, p. 56) (note 21).

[31] See Dreyfus, H.L. (1991). *Being-in-the-World* (Cambridge, MA: The MIT Press) as well as McManus, D. (2008). Rules, regression and the 'background': Dreyfus, Heidegger and McDowell. *European Journal of Philosophy*, **16**(3), 432–458.

[32] See Dreyfus (1992) (note 15) as well as Dreyfus, H.L. (1972). *What Computers Can't Do* (New York, NY: MIT Press).

[33] See Merleau-Ponty, M. (1962). Phenomenology of Perception, London: Routledge & Kegan Paul.

[34] Freeman, W.J. (1991). The physiology of perception. *Scientific American*, **264**(2), 78–85.

[35] See Dreyfus (2007) (note 2).

[36] See Reuter, M. (1999). Merleau-Ponty's notion of pre-reflective intentionality. *Synthese*, **118**(1), 69–88.

[37] Citing Reuter (1999, p. 73) (note 35).

[38] Citing Freeman, W.J. (1991). The physiology of perception. *Scientific American*, **264**(2), 78–85.

[39] Citing Freeman, W.J. (2000). *How Brains Make Up Their Minds* (New York: Columbia University Press).

[40] Citing Dreyfus (2007, p. 1154) (note 2).

[41] Citing Varela *et al.* (2017, p. 149) (note 4).

[42] See Freeman (1991) (note 32).

[43] See Dietrich, E. and Fields, C. (1996). The Role of the Frame Problem in Fodor's Modularity Thesis: A Case Study of Rationalist Cognitive Science. In *The Robot's Dilemma Revisited: The Frame Problem in Artificial Intelligence*, K. M. Ford and Z. W. Pylyshyn (eds.) (Norwood, NJ: Ablex), pp. 9–24.

[44] See Fodor, J. (2000). *The Mind Doesn't Work That Way: The Scope and Limits of Computational Psychology* (Cambridge, MA: MIT Press).

[45] Citing Samuels, R. (2010). Classical computationalism and the many problems of cognitive relevance. *Studies in History and Philosophy of Science*, **41**, 280–293.

[46] See Dietrich, E. and Fields, C. (1996). The Role of the Frame Problem in Fodor's Modularity Thesis: A Case Study of Rationalist Cognitive Science. In *The Robot's Dilemma Revisited: The Frame Problem in Artificial Intelligence*, K.M. Ford and Z. W. Pylyshyn (eds.) (Norwood, NJ: Ablex), pp. 9–24.

[47] Citing Samuels (2010, p. 285) (note 44).

[48] Citing Maguire, P., Moser, P., Maguire, R. and Griffith, V. (2014). Is Consciousness Computable? Quantifying Integrated Information Using Algorithmic Information Theory? In *Proceedings of the 36th Annual Conference of the Cognitive Science Society*, P. Bello, M. Guarini, M. McShane, & B. Scassellati (eds.) (Austin,

TX: Cognitive Science Society), pp. 2615–2620) on Tononi, G. (2008). Consciousness as integrated information: A provisional manifesto. *The Biological Bulletin*, **215**(3), 216–242.

[49] See Macguire *et al.* (2014) (note 47) and Fodor (2000) (note 43).

[50] See Freeman (1991) (note 37) and Fodor, J.A. (2005). Reply to Steven Pinker 'So How Does the Mind Work? *Mind and Language*, **20**, 25–32.

[51] See Tononi, G., Boly, M., Massamini, M. *et al.* (2016). Integrated information theory: From consciousness to its physical substrate. *Nature Review Neuroscience*, **17**, 450–461.

[52] See MacLennan, B.J. (2001). Connectionist Approaches. In *International Encyclopedia of the Social and Behavioral Sciences*, N.J. Smelser and P.B. Baltes (eds.) (Oxford: Elsevier), pp. 2568–2573.

[53] Citing McClelland, J. *et al.* (2010). Letting structure emerge: Connectionist and dynamical systems approaches to cognition. *Trends in Cognitive Sciences*, **14**, 348–356.

[54] See Gallistel, C.R. and King, A. (2009). *Memory and the Computational Brain* (Malden: Wiley-Blackwell).

[55] See Piccinini, G. (2008). Some neural networks compute, others don't. *Neural Networks*, **21**, 311–321.

[56] See Fodor (2000) (note 43), also Fodor (2005) (note 49), as well as Patokorpi, E. (2009). What could abductive reasoning contribute to human computer interaction? A technology domestication view. *PsychNology*, 7(1), 113–131, and finally, Boden, M.A. (2010). *Creativity and Art: Three Roads to Surprise* (Oxford: Oxford University Press).

[57] See Lorino P., Tricard B. and Clot Y. (2011). Research methods for non-representational approaches to organizational complexity: The dialogical mediated inquiry. *Organization Studies*, **32**(6), 769–801.

[58] Citing Adloff, F., Gerund K. and Kaldewey, D. (2015). *Revealing Tacit Knowledge: Embodiment and Explication* (Germany: Deutsche Nationalbibliothek), p. 133.

[59] Citing Peirce, C.S. (1935). *Collected Papers of Charles Sanders Peirce*, Volume 5, C. Harshorne and P. Weiss (eds.) (Cambridge: Harvard University Press).

[60] Citing Peirce (1935, p. 171) (note 58).

[61] See Anderson, D. (1986). The evolution of Peirce's concept of abduction. *Transactions of the Charles S. Peirce Society*, **22**(2), 145–164.

[62] Citing Peirce (1935, p. 171) (note 59) and Peirce, C.S. (1958). *Collected Papers of Charles Sanders Peirce*, Volume 7, Burks, A.W. (ed.) (Cambridge: Harvard University Press), p. 219.

[63] Citing Peirce (1935, p. 189) (note 58).

[64] Citing Patokorpi (2009, p. 123) (note 55)

[65] Citing Patokorpi (2009, p. 123) (note 55); also see Tsoukas, H. (2003). Do We Really Understand Tacit knowledge. In *The Blackwell Handbook of Organizational Learning and Knowledge Management*, M. Easterby-Smith and M. Lyles (eds.) (New York: Blackwell), pp. 410–427.

[66] See Patokorpi (2009) (note 55) as well as Pretz, J.E. (2011). Types of Intuition: Inferential and Holistic. In *Handbook of Intuition Research*, Sinclair, M. (ed.) (Cheltenham, UK: Edward Elgar Publishing), pp. 17–27.

[67] See Tversky, A. and Kahneman, D. (2008). Extensional Versus Intuitive Reasoning: The Conjecture Fallacy in Probability Judgement. In *Reasoning: Studies of Human Inference and its Foundations*, Adler, J.E. and Rips, L.J. (eds.) (New York: Cambridge University Press), pp. 114–135.

[68] See Peirce (1935, p. 181) (note 58).

[69] See both Moriarty, S.E. (1996). Abduction: A theory of visual interpretation. *Communication Theory*, **6**(2), 167–187 as well as Pretz (2011) (note 65).

[70] See Patokorpi (2009) (note 55).

[71] See Wood, N. (2014). Silent witness, using video to record and transmit tacit knowledge in creative practices. Sheffield Hallam University Research Archive, 1–15.

[72] Citing Brödner, P. (2019). Coping with Descartes' error in information systems. *AI & Society*, **34**, 203–213.

[73] For example, see both Morse, A., Herrera, C., Clowes, R., Montebelli, A. and Ziemke, T. (2011). The role of robotic modeling in cognitive science. *New Ideas Psychology*, **29**(3), 312–324 as well as Flusberg, S.J., Thibodeau, P.H., Sternberg, D.A. and Glick, J.J. (2010). A connectionist approach to embodied conceptual metaphor. *Frontiers in Psychology*, **1**, 197. doi: 10.3389/fpsyg.2010.00197.

[74] See Wheeler (2005) (note 9).

[75] Citing McClelland *et al.* (2010, p. 348) (note 52).

[76] Harnad, S. (1990). The symbol grounding problem. *Physica D*, **42**, 335–346.

[77] See Flusberg *et al.* (2010) (note 62).

[78] See Ziemke, T. (2016). The body of knowledge: On the role of the living body in grounding embodied cognition. *BioSystems*, **148**, 4.

[79] See both Brooks, R.A. (1991). Intelligence without reason. In *Proceedings of the Twelfth International Joint Conference on Artificial Intelligence (IJCAI-91)* (San Mateo, CA: Morgan Kauffmann), pp. 569–595 as well as Brooks, R.A. (1993). The engineering of physical grounding. In *Proceedings of The Fifteenth Annual Conference of the Cognitive Science Society* (Boulder, CO: Lawrence Erlbaum Associates, Inc.), pp. 153–154.

[80] See Ziemke (2016) (note 77) in regards to Searle (1983) (note 21).

[81] See Searle (1984) (note 22).

[82] See Damasio (2003) (note 1).

[83] See Negru (2013) (note 21), Ziemke (2016) (note 77), and especially Maturana, H.R. and Varela, F.J. (1980). *Autopoiesis and Cognition* (Dordrecht: Reidel), as well as Maturana, H.R. and Varela, F.J. (1987). *The Tree of Knowledge — The Biological Roots of Human Understanding* (Boston, MA: Shambhala).

[84] Citing Ziemke (2016, p. 7) (note 77).

[85] Citing Ziemke (2016, p. 9) (note 77).

[86] See Johnson, M. (2007). *The Meaning of the Body: Aesthetics of Human Understanding* (Chicago: University of Chicago Press).

[87] See Wilson, R. (2004). *Boundaries of the Mind: The Individual in the Fragile Sciences* (Cambridge, England: Cambridge University Press).

[88] Citing Chemero, A. (2013). Radical embodied cognitive science. *Review of General Psychology*, **17**(2), 145–150.

[89] See Dreyfus (2007) (note 2), Gibson, J. J. (1979). *The Ecological Approach to Visual Perception* (Boston, MA: Houghton Mifflin), and Chemero, A. (2009). *Radical Embodied Cognitive Science* (Cambridge, MA: The MIT Press).

[90] See Brödner (2019) (note 71).

[91] See Wallén, J. (2008). The history of the industrial robot. Technical report from Automatic Control at Linköpings Universitet, Report no.: LiTH-ISY-R-2853.

[92] See Bolmsjö, G.S. (1992). *Industriell robotteknik* (Lund: Studentlitteratur).

[93] See both Craig, J.J. (1989). *Introduction to Robotic Mechanics and Control* (New York: Addison-Wesley Publishing Company) as well as Spong, M.W., Hutchinson, S. and Vidyasagar, M. (2006). *Robot Modeling and Control* (New York: John Wiley & Sons).

[94] See Jarrahi, M.H. (2018). Artificial Intelligence and the future of work: Human--AI symbiosis in organizational decision making. *Business Horizons.* https://doi.org/10.1016/j.bushor.2018.03.007.

[95] See both Parry, K., Cohen, M. and Bhattacharya, S. (2016). Rise of the machines: A critical consideration of automated leadership decision making in organizations. *Group and Organization Management*, **41**(5), 571–594, as well as Marwala, T. (2015). *Causality, Correlation and Artificial Intelligence for Rational Decision Making* (Singapore: World Scientific).

[96] See Jarrahi (2018) (note 93).

[97] See Autor, D.H. (2015). Why are there still so many jobs? The history and future of workplace automation. *Journal of Economic Perspectives*, **29**(3), 3–30.

[98] Citing Faraj, S., Pachidi, S. and Sayegh, K. (2018). Working and organizing in the age of the learning algorithm. *Information and Organization*, **28**, 62–70.

[99] Citing Dewey, J. (1929). *The Quest for Certainty: A Study of the Relation of Knowledge and Action* (New York: Putnam), p. 173; also see Winther, R.G. (2014). James and Dewey on abstractions. *The Pluralist*, **9**(2), 1–28.

[100] See Holford, W.D. (2020). An ethical inquiry of the effect of cockpit automation on the responsibilities of airline pilots: Dissonance or meaningful control?

Journal of Business Ethics, https://doi.org/10.1007/s10551-020-04640-z; also see Moore, P. and Robinson, A. (2015). The quantified self: What counts in the neoliberal workplace. *New Media & Society*, online first); as well as Oliver, N., Calvard, T. and Potocnik, K. (2017). Cognition, technology and organizational limits: Lessons from the Air France 447 disaster. *Organization Science*, **28**(4), 597–780.

[101] See Holford (2020) (note 99), Oliver *et al.* (2017) (note 99), Chialastri, A. (2012). Automation in Aviation. In *Automation*, Kongoli, F. (ed.), pp. 79–102, InTech, doi: 10.5772/49949, Strauch, B. (2017). The automation-by-expertise-by-training interaction: why automation-related accidents continue to occur in sociotechnical systems. *Human Factors*, **59**(2), 204–228, and Gawron, V. (2019). Automation in aviation accident analyses. Center for Advanced Aviation System Development — MITRE Technical Report MTR190013. The MITRE Corporation. 20 pp.

[102] See both Pope, S. (2014). Fly by wire: Fact versus science fiction. *Flying Magazine*, 23 April. Available at: https://www.flyingmag.com/aircraft/jets/fly-by-wire-fact-versus-science-fiction/ as well as Harford, T. (2016). Crash: How computers are setting us up for disaster. *The Guardian*, October 11. Available at: https://www.theguardian.com/technology/2016/oct/11/crash-how-computers-are-setting-us-up-disaster.

[103] See Oliver *et al.* (2017) (note 99).

[104] *Ibid.*

[105] Citing Amalberti, R. (1998). Automation in Aviation: A Human Factors Perspective. In *Handbook of Aviation Human Factors*, Wise, J.A., Hopkin, V.D. and Garland, D.J. (eds.) (Boca Raton, FL: CRC Press), pp. 173–192.

[106] See *Ibid.* as well as Roe E. and Schulman P.R. (2008). *High Reliability Management: Operating on the Edge* (Palo Alto, CA: Stanford University Press).

[107] See Oliver *et al.* (2017) (note 99).

[108] See Greenhalgh, T., Howick, J. and Maskrey, N. (2014). Evidence based medicine: A movement in crisis? *BMJ*, **348**, g3725.

[109] See Sackett, D.L., Rosenberg, W.M., Gray, J.A., Haynes, R.B. and Richardson, W.S. (1996). Evidence based medicine: What it is and what it isn't. *BMJ*, **312**, 71–72.

[110] See Timmermans, S. and Berg, M. (2003). *The Gold Standard: The Challenge of Evidence-Based Medicine and Standardization in Health Care* (Philadelphia: Temple University Press).

[111] See Glasziou, P., Moynihan, R., Richards, T. and Godlee, F. (2013). Too much medicine; too little care. *BMJ*, **347**, f4247.

[112] See Marwala (2015) (note 94) as well as Elish, M. and Boyd, D. (2018). Situating methods in the magic of Big Data and AI. *Communication Monographs*, **85**(1), 57–80.

[113] See Faraj *et al.* (2018) (note 97) as well as Dejoux, C. and Léon, E. (2018). *Métamorphose des managers*. First edition (Paris: Pearson).

[114] See Faraj *et al.* (2018) (note 97), Dreyfus (2007) (note 2) as well as Dourish, P. (2016). Algorithms and their others: Algorithmic culture in context. *Big Data & Society*, **3**(2) (2053951716665128).

[115] Citing Faraj *et al.* (2018, p. 66) (note 97).

[116] See Mukherjee, S. (2017). AI v. MD. *New Yorker*, April 3.

[117] See Faraj *et al.* (2018) (note 97).

[118] See Faraj *et al.* (2018) (note 97) as well as Holford, W.D. (2020). The algorithmic workplace and its enactive effect on the future of professions. *Futures*, **122**, 1–11. https://doi.org/10.1016/j.futures.2020.102609.

[119] See Gibson, J.J. (1979). *The Ecological Approach to Visual Perception* (Boston, MA: Houghton Mifflin).

Chapter 6

Radical Embodied Cognitive Science and Certain Irreducible Phenomena Associated with Adaptive Expertise (*Mètis*)

6.1. Introduction

Radical embodied cognitive science (RECS) is a form of Jamesian perspective that fully rejects representationalism. This is in contrast to representational approaches to embodied cognitive science (discussed in the previous chapter), which is a "watering down" of RECS, in that it attempts to combine Jamesian theory with the computational theory of mind. In this chapter, we first examine RECS, which considers a theory of the relationship between mind and world as general, taking inspirations from Gibson's[1] ecological psychology as well as analytical interpretations of Heidegger's and Merleau-Ponty's phenomenology. RECS also incorporates the "enactive view" as first proposed by Maturana and Varela,[2] in which cognition depends constitutively on the living body. We then briefly look at RECS's role toward more human-centric, socio-technical designs within organizations, thus allowing human adaptive expertise (*mètis*) to better flourish. We also critically examine the potential pitfalls of RECS by way of various reminders of phenomenology's irreducible nature. Finally, through language and conversation (as a perfect example of human adaptive expertise in action), we argue that we must remain not only pluralistic in our attempt at explaining human behavior and practices but also open to irreducible phenomenological dimensions such as metaphors which resist being explicated and modeled in an analytical fashion.

6.2. RECS and its Ecological, Dynamic, and Enactive Perspectives

RECS is a relatively new branch of cognitive science that is "radical" in proposing new conceptual tools which help scientists understand how cognition depends on, and is a part of, the body in its interaction with the environment.[3] As such[4]:

> "The explanatory tools cognitive science deploys must do justice to the essential contributions of bodily skills and environmental affordances to cognitive behavior. They must account for the ways in which the individual is able to expertly coordinate their behavior with a dynamically changing environment. Ecological psychology and dynamical systems theory provide the tools to meet this challenge."

Cognitive neuroscientists have attempted to map emotional and cognitive functions onto discrete and separate structures of the brain. RECS, on the other hand, views structure–function mappings as not being fixed and static properties of networks.[5] Rather, structure–function relationships change with time, in which the way a function of a given network performs is adaptive and context-dependent. In turn, the functional aspect "of a network is determined by the whole organism in its interaction with an environment that is rich with possibilities for actions."[6]

RECS seeks to explain cognitive phenomena by way of a "dynamic coupling of information in the environment, sensory experience, body features, and opportunities for behavior. Moreover, once all constraints within this system are known, those constraints provide sufficient information to guide action, without the need for complex calculation."[7] As such, adherents of RECS argue that cognitive phenomena can be explained without the use of mediating representations.[8] In this spirit, Chemero explains that cognition's *primary* task is entirely different from "construction, manipulation, and use of representations of the world."[9] RECS taps into both the Jamesian perspective of ecological psychology, as put forward by Gibson, and phenomenology's embodied and embedded streams, as conceptualized by Heidegger and Merleau-Ponty.[10] Here, Chemero draws upon Gibson's[11] three major ideas:

(1) Perception is direct. When we perceive something, we perceive it directly — we are in direct contact with it. This means that perception "is not the result of inferences performed on sensory representations." Hence, no internal information is computed (or represented) going from sensation to perception. "This implies, of course, that the perceiving isn't inside the animal, but rather is part of a system that includes both the animal and the perceived object. This just is Jamesian radical empiricism."[12]

(2) Perception is for action.[13] This mutual relationship between perception and action means that "we perceive the world in order to act in it ... [yet] a good deal of action is also for perception or cognition. We lean to the left in order to get a better view."[14]

(3) People directly perceive affordances of environmental opportunities for action. Again, such a direct perception means that there is "no mediation of representational constructs or computations."[15] Affordances are both features of the environment and dependent on the perceiver.

Gibson's ontological position of affordance cuts across the subject–object dichotomy:

> "[A]n affordance is neither an objective property nor a subjective property; or it is both if you like. An affordance cuts across the dichotomy of subjective-objective and helps us to understand its inadequacy. It is equally a fact of the environment and a fact of behavior. It is both physical and psychical, yet neither. An affordance points both ways, to the environment and to the observer."[16]

Implicitly, Gibson's "two-way street" or relational perspective allows for structuration or enactment to occur both ways.[17] As such, humans are given the leeway to creatively "enact their human agency in response to technology's material agency."[18] We shall return to this in the next section, as we see how the enactive stream of embodied cognitive sciences complements and merges with the ecological stream.

The phenomenological aspect of embodied cognition can be argued through Heidegger's "ready-to-hand" and "unready-to-hand" interactions with tools. In paraphrasing Dreyfus'[19] interpretation of Heidegger's work, Chemero explains[20]:

> "Heidegger argued that most of our experience of tools is unreflective, smooth coping with them. When we ride a bicycle competently, for example, we are not aware of the bicycle but of the street, the traffic conditions, and our route home. The bicycle itself recedes in our experience, and becomes the thing through which we experience the road. In Heidegger's language, the bicycle is ready-to-hand, meaning that we experience it as a part of us, no different than our shoulders or knees. Sometimes, however, the brakes grab more forcefully than usual or the chain slips, and the bicycle becomes temporarily prominent in our experience. We notice the bicycle. Heidegger would say that the bicycle has become unready-to-hand, in that our smooth use of it has been interrupted temporarily and it has become, for a short time, the object of our experience."

Dotov *et al.* justify this transition from ready-to-hand to unready-to-hand by way of a cognitive experiment involving a video game requiring the use of a mouse to control a cursor on a monitor.[21] Across the use of the cursor, participants had to "herd" moving objects inside a circle. During the trial, the connection between the mouse and cursor was sometimes disrupted such that cursor movements did not correspond to those of the mouse — after which, connection and control was returned to normal. Motion-tracking equipment was used to record the trajectory of the hand-tool system. The fluctuations in the movements of the hand-tool before, during, and after the power disruptions (i.e. perturbations) were measured and characterized, showing fluctuations before and after the power disruptions to follow a $1/f^\beta$ (f = frequency and $0 \leq \beta \leq 1$), or more precisely, a $1/f$ noise pattern. A $1/f$ pattern in physiological systems indicates that the mouse is being treated as part of a single system with the rest of their body.[22] Such a noise pattern is the "signature of a softly assembled system exhibiting and sustained by interaction-dominant dynamics" involving coordinated processes which "alter one another's dynamics, with complex interactions extending to the body's periphery and, sometimes, beyond."[23] During the power disruption however, the noise pattern approached that of pure white noise, which is typical of component-dominant dynamics behavior, which "is the product of a rigidly delineated architecture of modules, each with pre-determined functions."[24] To summarize the experiment, "while participants were smoothly playing the video game, they were part of a human-computer system that had the same pattern of variability as a well-functioning physiological system; when we temporarily disrupted performance, that pattern of variability temporarily disappeared. This is evidence that the mouse was experienced as ready-to hand while it was working correctly, and became unready-to-hand during the perturbation."[25]

Consistent with RECS's holistic body–brain–environment perspective is that cognition is best understood as a dynamic system.[26] Although "the ability to think about the outcome of a yet to be performed action seems to necessitate a representational explanation," proponents of RECS often "rely on dynamical systems theory as an explanatory tool to substantiate their claims."[27] By representation, we refer to Haugeland's definition[28]:

"A sophisticated system (organism) designed (evolved) to maximize some end (e.g., survival) must in general adjust its behavior to specific features, structures, or configurations of its environment in ways that could not have been fully prearranged in its design. [...] But if the relevant features are not always present (detectable), then they can, at least in some cases, be represented; that is, something else can stand in for them, with the power to guide behavior in their stead. That which stands in for something else in this way is a representation; that which it stands for is its content; and its standing in for that content is representing it."

We also refer to Newell's interpretation[29]:

"An entity X designates an entity Y relative to a process P, if, when P takes X as input, its behavior depends on Y."

Hence, as van Roouij *et al.* argue, representation for traditional cognitive science "play a double role: they carry content and they cause behavior."[30] Yet, a representational account of behavior quickly leads us to the frame problem and the issue of infinite regress,[31] and all its associated practical limitations and consequent oversimplifications of contexts-at-hand.

Conversely, the preceding video game experiment by Dotov, Nie, and Chemero is an example of dynamic systems theory (DST) used to empirically support Heidegger's claims about phenomenology through descriptive means of a given situation and context, rather than through normative explanations and generalizations.[32] Indeed, Richardson and Chemero have shown that $1/f$ scaling is observed across a wide range of human activities.[33] "In part, this reflects the motor component of the activity being studied and the ability of people to adapt to situational demands as embodied systems ... While the patterns that $1/f$ scaling provides a means of analysing the temporal dynamics of activity, they do not provide clues as to how actions might be coordinated or controlled."[34] On this latter point, however, we shall return regarding the use of DST as an explanatory tool and possible predictive model later in this chapter with respect to the possible pitfalls of RECS, which re-echo the frame regress issues of context stripping and generalizations encountered within the representational approaches we have critically examined in previous Chapters 2, 4, and 5. For now, suffice to say that, as van Roouij *et al.* explain,[35] certain adherents of DST within RECS see it as a non-representational manner of understanding and accounting for behavior.[36] Across DST, whole-body behavior is studied as an emergent property of the interactions between its subsystems both within and beyond its periphery. DST typically describes behavior, "on the level of the whole system. On this account, behavior is seen as a self-organized pattern, emerging from the interaction among subsystems."[37]

Finally, RECS also incorporates enactivism, as first proposed by Maturana and Varela.[38] While "ecological psychology focuses on the nature of the environment that animals perceive and act in; enactivism focuses on the organism as an agent."[39] Baggs and Chemero remind us of both the ecological (or "pre-given") and relational aspects of Gibsonian affordance to justify how both ecological psychology and enactivism can co-exist together.[40] Specifically beyond what the environment "offers the animal,"[41] the relational view of affordance implies the relative skills and learning capabilities that the organism possesses, thus allowing to account for differences in behavior between members of the same species.[42] A potential conflict between what is pre-given and what is locally created or enacted is avoided, and in fact becomes complementary, through Reed's argument that "an affordance becomes a relation only when a given animal uses it; until that point it is to be understood as a resource (i.e., a property of the habitat, in our terms). This resolution allows us to talk about inter-individual variation while avoiding a solipsistic view of perception in the individual (because the umwelt [or perceived/actioned experience] is still conceived as a lived perspective on a common habitat)."[43] Adding to this, Baggs and

Chemero explain how in complementary fashion, phenomenologists (and enactivists) describe the umwelt through experience while ecological psychologists (and enactivists) describe the umwelt as being perceived directly — and that finally, enactivists tend to use the two terms interchangeably. To which they add[44]:

> "This makes sense since both 'given in experience' and 'perceived directly' imply that access to the umwelt is not mediated by representations or inferential processes. It is important to be clear that, despite the connotations of 'given', directly perceiving the umwelt typically takes work. As Gibson (1966) pointed out, the human visual system includes the eyes, brain, head, neck, torso, and legs, and direct visual perception requires moving."

Finally, we repeat (as previously mentioned in Chapter 5) that phenomenologists such as Dreyfus describe one's direct perception with reality through enactment phenomena, that is a coupling between body and environment which bridges the embedded character of Hedeigger's "throwness" of one's self into a given context, or Merleau-Ponty's "inseperateness with one's environment," with the enactive aspect of embodiment as proposed by Varela *et al.* — i.e. "the enactment or bringing forth of meaning from a background of understanding."[45] As we enact a world, we are also embodied in it, i.e. it involves the necessity of a physical body whose sensory–motor experiences result in cognition. This non-representational intelligence not only adaptively detects but also *creates* what is significant within one's perceptual world.[46]

6.3. So What?

While we do not believe RECS provides an answer to every aspect of human behavior and cognition, and that furthermore, there is definitely room for representational approaches whereby both approaches have there strengths and pitfalls (in this regard, we discuss the potential pitfalls of RECS in the next section), the factoring in of phenomenological enactive aspects of human adaptive expertise within RECS further legitimizes more human-centric, socio-technical design approaches in which human operators in interaction with "intelligent" technologies, retain meaningful control of the socio-technical organizational context-situation at hand.[47]

Control is "the power to influence [...] the course of events ... to have control means to influence the situation so that it develops or keeps in a way preferred by the controlling entity."[48] As such, the term control in a real or actual sense implies not just the actual authority (or allowance) to act appropriately toward an aim established by the controller (agent) but also the actual *ability* to do so.[49] Authority *allows* or permits the agent to control the course of events, while ability *enables* (through skills and resources) the agent to control the course of events[50]:

$$\text{Control (Actual)} \rightarrow \text{Authority (Actual)} + \text{Ability (Actual)}$$

In turn, determining what is relevant and meaningful is key toward maintaining full control. However, toward the attainment of a meaningful control of a human–technology system at hand, it is not sufficient to simply have a human presence or "being in the loop."[51] The human operator must be able to influence (enact) all parts of the system in a relevant or meaningful manner. This includes having sufficient information and options over the socio-technical system in question which goes beyond merely physico-cognitive reactions of "merely pushing a button in a reflex when a light goes on."[52] Maintaining a meaningful control means maintaining an *optimal grip*.[53] As we argued in Chapter 5, Heidegger[54] brings forward the non-representational aspect of being in the moment, i.e. no guidelines or rules, unless you merely want to be leveled out to a competent and standard way of doing things (i.e. "unauthentic").[55] Reaching a mastery of skills requires a direct embeddedness or "thrown-ness" into the context at hand in which there are no rules or guidelines to follow (i.e. being "authentic"). Merleau-Ponty then builds upon Heidegger's account by stressing the body: "when you're skillfully coping ... without thinking, without rules, your body and its skills are drawing you to get this optimal grip on the situation."[56] In Chapter 2, this allowed us to deconstruct human adaptive expertise in terms of its embodied, embedded, and non-representational nature and compare this to AI's more abstractive representational frames and *limitations*. More precisely, it allowed us to highlight the relevance of relevance within human adaptive expertise, something which AI cannot do in new or unforeseen situations. Determining, as well as enacting, what is relevant also becomes the basis of sufficient control, i.e. human meaningful control, in that he/she cannot exert control unless he/she can detect/enact what is relevant, and then take relevant decisions and relevant actions in regards to these relevant cues:

Meaningful Control → Actual decision-making authority + Ability (detect/enact relevant cues and take relevant actions)

The ability to detect/enact relevant cues and take relevant actions is the basis of adaptive expertise. Adaptive expertise has been recognized as a key characteristic in expert performance within various domains such as aircraft piloting, medical care, and engineering.[57] For example, Adams and Ericsson speak of expert pilots' "adaptive" expertise in regards to developing successful solutions in the face of "untrainable emergency situations"[58]; Pusic *et al.* refer to the criticality of adaptive expertise of expert medical practitioners in the face of "complex patients with complex needs requiring bespoke solutions"[59]; and Pierrakos *et al.* speak of how future engineers will require the ability to adapt quickly and engage in novel problem solving.[60]

In turn, Adams and Ericsson's[61] description of expert pilot adaptive expertise rejoins *mètis'* "multiple, polymorphous,"[62] "variegated and multicolored"[63] qualities, as they relate its mixture of "knowing-how," "knowing when," and "knowing-what" by way of the following performance characteristics:

(1) Rapid cognitive access to a well-organized body of conceptual and procedural knowledge.
(2) Keen, quick decisions as well as a direct perception of the proper course of action to take in a rapid and effective manner.

Adaptive expertise, like *mètis* (see Chapter 3), is rapid, whereby relevant or meaningful relationships are quickly perceived, decisions made, and actions taken rapidly, based on insight and intuition.[64]

Hence, meaningful control for today's human operators becomes a matter of achieving a meaningful partnership between humans and technology.[65] One promising area within the domain of human–computer interaction (HCI) is that of continuous human–technology interaction integrating the concepts of manual and supervisory control.[66] Continuous human–technology interaction taps into both the ecological and enactive aspects of Gibsonian affordance theory found within RECS, i.e. on the one hand, closely tied to the material features of a technological object, yet also derives from the unique ways different users enact and make sense of the same technological object. As such, human operators are provided the leeway to creatively "enact their human agency in response to technology's material agency" through improvisation within a volatile and unpredictable work context on condition that they are both knowledgeable and are provided the power/authority to do so.[67] While the details of such manual and supervisory control design theory is beyond the scope of this book, the overall design approach attempts to reflect the structure and dynamics of humans (with their central nervous and neuromuscular systems), in which human operators (pilots) are kept actively engaged within the socio-technical system.[68] This is specifically achieved across two criteria: (1) maintaining a direct contact between the human operator and his/her environment through actual and simulated manual actions and feedbacks, and (2) maintaining overall human supervisory control of tasks carried out by algorithmic technologies.[69] Across the first criterion, the approach seeks to maintain human operator skills, by avoiding "operator hand-off" and subsequent "automation complacency" phenomena through haptic feedback support. Here, feedback to human senses (e.g. force, stiffness, etc.) is provided to reinstate the full-bodily engagement of the human operator.[70] Across the second criterion, supervisory control is maintained across the human operator freedom to override the system through a sufficiently broad range of circumstances.[71] Interestingly, haptic feedback also helps support this latter design criteria by providing an effective and seamless control override capability toward the operator through his/her full-bodily engagement.[72] In this manner, RECS has helped support more recent research in human perceptual judgement through bodily engagement with the development of enhanced haptic sensory affordances based on enactive vibro-tactile feedback.[73]

Finally, maintaining meaningful human operator control over socio-technical systems requires not just design approach changes on the part of designers and manufacturers but also changes in organizational protocols and rules which management need to enact. This requires meaningful *dialogue* between human operators, management and designers/manufacturers to achieve such human-centric designs.[74] Unfortunately, and as previously argued in Chapter 5, current techno-centric systems relying solely on algorithmic representational systems and protocols continue to contribute toward overall erosion of human adaptive expertise. Supporting this view, Parasuraman and Manzey, across their own studies as well as an exhaustive review of prior research, argue that such erosion of skills occurs through a positive reinforcement loop of "learned carelessness," which builds upon the repetition of no abnormal issues or events arising from automated operations.[75] Said another way, "higher reliability of automation and higher levels of automation have been associated with greater complacency, which can lead to worse error management."[76] As an influential spokesperson for airline pilots, Captain Sullenberger (hero of the successful NY, Hudson River landing of US Airways Flight 1549 in January 2009), ascertains what experts and researchers in human factor studies independently concluded[77,78]:

> "The paradox of cockpit automation is that it can...relegate the pilots to the role of monitor, something that humans are not good at ... Humans are much better 'doers' than monitors ... The problem with technology is ... it can only manage what has been foreseen and for which it's been programmed ... So one of the weaknesses of technology is that it has a hard time handling 'black swan' events ... We have to design our systems to require our engagement. We cannot design a system that's so hands off that we are simply required to sit there and watch it for 14 hours. That's simply not going to work."

Too many techno-centric approaches in which the human operators are not bodily engaged with the socio-technical system in question have overemphasized *short-term* and well-defined machine efficiency and reliability in lieu of adaptability to unexpected situations and outcomes. Such approaches view technology as a replacement to human operator skills and decision-making, basing themselves on well-defined reliability criteria and measured outputs — thus leading to the paradox of high efficiency, yet low adaptability (as a result of human skills erosion). Conversely, socio-technical design approaches, which emphasize human-centric meaningful human operator control as discussed in the previous paragraphs (and therefore full operator engagement and ability to override systems), brings the human operator back into the loop in an active and engaged fashion, thus combining machine reliability with human capacity for adaptability to situations which go beyond technology's defined envelopes.

6.4. Potential Pitfalls and Overextensions within RECS as a Reminder of Human Phenomenology

RECS is an attempt at describing and understanding "'the bulkiest parts of Intelligence': perception, action, motor control, and coordination."[79] This "bulky part" is what Dreyfus argues to be Heidegger's ready-to-handedness, i.e. where "all relations of mental states to their objects presuppose a more basic form of being-with-things which does not involve mental activity."[80] For Dreyfus, "Heidegger accepts intentional directedness as essential to human activity, but he denies that [all] intentionality is mental."[81] It is only when something becomes problematic or "breaks down" in our "normal, everyday dealings with familiar things" that "psychological states or experiences with any kind of mental or representational content arise."[82] As such, RECS has actively pursued the non-representational, ready-to-hand dimensions of human perception, actions, and practices, i.e. *understand* human embodied cognition within its non-representational mode. And, to this we can add Chemero's prudency[83]:

> "I do not believe that radical embodied cognitive science is the one true psychology of the future ... The mind, I submit, is just as complicated as the Mississippi River, and it would be shocking if just one style of explanation could account for all of it. For this reason, it is wise to adopt explanatory pluralism in psychology."

Along with such good words, an ambiguity to which we are not initially opposed to, is RECS's objective of modeling, more precisely dynamical modeling.[84] As we described earlier in this chapter in the video game experiment by Dotov, Nie and Chemero, DST was used to empirically support Heidegger's claims about phenomenology.[85] Here, we stress the term *support* as opposed to *prove* in any deterministic and positivistic sense. The $1/f$ scaling observed should be viewed as a descriptive indication — not a normative or prescriptive proof and predictor of ready-to-hand behavior. In this sense, we can speak of this mathematical relationship as a model *representating* reality — and thus, rejoin James[86] and Dewey[87] as being useful for specific interventions in, and representations of, complex processes. However, to this, both James and Dewey add that models can promise too much when viewing themselves (i.e. representations) *as reality*. This is exactly what certain proponents of RECS risk doing, despite their claims to the contrary.[88] Chemero's own reference to RECS's actual usage of dynamic modeling is explicitly ambitious, and perhaps, implicitly reductionist regarding future research to pursue[89]:

> "The use of dynamical systems theory as a modeling tool plays several crucial roles in radical embodied cognitive science. First, and perhaps most important, it does what modeling does throughout the sciences: it bridges the gaps between abstract theorizing and concrete data that can be gathered in the lab. Second, radical embodied cognitive science requires an explanatory tool that can span the agent_environment border. A dynamical system is a set of quantitative variables changing continually, concurrently, and interdependently over time in accordance with dynamical laws that can, in principle, be described by some set of equations. To say that cognition is best described using dynamical systems theory is to say that cognitive scientists ought to try to understand cognition as intelligent behavior and to model intelligent behavior using a particular sort of mathematics, most often sets of differential equations."

On this point, however, Alessandroni is adamantly unequivocal in pointing toward RECS's reductionist project[90]:

> "Chemero, like Thelen, states that human cognition can be understood in mathematical terms ... For Chemero, the best explanation of how these type of systems work is not the computational-representational explanation, but the self-regulatory explanation provided by DST ... By discovering the equations that regulate the system, Chemero argues, we can claim to have described the regulator behaviour. And if we agree with that (particularly in what relates to the definition of "behaviour"), we must also accept that finding the equations that regulate human mechanical action is equivalent to explaining human cognition."

Before addressing Alessandronni's pertinent point, another interrelated issue quickly comes to mind — namely the issue of representation. RECS has argued for a non-representational comprehension and approach toward understanding human behavior.[91] Yet, its *apparent* adherence to a fully mathematized (and modelizable) version of DST brings us to an epistemological "hiccup" to say the least — i.e. certain spheres of RECS seek to fully understand direct, realist, non-representational behavior by way of mathematical representations (in this case, differential equations), an issue not ignored by proponents of computational-representational theory of mind such as Eliasmith.[92] To use conceptual models (whether mathematical or otherwise), as an aid toward a pluralized descriptive process is one thing. To use or aim such modeling initiatives toward the full description of behavior is quite another. By doing the latter, one can no longer legitimately accuse the various streams of computational theory of mind of being overly reductionist in their own way. Granted, RECS is not a monolithic movement by any means.[93] Many of its adherents are not just open toward a "a pluralistic account of the variety of processes implied in embodied cognition" but actively integrate different theories of cognition such as found within Raab and Araujo's account of representational and non-representational embodied cognition through the lens of judgment and decision-making in sports.[94] Such approaches can be argued to be in accord with Dreyfus' interpretations of Heidegger's ready, unready, and present-to-handedness account of human behavior.[95] However, one issue still remains — i.e. the issue of phenomenology.[96]

While RECS has inspired itself from Heidegger and Merleau-Ponty (especially, as interpreted and rendered accessible by Dreyfus), phenomenology's foundation is based on the study of the body as lived experience — i.e. "from an experientialist perspective [whereby] the body should not be considered a biological entity but a phenomenological one, as a body lived through our experiences."[97] Phenomenology does not pretend to go into the cognitive business of "comprehension by excision," whether by way of computational or holistic theories.[98] Alessandroni sees it as an unfinished body–world dialectical interaction, and therefore as a not fully articulated (or articulable) story — i.e. "without the third dialectical term, synthesis."[99] For Masis, it is about the transcendental which is not explicable[100]:

> "Phenomenology does not postulate entities whatsoever, neither natural nor cultural, and it certainly does not concern itself with the law-like causality governing natural processes. Instead, its task is to investigate the very basis that makes it possible for science to construct theories populated by such objective invariances and the very constitution of the experience which allows for those objects to appear as meaningful.

Following Husserl, this transcendental field that is revealed by phenomenology also discloses a transcendental subjectivity that cannot simply be identified with any constituted entity, whether natural or cultural. The transcendental sphere is, then, always relied on when postulating theories about consciousness or the mind, 'while not realizing that we are doing so, since whether acknowledged or not, it is the unspoken concomitant of everything we think and believe' (citing Olafson, 1987: 256)."

Yet, one can also argue, as does Massis that cognitivists can still offer insights, albeit incomplete ones. To this we fully adhere. Human behavior can be partially explained through both representational and non-representational theories, whereby the aggregate summation of both offers us at best only a partial insight as to what constitutes daily human activities. The rest remains unfathomable transcendence and indeterminacy to which phenomenology's *mètis* embraces without needing to provide an account.[101] For it was never "Heidegger's intention in the first place to give an account of human cognition or to develop a theory of knowledge or a philosophy of mind."[102]

6.5. Language's Overlapping Dimensions of Representation, Non-Representation, and Phenomenology

For IBM's Watson, some have claimed that its "natural language" algorithms (as specific forms of machine learning), by way of approximations and probabilities, has "the ability to understand nuanced human-composed sentences, and assign multiple meanings to terms and concepts"; and, in turn, allows Watson to "develop intelligent solutions based on past experience" as well as to give it the ability to correctly "discern cancer patterns."[103]

Before deconstructing the above discourse, we first return to precursors of the term AI, i.e. Turing's[104] paper reflecting on the possibility of machines being intelligent. Turing proposed a method for evaluating whether machines could exhibit intelligent behavior equivalent or indistinguishable from that of a human by way of the well-known Turing Test. The rationale was that if a computer could imitate the sentience of a human being, would that not imply the computer itself was sentient? The test would consist of a human evaluator judging natural language conversations between a human and a machine, knowing in advance that one of the two partners was a machine. All participants would be hidden from one another with exchanges limited to a text-only channel. If the evaluator could not reliably distinguish the machine from the human, the machine would pass the test. To date no machine has passed the Turing Test.[105]

In returning to IBM'S Watson, it was first developed and deployed for a very narrowly defined task: searching and matching textual clues to answers in the game of Jeopardy! As IBM's Ferrucci points out, this differs immensely with human interpretative capabilities.[106] Words in isolation, or sentences and entire discourses stripped from its context in a particular culture, at a particular time do not mean the same.[107] The majority of questions in Jeopardy! ask for factoids, with over 90% of answers linked to Wikipedia titles, whereby the Watson team exploited a few "hooks" and identified certain keywords.[108] Watson, like all other machines, manipulates numbers, as opposed to social constructs.[109]

Language and conversation is inherently complex, uncertain, and ambiguous.[110] For example, McComb and Semple show the inter-relationship between social and language complexities,[111] while Maddieson presents the phonological and morphological complexities of language,[112] respectively. In turn, uncertainty phenomena in language/discourse and its own inherent complexities have been examined from different aspects, including syntactics, semantics, and pragmatics.[113] Weick makes a clear distinction between uncertainty and ambiguity, the former defined as a lack of information, and the latter consisting of too many interpretations of a situation.[114] Hence, in a "clear cut" world, "while uncertainty is located at the boundary between knowing and what is yet unknown within a certain frame, ambiguity is located at the boundaries between different frames of knowledge or different kinds of knowing."[115] Yet, Walker *et al.* also refer to a more nuanced overlap between uncertainty and ambiguity, in which context and conceptual uncertainty are shown to be strongly related to ambiguity through subjectivity and intersubjectivity.[116]

This overlap can also be extended to complexity. Complexity involves "situations ... characterized by an abundance of elements or variables."[117] In the case of complexity, where we all know and explicitly agree on the rules, AI's superior computational capabilities allow it to easily surpass humans — i.e. at tasks that are clearly defined, and in which the analytics within these systems tap onto dependable or "good" data.[118] Yet performing such tasks with known and agreed rules can only limit us to the syntactic (or representational) complexities of language.[119]

The complexities of semantics and pragmatics involve endless rules associated with both context and practice, which are uncertain beforehand and can only be determined after-the-fact, i.e. through immersion within the community of practice in question — and whereby each context is unique onto itself.[120] Another component of semantic complexity is the diversity of interpretive perspectives, hence ambiguity, in which "even if a common syntax is present, interpretations are often different" and "the problem then shifts from processing information to learning about the sources that create these semantic differences."[121] As such, meaning between interpreting subjects transcends mere syntactic units. When learning language, we each learn unique, tentative, and sometimes ambiguous "things that are never said."[122] As previously mentioned in Chapter 3, utterances are personal and reconstructed all the time and are also the product of interaction between interlocutors — i.e. "an utterance has a potential to mean, but ... its potential is realized through another's response."[123] As such, conversation cannot be reduced to IBM Watson's "'data' processing" — it is a "dialogical meaning-making process" transcending mere representational syntactics inherently involving both uncertainty and ambiguity.[124]

Also discussed in Chapter 3 is Searle's attempt to understand metaphors within language in which he concluded that they could not be analyzed in a representational manner[125]:

> "There are ... whole classes of metaphors that function without any underlying principles of similarity. It just seems to be a fact about our mental capacities that we are able to interpret certain sorts of metaphors without the application of any underlying "rules" or "principles" other than the sheer ability to make certain associations. I don't know any better way of describing these abilities than to say that they are nonrepresentational mental capacities."

As a postscript, Chomsky makes the distinction between rule-governed and rule-changing aspects of creativity within the use of language.[126] The former is a formal property of the syntactic system and creative in a mechanical sense only. Rule-governed creativity includes the production of new sentences and the infinite ability of language to produce such new sentences. The rule-changing creativity within the use of language involves aspects of the semantic system, which was left largely unexplored by Chomsky. Most importantly, the semantic nature of creativity includes the use of metaphors, in which linguistic relevance is made beyond the literal rules and elements of syntax and semantics, and yet can still produce a comprehensible utterance.[127]

Metaphors have been re-examined in various fields such as psychology, neuroscience, philosophy, and linguistics — with the growing consensus that they are fundamental to the process of thinking and communication.[128] According to Lakoff and Johnson,[129] "our conceptual system is largely metaphorical." On the other hand, while analytical cognitivists have attempted to reduce metaphors "to a system of literal and verifiable sentences," metaphors are "cognitively irreducible"[130] — i.e. it cannot be reduced to "statements of literal meaning" without losing its potency.[131] Finally, Modell suggests that "what makes us uniquely human is an unconscious metaphoric process. Unconscious autobiographical memory, the memory of the self and its intentions, is constantly recontextualized, and the link between conscious experience and unconscious memory is provided by metaphor."[132]

Finally, the use of metaphors is inherently phenomenological in nature, thereby further justifying its irreducible character.[133] Metaphors can serve as both a bridge and an un-bridge in that they "are two-way vehicles of transport simultaneously connecting and disconnecting, embedding and disembedding people as well as concepts and issues."[134] As such[135]:

> "Experiencing bridges in an embodied way not only provides a passageway but are part of being in an embodied place. According to Heidegger (1993), bridges are places that permit to experience the uniqueness and unity of space. They allow us to feel that we belong and can enter as well as how to dwell and live in a placed world ..."

More specifically, metaphors involve the bridging transfer from experience to more abstract domains, which must unavoidably pass through our bodily experience and embodied constructing thinking, feeling, interpreting, and acting.[136]

As a postscript, Sandberg and Tsoukas provides an interesting summary of language's irreducible nature across what, we ourselves, would qualify as overlapping (and therefore, not "pure" categories of) phenomenological (or pragmatic/direct realist), constructionist (or semantic ambiguous/non-representational) and cognitivist (or representational) dimensions[137]:

> "Acting in the world involves the use of language: a semantic space is carved out within which distinctions are drawn, meanings are created, and utterances are made (citing Dreyfus, 1995: 63; Heidegger, 1962). How language is used reflects the way in which agents engage with the world (citing Dreyfus, 1995: 65–66)."

More specifically, in a Heideggerian ready-to-hand or absorbed coping, language is primarily (although we ourselves would insist in the Latourian sense, *not purely*) used in a phenomenological or performative fashion — to get things done.[138] Here, Sandberg and Tsoukas refer to when "a surgeon, in the middle of an operation, shouts 'scalpel', she uses language performatively (citing both Blattner (2006, pp. 103–108 and Dreyfus (2000, p. 317)."[139] When absorbed coping interrupted, i.e. an individual undergoes Heidegger's unready-to-hand mode, he/she starts paying deliberate attention to what they do, whereby explicit beliefs, desires, and propositional attitudes are uttered/*constructed*.[140] "The surgeon may now say 'this scalpel is not sharp enough.'"[141] While the surgeon may still be in a primarily performative/phenomenological mode in which "utterance is articulated, implicitly requesting another scalpel,"[142] we would also add that there exists a constructionist aspect in which expectations have been violated whereby the surgeon must now attend to and bracket cues in the environment by way of an intersubjective meaning "through cycles of interpretation and action, thereby enacting a more ordered environment from which further cues can be drawn."[143] Finally, in abstract detachment, that is in a Heideggerian present-to-handedness,

> "after the operation is over, while reflecting on the equipment used in order to avoid encountering similar problems in the future, the very same statement ('this scalpel is not sharp enough') points to an abstract property (sharpness) and to the scalpel in a more general sense than before (i.e. not only to this particular scalpel, but to this type of scalpel in general). Although still in a practical context, language is used here in a representational way,[144] namely to refer to abstracted features of the object at hand and the regularities they imply (citing Gallagher, 2017: 83–84)."[145]

Again, here one would insist that this is in a *primarily* rather than a *purely* cognitivist/representational manner, in that intersubjective constructions are always mobilized in articulating such abstract concepts.[146] Yet, always in the background, even within this reflective mode, we argue that phenomenological aspects are always at work. Here we draw upon the experiential aspect of organizational communication, or more precisely, the "Merleau-Pontyian intersubjectivist account of praxis," in which "embodied communicating is intimately linked with implicit and tacit knowing and inter-knowing, and processes of organisational learning, respectively inter-learning."[147]

In the next chapter...

In the next chapter, we look at the negative side of enactment across the lens of *mindlessness*. More specifically, we look at how organizations typically fall into mindless "algorithmic assumptions," resulting in the materialization and structuring of work practices and actions within predominantly algorithmic perspectives or paradigms. The material consequences of such enactive discursive and embodied practices on human *mètis* are also briefly discussed.

References

Dreyfus, H.L. (1995). *Being-in-the-World: A Commentary On Heidegger's Being and Time, Division I* (Cambridge, MA: MIT Press).
Dreyfus, H.L. (2000). Responses. In *Heidegger, Coping, and Cognitive Science: Essays in Honor of Hubert L. Dreyfus*, M. Wrathall & J. Malpas (eds.) (Cambridge, MA: MIT Press), pp. 313–349.
Gallagher, S. (2017). *Enactivist Interventions: Rethinking the Mind* (New York: Oxford University Press).
Heidegger, M. (1962, orig. pub. 1927). *Being and Time*, J. Macquarrie & E. Robinson (trans.) (New York, NY: Harper and Row).
Heidegger, M. (1993). *Holzweg* (Pfullingen: Neske).
Olafson, F. (1987). *Heidegger and the Philosophy of Mind* (New Haven London: Yale University Press).

Endnotes

[1] See Gibson, J.J. (1966). *The Senses Considered as Perceptual Systems* (Boston, MA: Houghton Mifflin) and Gibson, J.J. (1979). *The Ecological Approach to Visual Perception* (Boston, MA: Houghton Mifflin).

2 See Maturana, H.R. and Varela, F.J. (1987). *The Tree of Knowledge: The Biological Roots of Human Understanding* (New York: New Science Library/ Shambhala Publications).

3 See Kiverstein, J. and Miller, M. (2015). The embodied brain: Towards a radical embodied cognitive neuroscience. *Frontiers in Human Neuroscience*, **9**, Article 237, 1–11.

4 Citing *Ibid.*, p. 2.

5 See Pessoa, L. (2014). Understanding brain networks and brain organization. *Physics of Life Reviews*, **11**, 400–435. doi:10.1016/j.plrev.2014.03.005.

6 Citing Kiverstein and Miller (2015, p. 2) (note 3).

7 Citing Beckes, L., IJzermanand, H. and Tops, M. (2015). Toward a radically embodied neuroscience of attachment and relationships. *Frontiers in Human Neuroscience*, **9**, article 266, 1–18.

8 See *Ibid.*, Chemero, A. (2009). *Radical Embodied Cognitive Science* (Cambridge, MA: MIT Press), as well as Wilson, A.D. and Golonka, S. (2013). Embodied cognition is not what you think it is. *Frontiers in Psychology*, **4**, 58. doi: 10.3389/fpsyg.2013.00058.

9 Citing Chemero (2009, p. 18) (note 8).

10 See Dreyfus, H.L. (2007). Why Heideggerian AI failed and how fixing it would require making it more Heidegerrian. *Artificial Intelligence*, **171**(18), 1137–1160.

11 See Gibson (1979) (note 1).

12 Citing Käufer, S. and Chemero, A. (2016). Pragmatism, Phenomenology, and Extended Cognition. In *Pragmatism and Embodied Cognitive Science: From Bodily Intersubjectivity to Symbolic Articulation*, M. Jung and R. Madzia (eds.) (Berlin: De Gruyter), pp. 57–72.

13 See James, W. (1884). What is an emotion? *Mind*, **9**, 188–205. doi:10.1093/mind/os-IX.34.188.

14 *Ibid.*

15 Citing Beckes *et al.* (2015, p. 3) (note 7).

16 Citing Gibson (1979, p. 129) (note 1).

17 See Stoffregen, T.A. (2003). Affordances as properties of the animal-environment system. *Ecological Psychology*, **15**(2), 115–134.

18 Citing Kallinikos, J., Leonardi, P.M. and Nardi, B.A. (2012). The Challenge of Materiality: Origins, Scope, and Prospects. In *Materiality and Organizing: Social Interaction in a Technological World*, P. Leonardi, B. Nardi and J. Kallinikos (eds.) (Oxford: Oxford University Press), pp. 1–22; also see Boudreau, M.-C. and Robey, D. (2005). Enacting integrated information technology: A human agency perspective. *Organization Science*, **16**(1), 3–18. doi:10.1287/orsc.1040.0103.

19 Dreyfus, H.L. (1991). *Being-in-the-World* (Cambridge, MA: The MIT Press).

20 Citing Chemero, A. (2013). Radical embodied cognitive science. *Review of General Psychology*, **17**(2), 145–150.

21 See Dotov, D.G., Nie, L. and Chemero, A. (2010). A demonstration of the transition from ready-to-hand to unready-to-hand. *PLoS ONE*, **5**(3), e9433, doi:10.1371/journal.pone.0009433.

22 See both Riley, M.A. and Holden, J.G. (2012). Dynamics of cognition. *WIRES Cognitive Science*, **3**, 593–606. doi:10.1002/wcs.1200 as well as West, B.J. (2006). Fractal Physiology, Complexity, and the Fractional Calculus. In *Fractals, Diffusion and Relaxation in Disordered Complex Systems*, W.T. Coffey and Y.P. Kalmykov (eds.), Vol. 133, Part B (Hoboken, NJ: John Wiley & Sons), pp. 1–92. doi:10.1002/0470037148.ch6.

23 Citing Dotov *et al.* (2010, p. 3) (note 21).

24 *Ibid.*

25 Citing Chemero (2013, p. 149) (note 20).

26 See Thompson, E. and Varela, F.J. (2001). Radical embodiment: Neural dynamics and consciousness. *Trends in Cognitive Sciences*, **5**, 418–425. doi: 10.1016/S1364-6613(00)01750-2.

27 Citing both Van Roouij, I., Bongers, R.M. and Haselager, W.F.G. (2002). A nonrepresentational approach to imagined action. *Cognitive Science*, **26**, 345–375, as well as Chemero, A. and Silberstein, M. (2008). After the philosophy of mind: Replacing scholasticism with science. *Philosophy of Science*, **75**(1), 1–27.

28 Citing Haugeland, J. (1991). Representational genera. In *Philosophy and Connectionist Theory*, W.M. Ramsey, S.P. Stich and D.E. Rumelhart (eds.) (Hillsdale, NJ: Lawrence Erlbaum Associates), pp. 61–90.

29 Citing Newell, A. (1980). Physical symbol systems. *Cognitive Science*, **4**, 135–183.

30 Citing Van Roouij *et al.* (2002, p. 350) (note 27).

31 See Dreyfus (2007) (note 10).

32 See Dotov *et al.* (2010) (note 21).

33 See Richardson, M.J. and Chemero, A. (2014). Complex Dynamical Systems and Embodiment. In *The Routledge Handbook of Embodied Cognition*, L. Shapiro (ed.) (London: Routledge), pp. 39–50.

34 Citing Baber, C., Chemero, A. and Hall, J. (2019). What the jeweller's hand tells the jeweller's brain: Tool use, creativity and embodied cognition. *Philosophy & Technology*, **32**, 283–302.

35 See Van Roouij *et al.* (2002) (note 27).

36 See both Van Gelder, T. (1995). What might cognition be, if not computation? *Journal of Philosophy*, **92**, 345–381, as well as Van Gelder, T. (1998). The dynamical hypothesis in cognitive science. *Behavioral and Brain Sciences*, **21**, 615–665.

37 Citing Van Roouij *et al.* (2002, p. 351) (note 27).

38 See Maturana and Varela (1987) (note 2).

39 Citing Baggs, E. and Chemero, A. (2018). Radical embodiment in two directions. *Synthese*. https://doi.org/10.1007/s11229-018-02020-9.

[40] *Ibid.*
[41] Citing Gibson (1979, p. 127) (note 1).
[42] See both Chemero, A. (2003). An outline of a theory of affordances. *Ecological Psychology*, **15**(2), 181–195, as well as Rietveld, E. and Kiverstein, J. (2014). A rich landscape of affordances. *Ecological Psychology*, **26**(4), 325–352.
[43] Citing Reed, E.S. (1996). *Encountering the World: Toward an Ecological Psychology* (New York: Oxford University Press), p. 26.
[44] Citing Baggs and Chemero (2018, pp. 12–13) (note 39).
[45] Citing Varela, F.J., Thompson, E. and Rosch, E. (2017). *The Embodied Mind: Cognitive Science and Human Experience* (New York, NY: MIT Press), p. 149.
[46] See Dreyfus (2007) (note 10).
[47] See Holford, W.D. (2020). An ethical inquiry of the effect of cockpit automation on the responsibilities of airline pilots: Dissonance or meaningful control? *Journal of Business Ethics*. https://doi.org/10.1007/s10551-020-04640-z.
[48] Citing Flemisch, F. *et al.* (2012). Towards a dynamic balance between humans and automation: Authority, ability, responsibility and control in shared and cooperative control situations. *Cognition, Technology & Work*, **14**, 3–18.
[49] *Ibid.*
[50] *Ibid.*
[51] See Santonio de Sio, F. and van den Hoven, J. (2018). Meaningful human control over autonomous systems: A philosophical account. *Frontiers in Robotics and AI*, **5**(15), 1–14.
[52] See both Horowitz, M.C. and Scharre, P. (2015). Meaningful human control in weapon systems: A primer. Available at: https://www.cnas.org/publications/reports/meaningful-human-control-in-weapon-systems-a-primer) as well as Schultz, T.P. (2018). *The Problem with Pilots: How Physicians, Engineers and Airpower Enthusiasts Redefined Flight* (Baltimore, MA: John Hopkins University Press).
[53] See Dreyfus (2007) (note 10).
[54] See Heidegger, M. (1962, orig. pub. 1927). *Being and Time*, J. Macquarrie and E. Robinson (trans.) (New York, NY: Harper and Row).
[55] See Dreyfus, H.L. and Dreyfus, S.E. (2005). Peripheral vision expertise in real world contexts. *Organization Studies*, **26**(5), 779–792.
[56] Citing conversation between Dreyfus, H.L. and Kreisler, H. (2005). Meaning, relevance and the limits of technology — conversation with H.L. Dreyfus. Conversations with History, Institute of International Studies, UC Berkeley; also see Dreyfus, H.L. (2014). *Skillful Coping: Essays on the Phenomenology of Everyday Perception and Action* (Oxford, UK: Oxford University Press).
[57] See Adams, R.J. and Ericsson, A.E. (2000). Introduction to cognitive processes of expert pilots. *Journal of Human Performance in Extreme Environments*, **5**(1), 44–62. doi: 10.7771/2327-2937.1006; also Pierrakosa, O., Welch, C.A. and Anderson, R.D. (2016). Measuring adaptive expertise in engineering education, *2016 ASEE Southeast Section Conference, American Society for Engineering*

Education, Paper ID. 17095; and finally, Pusic, M.V. *et al.* (2018). Learning to balance efficiency and innovation for optimal adaptive expertise. *Medical Teacher*, **40**(8), 820–827. https://doi.org/10.1080/0142159X.2018.1485887.

[58] Citing Adams and Ericsson (2000, p. 48) (note 57).

[59] Citing Pusic *et al.* (2018, p. 820) (note 57).

[60] See Pierrakos *et al.* (2016) (note 57).

[61] See Adams and Ericsson's (2000, p. 58, 60) (note 57) description of "knowing how," "knowing when" and "knowing what," citing Dreyfus H.L. and Dreyfus S.E. (1986). *Mind Over Machine* (New York: The Free Press).

[62] See Baumard, P. (1999). *Tacit Knowledge in Organizations* (London: Sage Publications), p. 65.

[63] See Raphals, L. (1992). *Knowing Words. Wisdom and Cunning in the Classical Tradition of China and Greece* (Ithaca, NY: Cornell University Press), p. 6.

[64] See Adams and Ericsson (2000, p. 60) (note 57) and also Li, W.-C., Chiu, F.-C., Kuo, Y. and Wu, K.-J. (2013). — The investigation of visual attention and workload by experts and novices in the cockpit. In *International Conference on Engineering Psychology and Cognitive Ergonomics*, Springer, pp. 167–176.

[65] See Santonio and van den Hoven (2018) (note 51).

[66] See Gaffary, Y. and Lécuyer, A. (2018). The use of haptic and tactile information in the car to improve driving safety: A review of current technologies. *Frontiers in ICT*, **5**(5), 1–11; also see Abbink, D.A. and Mulder, M. (2009). Exploring the dimensions of haptic feedback support in manual control. *Journal of Computing and Information Science in Engineering*, **9**(1), 011006-1–011006-9; and finally also see Doherty, G. and Massink, M. (1999). Continuous Interaction and Human Control. In *Proceedings of the XVIII European Annual Conference on Human Decision Making and Manual Control*, Alty, J. (ed.), pp. 80–96.

[67] Citing Kallinikos *et al.* (2012, p. 35) (note 18) and also see Boudreau and Robey (2005) (note 18).

[68] See Gaffary and Lécuyer (2018) (note 66); also see Abbink and Mulder (2009) (note 66); as well as Abbink, D.A., Mulder, M. and Boer, E.R. (2012). Haptic shared control: Smoothly shifting control authority? *Cognition Technology and Work*, **14**, 19–28); and finally, see Oguz, S.O., Kucukyilmaz, A., Sezgin, T.M. and Basdogan, C. (2010). Haptic negotiation and role exchange for collaboration in virtual environments. In: *IEEE Haptics Symposium*, pp. 371–378. doi:10.1109/HAPTIC.2010.5444628.

[69] See Abbink and Mulder (2009) (note 66); also see Doherty and Massink (1999) (note 66); and finally, see Abbink *et al.* (2012) (note 68).

[70] See both Gaffary and Lécuyer (2018) (note 66) as well as Abbink and Mulder (2009) (note 66).

[71] See Santonio and van den Hoven (2018) (note 51).

[72] See Abbink *et al.* (2012) (note 68).

[73] See Favela, L.H., Riley, M.A., Shockley, K. and Chemero, A. (2018). Perceptually equivalent judgments made visually and via haptic sensory-substitution devices. *Ecological Psychology*, **30**(4), 326–345. doi: 10.1080/10407413.2018.1473712.

[74] See Holford (2020) (note 47); also see Flemisch *et al.* (2012) (note 48); as well as Chialastri, A. (2012). Automation in Aviation. In *Automation*, Kongoli, F. (ed.) (InTech), pp. 79–102. doi: 10.5772/49949); and finally, see Elish, M. and Boyd, D. (2018). Situating methods in the magic of Big Data and AI. *Communication Monographs*, **85**(1), 57–80.

[75] See Parasuraman, R. and Manzey. D.H. (2010). Complacency and bias in human use of automation: An attentional integration. *Human Factors*, **52**(3), 381–410.

[76] Citing McBride, S.E., Rogers, W.E. and Fisk, A.D. (2014). Understanding human management of automation errors. *Theoretical Issues Ergonomic Sciences*, **15**(6), 545–577.

[77] See Wachter, B. (2015). My interview with Capt. Sully Sullenberger: On aviation, medicine and technology. *The Hospital Leader*, February 23. Available at: https://thehospitalleader.org/my-interview-with-capt-sully-sullenberger-on-aviation-medicine-and-technology/.

[78] See Parasuraman and Manzey (2010) (note 75) and also Strauch, B. (2017). The automation-by-expertise-by-training interaction: Why automation-related accidents continue to occur in sociotechnical systems. *Human Factors*, **59**(2), 204–228.

[79] Citing Chemero (2013, p. 149) (note 20).

[80] Citing Dreyfus (1991, p. 52) (note 19).

[81] Citing Dreyfus (1991, p. 51) (note 19).

[82] Citing Dreyfus (1991, p. 76) (note 19).

[83] Citing Chemero (2013, p. 149) (note 19).

[84] See both Chemero (2013) (note 20) as well as Alessandroni, N. (2018). Varieties of embodiment in cognitive science. *Theory and Psychology*, **28**(2), 227–248.

[85] See Dotov, Nie and Chemero (2010) (note 21).

[86] See James, W. (1955, orig. pub. 1907). *Pragmatism* (Cleveland, NY: Meridian Book).

[87] See Dewey, J. (1929). *The Quest for Certainty: A Study of the Relation of Knowledge and Action* (New York: Putnam).

[88] See Alessandroni (2018) (note 86) as well as Eliasmith, C. (1997). Computation and dynamical models of mind. *Minds and Machines*, **7**, 531–541. https://doi.org/10.1023/A:1008296514437.

[89] Citing Chemero (2013, pp. 148–149) (note 21).

[90] Citing Alessandroni (2018, pp. 236–237) (note 86).

[91] As per Chemero (2013) (note 21).

[92] See Eliasmith (1997) (note 88).

[93] For example, see Raab, M. and Araujo, D. (2019). Embodied cognition with and without mental representations: The case of embodied choices in sports. *Frontiers in Psychology*, **10**, Article 1825, pp. 1–12, doi: 10.3389/fpsyg.2019.01825, as well as Chemero (2019) (note 88).

[94] Citing Raab and Araujo (2019, p. 10) (note 93).

[95] See Dreyfus (1991) (note 21).

[96] As pointed out by Alessandroni (2018) (note 86).

[97] Citing Alessandroni (2018, p. 237) (note 86).

[98] See both Alessandroni (2018) (note 86) as well as Masis, J. (2014). Naturalizing dasein. Aporias of the neo-heideggerian approach in cognitive science. *Cosmos and History: The Journal of Natural and Social Philosophy*, **10**(2), 158–181.

[99] Citing Alessandroni (2018, p. 239) (note 86).

[100] Citing Masis (2014, p. 178) (note 98).

[101] See Scott, J.C. (1998). *Seeing like a State: How Certain Schemes to Improve the Human State have Failed* (Binghamton, NY: Vail-Ballou Press).

[102] Citing Masis (2014, p. 177) (note 98).

[103] Citing Jarrahi, M.H. (2018). Artificial Intelligence and the future of work: Human-AI symbiosis in organizational decision making. *Business Horizons*, p. 578. https://doi.org/10.1016/j.bushor.2018.03.007.

[104] See Turing, A. 1950. Computing Machinery and Intelligence. *Mind*, **49**(236), pp. 433–460.

[105] See both Proudfoot, D. (2011). Anthropomorphism and AI: Turing's much misunderstood imitation game. *Artificial Intelligence*, **175**(5–6), 950–957; as well as Russell, S. and Norvig, P. (2010). *Artificial Intelligence: A Modern Approach*, 3rd Edition (Upper Saddle River, NJ: Prentice Hall).

[106] See Ferrucci, D.A. (2012). Introduction to 'This is Watson'. *IBM Journal of Research and Development*, **56**(3.4) May–June.

[107] As per both Weick, K. (2009). *Making Sense of the Organization (Volume 2): The Impermanent Organization* (West Sussex, UK: John Wiley and Sons) as well as Collins, H. (2010). *Tacit and Explicit Knowledge* (Chicago, IL: University of Chicago Press).

[108] See Ferrucci (2012) (note 105).

[109] See Elish and Boyd (2018) (note 74).

[110] See Marneffe, M.-C., Manning, C.D. and Potts, C. (2012). Did it happen? The pragmatic complexity of veridicality assessment. *Computational Linguistics*, **38**: 301–333.

[111] See McComb, K. and Semple, S. (2005). Coevolution of vocal communication and sociality in primates. *Biology Letters*, **1**: 381–385. doi:10.1098/rsbl.2005.0366.

[112] See Maddieson I. (1984). *Patterns of Sounds* (Cambridge, UK: Cambridge University Press).

[113] See Marneffe *et al.* (2012) (note 109).

[114] See Weick, K.E. (2015). Ambiguity as grasp: The reworking of sense. *Journal of Contingencies and Crisis Management*, 23(2), 117–123.

[115] Citing Dewulf, A., Craps, M., Bouwen, R., Taillieu, T. and Pahl-Wostl, C. (2005). Integrated management of natural resources: Dealing with ambiguous issues, multiple actors and diverging frames. *Water Science and Technology*, 52(6): 115–124.

[116] See Walker, W., Harremoe''s, P., Rotmans, J., Van der Sluijs, J., Van Asselt, M., Jansen, P. and Krayer von Krauss, M.P. (2003). Defining uncertainty: A conceptual basis for uncertainty management in model-based decision support. *Journal of Integrated Assessment*, 4(1), 5–17.

[117] Citing Jarrahi (2018, p. 5) (note 103).

[118] See both Marwala, T. (2015). *Causality, Correlation and Artificial Intelligence for Rational Decision Making* (Singapore: World Scientific) as well as Elish and Boyd (2018) (note 74).

[119] See Lorino, P., Tricard, B. and Clot, Y. (2011). Research methods for non-representational approaches to organizational complexity: The dialogical mediated inquiry. *Organization Studies*, 32(6), 769–801.

[120] See both Collins (2010) (note 106) as well as Dreyfus and Dreyfus (2005) (note 56).

[121] Citing Carlile, P.R. (2002). A pragmatic view of knowledge and boundaries: Boundary objects in new product development. *Organization Science*, 13(4), 442–455.

[122] Citing Collins (2010, p. 280) (note 106).

[123] Citing Tsoukas, H. (2009). A dialogical approach to the creation of new knowledge in organizations. *Organization Science*, 20(6), 941–953.

[124] Citing Lorino *et al.* (2011, p. 793) (note 118); also see Ferrucci (2012) (note 105).

[125] Citing Searle, J.R. (1983). *Intentionality: An Essay in the Philosophy of Mind* (Cambridge, UK: Cambridge University Press).

[126] See Pedriali, W.B. (2017). Speaking images: Chomsky and Ricoeur on linguistic creativity. *Ricoeur Studies*, 8(1), 83–110.

[127] For the use of metaphors in language and conversation, see Ortony, A. (1979). *Metaphor and Thought* (Cambridge, UK: Cambridge University Press); Mooij, J.J.A. (1976). *A Study of Metaphor* (Amsterdam: North Holland); Ricoeur, P. (1978). *The Rule of Metaphor* (London, UK: Kegan Paul); as well as Pedriali (2017) (note 125).

[128] See Lake, R.L. (2011). Metaphor: The language of the imagination. *Journal of the Imagination in Language Learning*, 9, 119–125. Available at: https://digitalcommons.georgiasouthern.edu/curriculum-facpubs/10.

[129] Citing Lakoff, G. and Johnson, M. (1980). *Metaphors We Live By* (Chicago: Chicago University Press), p. 3.

[130] Citing Johnson, M. (1981). *Philosophical Perspectives on Metaphor* (Minneapolis: University of Minnesota Press), p. 17, 19.

131 See Lake (2011) (note 127).
132 Citing Modell, A. (2003). *Imagination and the Meaningful Brain* (Boston: MIT Press), p. 25.
133 See Küpers, W., Deeg, J. and Edwards, M. (2015). "Inter bridging" bridges and bridging as metaphors for "syn integrality" in organization studies and practice. *Integral Review*, **11**(3), 117–137.
134 *Ibid.*, p. 118.
135 *Ibid.*, p. 120.
136 See *Ibid.* as well as Lakoff, G. and Johnson, M. (1999). *Philosophy in the Flesh: The Embodied Mind and Its Challenge to Western Thought* (New York: Basic Books).
137 Citing Sandberg J. and Tsoukas H. (2020). Sensemaking reconsidered: Towards a broader understanding through phenomenology. *Organization Theory*, p. 8. doi:10.1177/2631787719879937
138 See Ford, J.D. and Ford, L.W. (1995). The role of conversations in producing intentional change in organizations. *Academy of Management Review*, **20**, 541–570; also see Cooren, F. (2007). *Interacting and Organizing* (Mahwah, NJ: Lawrence Erlbaum); and finally see Whittle, A., Mueller, F., Gilchrist, A. and Lenney, P. (2016). Sensemaking, sense-censoring, and strategic inaction: The discursive enactment of power and politics in a multinational corporation. *Organization Studies*, **37**, 1323–1351.
139 Citing Sandberg and Tsoukas (2020, p. 8) (note 135).
140 See both Schatzki, T.R. (2000). Coping with Others with Folk Psychology. In *Heidegger, Coping, and Cognitive Science: Essays in Honor* of Hubert L. Dreyfus, M. Wrathall and J. Malpas (eds.) (Cambridge, MA: MIT Press), pp. 29–52; as well as Gallagher, S. (2017). *Enactivist Interventions: Rethinking the Mind* (New York: Oxford University Press).
141 Citing Sandberg and Tsoukas (2020, p. 8) (note 135).
142 *Ibid.*
143 Citing Maitlis, S. and Christianson, M. (2014). Sensemaking in organizations: Taking stock and moving forward. *Academy of Management Annals*, **8**, 57–125.
144 Citing Dreyfus, H.L. (2000). Responses. In *Heidegger, Coping, and Cognitive Science: Essays in Honor* of Hubert L. Dreyfus, M. Wrathall and J. Malpas (eds.) (Cambridge, MA: MIT Press), pp. 313–349.
145 Citing Sandberg and Tsoukas (2020, p. 8) (note 135).
146 See Boje, D.M. (2014). *Storytelling Organizational Practices* (London: Routledge).
147 Citing Küpers, W. (2012). "Inter-communicating": Phenomenological perspectives on embodied communication and contextuality. *Journal for Communication and Culture*, **2**(2), 114–138.

Chapter 7

Human Mindlessness and Technology

7.1. Introduction

In the previous chapter, we highlighted the significance of enactive action within a radical embodied cognitive perspective. As past researchers in organization studies have highlighted, enactments often appear as "the way things occur."[1] Enactive actions can either be mindful or mindless in nature.[2] While mindfulness was previously discussed and associated to situational awareness, human adaptive expertise, and *mètis* (Chapter 3), mindless acts are when we "treat information as if it were contextfree — true regardless of circumstances."[3] We commonly drift toward mindlessness without realizing it through repetition and familiar situations. Burgoon and Langer define mindlessness as "limited information processing, rigid categorical thinking, single perspectives, and failure to recognize context."[4] This chapter examines how we have often fallen for mindless "algorithmic assumptions," resulting in the materialization and structuring of work practices and actions within a predominantly algorithmic perspective or paradigm. Such mindlessness is brought about by entrenched metaphors, one of which is the technology-as-tool metaphor. Mindlessness leads to unintended consequences,[5] in this case being the erosion/loss of human adaptive expertise (*mètis*). Finally, we look at technology's own enactive effect on us, to which we are also mindless towards, thus completing our mindless dialectic, while also vindicating Suppe's argument[6] — i.e. we typically interpret and react to events within our environment according to the system already inscribed within us. Yet, the key word here is typically — *not* inevitably.

7.2. Intra-Enactive Agency, Embodiment, and the Pertinence of Metaphors

As we have discussed in the previous chapter, human behavior is enactive. On the one hand, Morgan offers a concise human-centric explanation on enactment: "Although we often see ourselves as living in a reality with objective characteristics, life actually demands much more of us than this. It requires that we take an active role in bringing our realities into being through various interpretive schemes, even though these realities may then have a habit of imposing themselves on us as 'the way things are.'"[7] On the other hand, Weick cites Follett[8] to provide a Jamesian description on the *reciprocal* shaping processes occurring between the environment (in the most general sense) and the individual[9]:

> "... the activity of the individual is only in a certain sense caused by the stimulus of the situation because that activity is itself helping to produce the situation which causes the activity of the individual ... My farmer neighbours know this: we prune and graft and fertilize certain trees, and as our behaviour becomes increasingly that of behaviour towards apple-bearing trees, these become increasingly apple-bearing trees. The tree releases energy in me and I in it; it makes me think and plan and work, and I make it edible fruit. It is a process of freeing on both sides. And this is a creating process."

Enactment has been studied in various contexts: these include organizational change,[10] entrepreneurship,[11] organizing and sensemaking,[12] personal as well as corporate identities,[13] and firm capabilities,[14] just to name a few. Enactment within organizations is a fundamental process in that "a pattern of enactment establishes the foundation of organizational reality, and in turn has effects in shaping future enactments."[15] According to Weick, enactment involves all actions and sensemaking: "enactment drives everything else in an organization. How enactment is done is what an organization will know."[16]

Building on the principle that enactment involves reciprocal shaping processes between the environment and the individual, enactment is both social and material.[17] Shaping between individuals is, on the one hand, a social process involving social actors whose activities bring structures and events into existence and set these in action.[18] Yet, human activity and behavior is also affected by material artefacts (including technology), in that the latter provide "focus" for activity and thus "orient" human actions.[19] As such, human activity and behavior is "connected and related to material artifacts."[20] To this, Svabo adds, "they are the objects for meaningful action."[21] However, we argue that this last statement be modified to read "they are the objects for both *meaningful and meaningless* action" (which we shall return to through the notion of mindlessness). The reciprocal shaping process occurring between humans and technology can be found across examples of technology's designs and "subsequent" shaping of work practices.[22] On the one hand, technologies are in themselves "imbued with the value choices of their designers," which "reflect valuation schemes, beliefs, and ethical standards ... often made in an informal, intuitive, and idiosyncratic way by the individual who designs the algorithm."[23] On the other hand, learning algorithms have taken over many of the "repetitive and routine tasks that comprise most knowledge jobs."[24] Faraj *et al.* provide the example of heart and lung image recognition algorithms, which are already "guiding radiologists toward certain diagnoses, by identifying suspicious tissue and attaching specific probabilities of malignancy to them."[25] Yet, even this rendition of reciprocal enactment on our part is simplistic. Here, we turn to Orlikowski's[26] "sociomateriality" in organization studies, a term in reference to the onto-epistemology of Karen Barad.[27] This involves the concept of "entanglement" or "generative entanglement," whereby within a practice or behavior, the social and the technological are not only inseparable but constitute (enact) one another within a "texture" of situated action.[28] By texture, Gherardi refers to an endless series or networking of relationships which "continually move into" one another.[29]

At this point, we open an important parenthesis to specify that through Gherardi's[30] complexity of relationships, we can also tap into phenomenology and the "embodied turn" in social and organizational studies to argue that, from the human agents' perspective, the body and embodiment are the media of organizational practice.[31] As such, it is "through their embodied selves that 'subjects' ... are situated in their life-world in tactile, visual, olfactory and auditory way."[32] Complexity of relationships for human agents involves a "synchronised field of inter-related senses," whereby it is through the living body that organizational life "is being experienced and realised."[33]

Returning to Barad's sociomateriality, culture and nature are entangled. Barad coins her epistemological position as "agential realism."[34] Barad uses the term "intra-action" to denote the ontological inseparability of all language, text, conversation-as-discursive-practice (culture) and all things (nature).[35] For Barad, realism is non-representational, in that it is not "about representations of an independent reality but about the real consequences, interventions, creative possibilities, and responsibilities of intra-acting within and as part of our world."[36] Actors do not simply inter-act with the environment, but shape (enact) it by being affected and *changed* by it.[37] Within such an agential realist perspective is "a dynamic reality in ceaseless, unfolding movement" consisting "of continuously intermingling, flowing lines or strands of unfolding, agential activity, in which nothing (no thing) exists in separation from anything else, a reality within which we are immersed both as participant agencies and to which we also owe significant aspects of our own natures."[38] Agential realism is the entanglement of the material and the social through intra-activity of materiality with discursive practice. A specific intra-action enacts an out-come in the form of an agential "cut."[39] According to Barad, any act of "observation" (or more precisely, an interpretation) makes a "cut" between what is included and excluded from what is being considered. Agencies can be human or non-human, are entangled, and mutually con-stitute one another through intra-actions.[40] As agents make these tempo-rary cuts, further actions and re-entanglements ensue to generate new or modified "cuts" in a never-ending process, making up the phenomenon in question.[41] In a manner similar to Latour's[42] temporary, imperfect, incom-plete, and pragmatic "state of affairs," Barad's[43] "cuts" do not mark some absolute separation, but rather, allows for "certain phenomena to be momentarily distinguished," thus allowing phenomena and specific embodied concepts to become meaningful.[44] As such, agential cuts are also reconfigurings of organizational systems.[45] In this sense, materiality is constitutively entangled with discourse-in-practice, whereby the focus is on enactment and on how specific materializations of discourse make a difference in practice, and with what performative consequences.[46] Furthermore, technologies or objects will trigger, provoke, and stimulate (i.e. enact) reactions (both as practice and conceptual ideas) on the part of human agencies, while the latter, in turn, reshape the former.[47]

Here, it is important to remind ourselves that discursive practise is not just about representational aspects of language and conversation but, and as previously discussed in Chapter 6, is also about its non-representational subjective and phenomenological dimensions. In remaining coherent with our previous phenomenological "parenthesis," we especially emphasize human agency as involving the act of experiencing and realizing organizational life across the living and embodied self that is situated in the real world through his/her senses.[48] It is also here that we reintroduce the importance of metaphors (as well as narratives) across Küpers' following words[49]:

> "For Merleau-Ponty embodied practitioners are situated and know metaphorically and narratively through their bodies and embodiment. Their living bodies mediate between internal and external as well as subjective and objective dimensions of experience and meaning, as these are processed and expressed in metaphors and stories (referencing Merleau-Ponty, 1962: xii)."

Sensemaking of and through metaphors and stories is not merely a cognitive mechanism but a sensual process able to handle complex informational data, knowledge, as well as multiple meaning (i.e. ambiguity).[50] More specifically, through Lakoff and Johnson's[51] "embodied realism," abstract conceptualizations and thought, symbolic expressions, as well as daily interactions (as both routine and non-routine experiences) are intimately related to our embodied experience as well as to the pervasive aesthetic characteristics of these experiences. As such, metaphors both enact the structure of bodily experiences as well as emerge from these same experiences.[52]

Finally, as we shall see through both the following section and following chapter, metaphors are "multiple-edged swords," in that they can be used in either a co-active or autocratic, creative or destructive, mindful or mindless manner to enact changes/transformations of (or reinforce existing status quo's on) practices and outcomes in both overt and covert ways. In the next section, we look at specific examples of mindless enactments and material consequences regarding the use of, and intra-action with, "intelligent" technologies within organizations.

7.3. Human Mindlessness Through the "Technology is a Tool" Metaphor

Timmerman succinctly describes mindlessness as "a state in which one does not attend to information in the environment, but rather behaves in an automatic fashion, minimally attentive to behavior."[53] While "the drawing of novel distinctions" are mindful behaviors, "once distinctions are created, they take a life of their own ... and are very hard to overthrow."[54] No one, or at least not many amongst us, is always able to discern pertinent cues and behave in a mindful manner 100% of the time. For example, much interpersonal communication as well as repetitive tasks such as checking emails are carried out in a mindless manner.[55] Ashforth and Fried go further by arguing that much of our organizational activities are mindless due to their repetitive nature.[56] In the best of cases, we enact both mindful and mindless discernments and behavior.[57] Mindlessness is essentially the opposite of human *mètis*, which is at the heart of adaptive expertise. Here, rather than being situationally aware of pertinent cues, we attend only to a limited number of cues, while ignoring others which may otherwise have allowed us to draw novel distinctions.[58]

Studies in Human Factor Research have shown that poorer detection of cues can be associated to what is often referred to as "inattentional blindness" — i.e. "reduced visual attention to the primary information sources feeding automation which must be monitored to detect an abnormal event."[59] Of interest is a specific form of inattentional blindness known as attentional tunneling, sometimes referred to as "cognitive tunneling."[60] Attentional tunneling involves "the allocation of attention to a particular channel of information, diagnostic hypothesis, or task goal, for a duration that is longer than optimal, given the expected cost of neglecting events on other channels, failing to consider other hypotheses, or failing to perform other tasks."[61] Inattentional blindness caused by such attentional tunneling, in turn, leads to a loss in situational awareness, and as such, a loss in overall adaptive expertise amongst human operators.[62] Interestingly, such inattentional blindness can result from human operator complacency caused by unduly low expectations of system failures regarding the highly reliable (yet, never perfect) nature of the automation systems with which they work with.[63] Such unduly low expectations of systems failures is known as automation bias.[64] More importantly, Parasuraman and Manzey,[65] through their own studies as well as an exhaustive review of prior research, argue that the overriding factor determining the onset (and maintenance) of automation bias (and loss of situational awareness), irrespective of training and accountability factors, is through a positive reinforcement loop of "learned carelessness" which builds upon the repetition of no abnormal issues or events arising from automated operations. Said another way, "higher reliability of automation and higher levels of automation have been associated with greater complacency, which can lead to worse error management."[66]

Langer explains that mindlessness comes about by being entrapped within categories. More specifically, "the categories we make gather momentum."[67] Institutions evidently play a role in this in that once they adopt a given category, they impose "cognitive constraints on the actors who do the sensemaking."[68] Roles identified with such sensemaking "become embodied in actors as habitus or tastes and dispositions (citing Bourdieu 1990[1980]), encoded into action scripts that are enacted (citing Barley and Tolbert 1997), or habitually repeated without much mediating processes (citing Zucker 1991)."[69] In turn, such mindless reinforcement of categories can come about through the use of powerful metaphors. Metaphors, as we shall examine in more detail in the following chapter, are pervasive not just in language, but in everyday actions and thought. Wilken,[70] in particular, explains that technological metaphors are highly ubiquitous yet "never innocent" and, "when deployed as part of deliberate rhetorical strategies, have the potential to profoundly shape cultural and social practices."[71] Such metaphors "both illuminate and obscure the relationships between people and technology."[72] One popular metaphor we often hear is that "technology is a tool".[73] The term "tool" in itself connotes effectiveness in that it is a "device-used-by-an-individual-to-get-something-done."[74]

In parallel, a dominant social imaginary associated with technology is that it consists of an *efficient method* to reach one's objective.[75] Dominant social imaginaries, in themselves, involve "producing authoritative representations of how the world works — as well as how it should work."[76] In this manner, technology on the one hand emerges from the notion of efficiency in that its essence is to seek more and more efficiency for its own sake — i.e. producing the most with the least energy possible,[77] whereby "expediting is always itself directed from the beginning ... towards driving on to the maximum yield at minimum expense."[78] In a similar, complementary vein, Ellul's technological society is a society of techniques requiring that we always choose the most rationally efficient techniques for every endeavour.[79] In this manner, technology becomes a mindset or ideology which values efficiency over all other things.[80] In turn, this logic of efficiency is part of a greater "cultural logic" which "values the fastest and least expensive production and distribution of any product, as well as fast and inexpensive modes, technologies, and behaviors."[81] By cultural logic, Clair refers to a "construct that has been used by many but defined by few ... as a shared and collectively imagined prescription for individual or collective social action ... They are prescriptions and practices picked up and used by individuals in varying circumstances and contexts."[82] Along these lines, more recent manifestations of efficiency's ever-present cultural imaginary is the powerful socio-economic prescription and mantra of "doing more with less".[83]

Returning to our "tool" metaphor, technology can be mindlessly viewed as not just an effective but also an efficient means (or device). Paradoxically, a mindless obsession with efficiency will often undermine effectiveness.[84] More importantly, the "technology as tool" metaphor, by way of our cultural imaginary/obsession on efficiency, is reduced or literalized to a "tool of efficiency," thus providing an impoverished picture of what humans in the presence of technology could truly attain.[85] This impoverished picture reinforces our mindless view toward technology as an efficient means — full stop. As such, we already saw in Chapter 6 how techno-centrically designed airline cockpit technologies mindlessly overemphasize well-defined machine efficiency and reliability through imposed algorithmic rules and decision-making, which in turn leads to the unintended consequence of erosion or loss of human pilot adaptive expertise.[86] In this manner, we end up having highly efficient socio-technical systems that are essentially ineffective in dealing with new unexpected situations. Interestingly, people who view technology as a "tool" very often see themselves controlling it.[87] Yet, as already discussed in Chapter 6, human operators are often no longer fully in control (control being a combination of *both* the necessary skills and the authority to successfully carry out a task) of socio-technical systems in question, thus further undermining the socio-technical systems to adaptively deal with novel situations at hand.[88]

The "efficient tool" metaphor is what typically drives various techno-centric design and implementation strategies in numerous socio-technical organizational contexts. One such example is presented by Bjørn and Balka regarding the electronic triage system ETRIAGE at the emergency department of British Columbia (Canada) Children's Hospital.[89] Triage is the process patients go through in which they are assessed according to the urgency of their need for care. Here, the authors had found that ETRIAGE's design involved externally imposed work categorizations in the form of standardized rules and protocols regarding the nature of nurses' work. More specifically, the design integrated four fallacious assumptions within its system:

(1) The triage process is objective and can be reduced to a set of rules and protocols;
(2) Triage work can be understood out of its specified context;

(3) Nurses do not do their work properly; and
(4) ETRIAGE is designed to support management.

As the authors explain, triage work requires complex knowledge about humans and symptoms. For this reason, triage is conducted by highly experienced nurses who have been specially trained. One of the problems identified was the mismatch between the assumptions about workflow embedded within the ETRIAGE system and actual triage interviews conducted by nurses. The electronic triage system required the nurses, by way of complicated scrolling and nested pull-down menus, to interrupt (and thereby risk losing) the patient's or parent's key conversational/descriptive flow. Also, the electronic input forms included fields which were not appropriate to the local context at hand. Other shortcomings included the inability to document and describe symptoms in more nuanced manners. For example, triage nurses often wrote "crying baby" as a presenting symptom on paper forms, yet the only way to capture this in ETRIAGE's classification system was by selecting the abstract category "altered level of consciousness." Moreover, the classification scheme did not reflect local terminology or practices and in some cases reflected a medical diagnosis (such as asthma) rather than presenting a complaint or a symptom (such as wheezing).

A consequence of such a system was that nurses' expertise was repressed through the disruption of natural workflows (practices) — for as Dreyfus and Dreyfus point out, with expertise comes fluid perfor-mance.[90] Here, Bjørn and Balka also add that standardized rules and procedures "makes it theoretically possible to monitor deviations from anticipated workflows, but in a manner that fails to take the continuous exception-handling of work into account ... Standardized categories do not have the power to capture the invisible [i.e. tacit and hard to explain], but often critically important, aspects of work."[91] Furthermore, from an overt power perspective, the system overspecified through standardized rules "what nurses should do, which can take discretion away from the individual ... Thus, building categories to capture the richness of collabo-ration, including the informal aspects of work, brings a risk of control and surveillance (citing Suchman, 1994)."[92] Hence, the entanglements of such knowledge and power constraints clearly led towards loss of meaningful control on the part of the nurses, and as such, risks and consequences of mis-triage.

In the next section, we further examine how operators lose such meaningful control across our mindlessness toward technology's own enactive effect on humans.

7.4. Technology's Enactive Effect

In the previous section, we spoke of human mindlessness resulting from, as well as leading to (i.e. the enactment of) established categories which we take "as the way things are"[93] — and more specifically, as a result of viewing technology through the metaphoric lens of "tool". Such mindlessness helps produce and reinforce the cycle of automation bias and learned carelessness amongst human operators within socio-technical systems, ultimately leading to a loss in human adaptive skills (*mètis*) — which ironically, technology cannot replace or substitute for. However, technology can also have an "enframing" or mesmerizing effect on humans.[94] This is what we refer to as the second leg of "an infernal dialectic," leading to the same end-resulting loss of adaptive expertise (*mètis*).

In Chapters 2 and 5, we spoke of algorithmic technology's limitations as a result of its representational frames (i.e. "frame problem" as a result of frame regression). Human operators do not simply interact with technology, but rather they intra-act with it in the sense that they work *through* it. This is not an obsessive attempt on our part to force fit Barad's sociomateriality into the picture.[95] On the contrary, Barad's concept of entanglement enlightens us as to how human and non-human things are "dependent on each other in ways that are entrapping and asymmetrical."[96] Modern day airline pilots "rarely 'hand-fly' the aircraft as they comply with company directives to surrender control to the auto-pilot except for takeoff and landing … Occasionally, they grip controls, jockey throttles, and apply manual stick and rudder skills, yet even these actions are adjudicated by computer logic in fly-by-wire aircraft … Increasingly, pilots serve as information managers and type commands into a computer as they monitor displays connected to various onboard sensors linked with Global Positioning Systems (GPS) … Pilots … commit to becoming … often hands-off managers, of a highly computerized and heavily automated system."[97] Yet, "pilots are expected to exert manual control if necessary during an emergency or unusual circumstance even though they rarely practice such control", whereby during such circumstances their actions are still limited by automatic systems.[98] In this manner, Schultz[99] argues that pilots have become "servants" to their technology rather than masters of it. However, with this overt control over human agency, is a more subtle or covert conditioning at work. Pilots, at the socio-technical interfaces, are presented representational accounts (or frames) of what is happening in reality.[100] Along with being cut-off from the direct reality of phenomenological senses (i.e. an indirect reality), pilots now fully interpret their surroundings through the lenses of algorithmic representations.[101] In other words, pilots have become disembodied from their surroundings across the blinkering effect of representational technologies — i.e. where representational accounts (or frames) impoverish their direct contact with the performative environment of the aircraft across the masking of their phenomenological senses.[102] The algorithmic or automated cockpit involves a mix of both symbolic and connectionist (or distributed) representations.[103] Frames are built by way of predefined symbolic or data representations.[104] To this, Dreyfus points out the issue of infinite regress — i.e. "if each context can be recognized only in terms of features selected as relevant and interpreted in a broader context, the AI worker is faced with a regress of contexts," and a resultant impoverishment (or loss) of relevant contextual knowledge.[105] This applies equally to symbolic and connectionist AI, whereby the latter simply consists of finer grade, discrete, and interrelated representational frames with all the representational frame problems that accompany them.[106] AI researchers such as Margaret Boden have also concluded that the various combinations of connectionist and symbolic approaches integrated or attempted by AI developers have been unsuccessful in identifying suitable knowledge representations that would avoid the frame problem, and as such are unable to determine what is relevant within new situations.[107] The difficulty, according to Boden, has been that being able to achieve something significant and relevant requires knowledge of social beliefs, values, and practices that are highly tacit through its embodied and embedded nature[108] — and to which many have argued cannot be reduced to explicit representations.[109] Hence, when pilots continuously interact with automated algorithmic technologies by way of technology's representational frames, they gradually lose their first brain's reflex of engaging directly with the environment through phenomenological senses, and as such, bypass a critical component that is required toward adaptively learning (and reacting to) one's environment.[110] Pilots, across current techno-centric design philosophies are, for the majority of the flight cycle, imposed representations of the environment according to the technology in question — *and*, are never allowed to adequately or sufficiently get back into direct contact with the reality in question across full freedom of practice of manual operations, in that automation prevents them to do so.[111] As such, pilots lose the ability to determine what is relevant, and through continued dependency and trust in technology, become complacent, thus eventually atrophying any acquired manual flying skills.[112] In a similar manner, human operators in general lose their control over the socio-technical systems in question through their loss in adaptive skills and decision-making authority through the imposition of algorithmic protocols.[113]

What has effectively been evacuated from the socio-technical system is human creativity, for as we saw in Chapter 3, determining what is relevant is a key part of not only adaptive expertise but also of human creativity involving the ability to find novel and meaningful ways of looking at things and taking actions. Furthermore, as we argued in Chapters 2, 3 and 5, technology and AI are unable to match such human creativity.[114] In this manner, we can also begin to appreciate Tenner's efficiency paradox — i.e. current socio-technical systems (which includes Big Data) can only improve themselves by way of rules that have already been defined or detected within existing sets of paradigms.[115] This is what is often referred to as incremental or continuous improvements within current ways of "doing things". Yet, turbulent environments can suddenly impose completely "new rules" which technologies have not been programmed to deal with or are outside of their current performance envelopes. Add to this that human operators having lost their own meaningful control over such systems through technology's own mesmerizing effect, entire systems risk not only losing their ability to remain effective but also lose their ability to remain efficient because of futile/irrelevant, yet, very energy-consuming attempts to algorithmically deal with the new rule-breaking situations at hand. Perhaps not so coincidently, is that increased use of AI and robotics within the economic workplace has been accompanied with consistently optimistic predictions in productivity improvements.[116] Yet,[117]

"In aggregate form, the data from the last 30 years in advanced economies actually suggest a worsening, rather than improving trend. US Conference Board data analysed by the economist Michael Roberts show us that between 1960 and 1980, average productivity growth per year in advanced economies was slightly over 4 per cent, it averaged approximately 2 per cent between 1980 and 2000 but fell further to 1 per cent and less after 2000."

Finally, by way of our own cognitive, epistemological, phenomeno-logical, and organizational arguments, we rejoin Arthur Molella's review commentary regarding Tenner's own more vulgarized examination of AI and Big Data: "computers, big data, and artificial intelligence are too often allowed to supersede human judgment and indeed undermine our very self-confidence as human beings.[118] Yet no electronic machine can match our capacity for the untidy human factors needed to balance the sanitized precision and tunnel vision of our digital devices: holistic think-ing, serendipity, and intuition."

In the next chapter...

As we previously showed in Chapter 3, it is only through creative human symbolic transformations that we can create new rule-breaking para-digms.[119] In the next chapter, we shall argue that getting there involves the use of metaphors — albeit, creative ones.

References

Barley, S.R., and Tolbert, P.S. (1997). Institutionalization and structuration: Studying the links between action and institution. *Organization Studies*, **18**, 93–117.

Bourdieu, P. (1990) [1980]. *The Logic of Practice* (Cambridge, UK: Polity Press).

Follett, M.P. (1924). *Creative Experience* (New York: Longmans, Green and Company).

Merleau-Ponty, M. (1962). *The Phenomenology of Perception*, C. Smith (trans.) (New York, NY: Routledge).

Suchman, L.A. (2009). *Human-Machine Reconfigurations: Plans and Situated Actions*. 2nd Edition (Cambridge, UK: Cambridge University Press).

Zucker, L.G. (1991). The Role of Institutionalization in Cultural Persistence. In *The New Institutionalism in Organizational Analysis*, W.W. Powell and P.J. DiMaggio (eds.) (Chicago, IL: University of Chicago Press), pp. 83–107.

Endnotes

[1] See both Morgan, G. (2006). *Images of Organizations* (Thousand Oaks, CA: Sage Publications) as well as Weick, K.E. (1995). *Sensemaking in Organizations* (Thousand Oaks, CA: Sage Publications).

[2] See both Weick (1995) (note 1) as well as Langer, E.J. (1989). *Mindfulness* (Cambridge, MA: Perseus Books).

[3] Citing Langer (1989, p. 3) (note 2).

[4] Citing Burgoon, J.K. and Langer, E.J. (1996). Language, fallacies, and mindlessness-mindfulness in social interaction. *Communication Yearbook*, **18**, 105–132.

[5] See Weick, K.E., Sutcliffe, K.M. and Obstfeld, D. (2005). Organizing and the process of sensemaking. *Organization Science*, **16**(4), 409–421.

[6] See Suppe, F. (1977). *The Structure of Scientific Theories* (Champaign, IL: University of Illinois Press).

[7] Citing Morgan (2006, p. 141) (note 1).

[8] Follett, M.P. (1924). *Creative Experience* (New York: Longmans, Green and Company).

[9] Citing Weick, K. (2009). *Making Sense of the Organization: The Impermanent Organization* (Chichester: John Wiley & Sons), p. 190, in turn citing from Follett, M.P. (1924). *Creative Experience* (New York: Longmans, Green and Company), pp. 118–119.

[10] See Orton, J.D. (2000). Enactment, sensemaking and decision making: Redesign processes in the 1976 reorganization of U.S. intelligence. *Journal of Management Studies*, **37**(2), 213–234.

[11] See Anderson, A.R. (2000). Paradox in the periphery: An entrepreneurial reconstruction? *Entrepreneurship & Regional Development*, **12**, 91–109.

[12] See Weick *et al.* (2005) (note 5).

[13] See both Marziliano, N. (1998). Managing the corporate image and identity: A borderline between fiction and reality. *International Studies of Management and Organization*, **28**(3), 3–11; as well as Beyer, J. and Hannah, D.R. (2002). Building on the past: Enacting established personal identities in a new work setting. *Organization Science*, **13**(6), 636–652.

[14] Prencipe, A. (2001). Exploiting and nurturing in-house technological capabilities: Lessons from the aerospace industry. *International Journal of Innovation Management*, **5**(3), 299–321.

[15] Citing Smircich, L. and Stubbard, C. (1985). Strategic management in an enacted world. *Academy of Management Review*, **10**(4), 724–736.

[16] Citing Weick, K.E. (2001). *Making Sense of the Organization* (Malden, MA: Blackwell), p. 187.

[17] See both Yanow, D. (2003). Seeing organizational learning: A cultural view. In *Knowing in Organizations: A Practice-based Approach*, D. Nicolini, S. Gherardi and D. Yanow (eds.) (New York, NY: M.E. Sharpe), pp. 32–52; as well as Yanow, D. (2006). Studying physical artifacts: An interpretive approach. In *Artifacts and Organizations — Beyond Mere Symbolism*, M.G. Pratt and A. Rafaeli (eds.) (Mahwah, NJ: Lawrence Erlbaum Associates), pp. 41–60.

[18] See Weick, K.E. (1969). *The Social Psychology of Organizing* (Reading, MA: Addison-Wesley).

[19] See Yanow (2003) (note 17); also see Engeström, Y., Puoni, A. and Seppänen, L. (2003). Spatial and temporal expansion of the object as a challenge for

reorganizing work. In *Knowing in Organizations: A Practice-based Approach*, Nicolini, D., Gherardi, S. and Yanow, D. (eds.) (New York, NY: M.E. Sharpe), pp. 151–186; and finally, see Svabo, C. (2009). Materiality in a practice-based approach. *The Learning Organization*, **16**(5), 360–370. https://doi.org/10.1108/09696470910974153.
[20] Citing Svabo (2009, p. 365) (note 19).
[21] *Ibid.*
[22] See Faraj, S., Pachidi, S. and Sayegh, K. (2018). Working and organizing in the age of the learning algorithm. *Information and Organization*, **28**, 62–70.
[23] Citing Faraj *et al.* (2018, p. 65) (note 22); also see Ananny, M. (2016). Toward an ethics of algorithms: Convening, observation, probability, and timeliness. *Science, Technology and Human Values*, **41**(1), 93–117; and finally see Introna, L.D. (2016). Algorithms, governance, and governmentality: On governing academic writing. *Science, Technology & Human Values*, **41**(1), 17–49.
[24] Citing Faraj *et al.* (2018, p. 66) (note 22); also see Frey, C.B. and Osborne, M.A. (2017). The future of employment: How susceptible are jobs to computerisation? *Technological Forecasting and Social Change*, **114**, 254–280; and finally, see Manyika, J., Lund, S., Chui, M., Bughin, J., Woetzel, J., Batra, P. and Ko, R. (2017). *Jobs Lost, Jobs Gained: Workforce Transitions in a Time of Automation*. McKinsey Global Institute, pp. 1–148.
[25] Citing Faraj *et al.* (2018, p. 66) (note 22).
[26] See Orlikowski, W. J. (2007). Sociomaterial practices: Exploring technology at work. *Organization Studies*, **28**(9), 1435–1448.
[27] See both Barad, K. (2003). Posthumanist performativity: Toward an understanding of how matter comes to matter. *Signs*, **28**, 801–831, as well as Barad, K. (2007). *Meeting the Universe Halfway: Quantum Physics and the Entanglement of Matter and Meaning* (Durham, NC: Duke University Press).
[28] See Gherardi, S. (2006). *Organizational Knowledge: The Texture of Workplace Learning* (Oxford: Blackwell).
[29] *Ibid.*
[30] *Ibid.*
[31] See both Kuepers, W. (2011). "Tran- + -form": Leader- and followship as an embodied, emotional and aesthetic practice for creative transformation in organizations. *Leadership and Organization Development Journal*, **32**(1), 20–40, as well as Hassard, J., Holliday, R. and Willmott, H. (2000). *Body and Organization* (London: Sage Publications), p. 12.
[32] Citing Kuepers (2011, pp. 23–24) (note 31).
[33] Citing Kuepers (2011, p. 24) (note 31).
[34] See Barad (2007) (note 27).
[35] *Ibid*; also see Barad (2003) (note 27).
[36] Citing Barad (2007, p. 37) (note 27).

[37] See Crossley, N. (2011). *Towards Relational Sociology* (New York: Routledge), p. 31.

[38] Citing Shotter, J. (2014). Agential realism, social constructionism, and our living relations to our surroundings: Sensing similarities rather than seeing patterns. *Theory & Psychology*, **24**(3), 305–325.

[39] See Barad (2007) (note 27).

[40] Citing Barad (2007, p. ix, 33) (note 27).

[41] See Barad (2007) (note 27).

[42] See Latour, B. (2006). A textbook case revisited: Knowledge as mode of existence. In *The Handbook of Science and Technology Studies*, Third Edition, E. Hackett, O. Amsterdamska, M. Lynch and J. Wacjman (eds.) (Cambridge, MA: MIT Press), pp. 83–112.

[43] See Barad (2007) (note 27).

[44] Citing Lynch, R. and Farrington, C. (2017). *Quantified Lives and Vital Data* (London, UK: Palgrave Macmillan), p. 117.

[45] See Orlikowski, W.J. and Scott, S. (2015). Exploring material-discursive practices. *Journal of Management Studies*, **52**(5), 696–705.

[46] *Ibid.*

[47] See Suchman, L.A. (2009). *Human-Machine Reconfigurations: Plans and Situated Actions*, 2nd Edition (Cambridge, UK: Cambridge University Press).

[48] Citing Merleau-Ponty, M. (1962). The Phenomenology of Perception, C. Smith (trans.) (New York, NY: Routledge), p. 207.

[49] Citing Küpers, W. (2013). Embodied transformative metaphors and narratives in organizational life-worlds of change. *Journal of Organizational Change Management*, **26**(3), 494–528.

[50] See Küpers (2013) (note 49).

[51] See both Lakoff, G. and Johnson, M. (1980). *Metaphors We Live By* (Chicago, IL: University of Chicago Press), as well as Lakoff, G. and Johnson, M. (1999). *Philosophy in the Flesh: The Embodied Mind and its Challenge to Western Thought* (Berkeley, CA: Basic Books).

[52] See Küpers (2013) (note 49).

[53] Citing Timmerman, C.E. (2002). The moderating effect of mindlessness/mindfulness upon media richness and social influence explanations of organizational media use. *Communication Monographs*, **69**(2), 111–131.

[54] Citing Langer (1989, p. 11) (note 2).

[55] See both Burgoon, J.K., Berger, C.R. and Waldron, V.R. (2000). Mindfulness and interpersonal communication. *Journal of Social Issues*, **56**(1), 105–127, as well as Sætre, A.S., Sørnes, J-O., Browning, L.D. and Stephens, K.K. (2007). Enacting media use in organizations. *Journal of Information, Information Technology, and Organizations*, **2**, 133–158.

[56] See Ashforth, B.E. and Fried, Y. (1988). The mindlessness of organizational behaviors. *Human Relations*, **41**(4), 305–329.

[57] See Sætre *et al.* (2007) (note 49).

[58] See both Sætre *et al.* (2007) (note 49), as well as Abougomaah, N.H., Schlacter, J.L. and Gaidis, W. (1987). Elimination and choice phases in evoked set formation. *The Journal of Consumer Marketing*, **4**(4), 67–73.

[59] Citing Parasuraman, R, and Manzey. D.H. (2010). Complacency and bias in human use of automation: An attentional integration. *Human Factors*, **52**(3), 381–410, as well as Wickens, C.D. and Alexander, A.L. (2009). Attentional tunneling and task management in synthetic vision displays. *The International Journal of Aviation Psychology*, **19**(2), 182–199. https://doi.org/10.1080/10508410902766549.

[60] Citing Wickens and Alexander (2009, p. 182) (note 59).

[61] *Ibid.*

[62] See Holford, W.D. (2020). An ethical inquiry of the effect of cockpit automation on the responsibilities of airline pilots: Dissonance or meaningful control? *Journal of Business Ethics* [Online]. https://doi.org/10.1007/s10551-020-04640-z.

[63] See both Parasuraman and Manzey (2010) (note 59), as well as Wickens and Alexander (2009) (note 59).

[64] See Mosier, K.L, Skitka, L.J., Heers, S. and Burdick M.D. (1998). Automation bias: Decision making and performance in high-tech cockpits. *The International Journal of Aviation Psychology*, 47–63.

[65] See Parasuraman and Manzey (2010) (note 59).

[66] McBride, S.E., Rogers, W.E. and Fisk, A.D. (2014). Understanding human management of automation errors. *Theoretical Issues Ergonomic Sciences*, **15**(6), 545–577.

[67] Citing Langer (1989, p. 11) (note 2).

[68] Citing Weber, K. and Glynn, M.A. (2006). Making sense with institutions: Context, thought and action in Karl Weick's theory. *Organization Studies*, **27**(11): 1639–1660.

[69] *Ibid.*

[70] Citing Wilken, R. (2013). An exploratory comparative analysis of the use of metaphors in writing on the Internet and mobile phones. *Social Semiotics*, **23**(5), 632–647. doi:10.1080/10350330.2012.738999.

[71] Citing Puschmann, C. and Burgess, J. (2014). Metaphors of big data. *International Journal of Communication*, **8**, 1690–1709, who in turn refer to Wilken (2013) (note 70).

[72] Citing Nardi, B.A. and O'Day, V.L. (1999). *Information Ecologies: Using Technology with Heart* (Cambridge, MA: MIT Press), p. 25.

[73] *Ibid.*

[74] *Ibid.* p. 28.

[75] See both Alexander, J.K. (2008). *The Mantra of Efficiency: From Waterwheel to Social Control* (Baltimore: John Hopkins University Press), as well as

Holford, W.D. (2019). The future of human creative knowledge work within the digital economy. *Futures*, **105**, 143–154.

[76] Citing Jasanoff, S. and Kim, S.-H. (2009). Containing the atom: Sociotechnical imaginaries and nuclear power in the United States and South Korea. *Minerva*, **47**(2), 119–146.

[77] See Heidegger, M. (1977). *The Question Concerning Technology and Other Essays* (New York: Garland Publishing); also see Hanks, C. (2010). *Technology and Values: Essential Readings* (Oxford: John Wiley/Blackwell Publishing); and finally, see Van Vleet, J.E. (2014). *Dialectical Theology and Jacques Ellul: An Introductory Exposition* (Minneapolis, MN: Fortress Press).

[78] Citing Heidegger (1977, p. 15) (note 77).

[79] See Ellul, J. (1964). *The Technological Society* (New York: Alfred A. Knopf Inc).

[80] *Ibid.*, pp. 1–20.

[81] Citing Clair, M. (2016). The limits of neoliberalism: How writers and editors use digital technologies in the literary field. *Communication and Information Technologies Annual*, **11**, 169–201; also see Gere, C. (2008). *Digital Culture* (London: Reaktion Books).

[82] Citing Clair (2016, pp. 173–174) (note 81).

[83] See Autor, D.H. (2015). Why are there still so many jobs? The history and future of workplace automation. *Journal of Economic Perspectives*, **29**(3), 3–30.

[84] See both Holford (2020) (note 62) as well as Holford, W.D. (2020). The algorithmic workplace and its enactive effect on the future of professions. *Futures*, **122**, article 102609. http://dx.doi.org/10.1016/j.futures.2020.102609.

[85] See Ryall, E. (2008). The language of genetic technology: Metaphor and media representation. *Continuum: Journal of Media & Cultural Studies*, **22**(3), 363–373. doi:10.1080/10304310701861556.

[86] See both Wickens and Alexandre (2009) (note 59) as well as Strauch, B. (2017). The automation-by-expertise-by-training interaction: Why automation-related accidents continue to occur in sociotechnical systems. *Human Factors*, **59**(2), 204–228.

[87] Citing Nardi and Day (1999, p. 27) (note 72).

[88] See Holford (2020) (note 62).

[89] See Bjørn, P. and Balka, E. (2007). Health care categories have politics too: Unpacking the managerial agendas of electronic triage systems, *ECSCW'07: Proceedings of the Tenth European Conference on Computer Supported Cooperative*, pp. 371–390.

[90] See Dreyfus, H.L. and Dreyfus, S.E. (1986). *Mind Over Machine* (New York: The Free Press).

[91] Citing Bjørn, P. and Balka, E. (2007, p. 375) (note 89).

[92] Citing Bjørn, P. and Balka, E. (2007, p. 376) (note 89).

[93] See Morgan (2006) (note 1).

[94] See both Holford (2020) (note 62) as well as Schultz, T.P. (2018). *The Problem with Pilots: How Physicians, Engineers and Airpower Enthusiasts Redefined Flight* (Baltimore, MA: John Hopkins University Press).

[95] See Barad (2007) (note 27).

[96] See Webb, S. (2020). Why agential realism matters to social work. *The British Journal of Social Work*, **106**, https://doi.org/10.1093/bjsw/bcaa106.

[97] Citing Schultz (2018, p. 122) (note 94).

[98] Citing Schultz (2018, p. 124) (note 94).

[99] Citing Schultz (2018) (note 94).

[100] See Schultz (2018) (note 94).

[101] *Ibid*; also see Dreyfus, H.L. (2007). Why Heideggerian AI failed and how fixing it would require making it more Heidegerrian. *Artificial Intelligence*, **171**(18), 1137–1160.

[102] *Ibid.*; also see Carr, N. (2015). *The Glass Cage — How Our Computers Are Changing Us* (New York: W.W. Norton and Company).

[103] See both Schultz (2018) (note 94) as well as Chialastri, A. (2012). Automation in aviation. In *Automation*, Kongoli, F. (ed.), InTech, pp. 79–102. doi: 10.5772/49949.

[104] See Dreyfus (2007) (note 101).

[105] Citing Dreyfus (2007, p. 1145) (note 101).

[106] See Dreyfus (2007, p. 1146–1147) (note 101).

[107] See Boden, M.A. (2016). *AI: Its Nature and Future* (Oxford, UK: Oxford University Press).

[108] See both *Ibid.* as well as Boden, M.A. (2010). *Creativity and Art: Three Roads to Surprise* (Oxford, UK: Oxford University Press).

[109] See both Gallagher, S. (2009). The Philosophical Antecedents of Situated Cognition. In *The Cambridge Handbook of Situated Cognition*, Robbins, P. and Aydede, M. (eds.) (Cambridge, UK: Cambridge University Press), as well as Collins, H. (2010). *Tacit and Explicit Knowledge* (Chicago, IL: University of Chicago Press).

[110] See Dreyfus (2007) (note 101); also see Carr (2015) (note 102); as well as Schultz (2018) (note 94).

[111] See both Carr (2015) (note 102) as well as Schultz (2018) (note 94).

[112] See both Schultz (2018) (note 94) as well as Strauch (2017) (note 86).

[113] See Oliver, N., Calvard, T. and Potocnik, K. (2017). Cognition, technology and organizational limits: Lessons from the Air France 447 disaster. *Organization Science*, **28**(4), 597–780.

[114] See Boden (2010) (note 107); also Boden (2016) (note 108); finally, see Boden, M.A. (2015). *Artificial Intelligence* (Boston: MIT Technology Review).

[115] See Tenner, E. (2018). *The Efficiency Paradox: What Big Data Can't Do* (New York: Knopf).

[116] See Upchurch, M. (2018). Robots and AI at work: The prospects for singularity. *New Technology, Work and Employment*, **33**(3), 205–218.
[117] Citing *Ibid.* p. 208.
[118] See Tenner (2018) (note 115).
[119] See Boden (2010) (note 107); also see Boden (2015) (note 104); as well as Boden (2016) (note 107); finally, see Holford, W.D. (2019). The future of human creative knowledge work within the digital economy. *Futures*, **105**, 143–154.

Chapter 8

Achieving Meaningful Human Control Through Mindfulness and Creative Metaphors

8.1. Introduction

The design of technology often reflects social factors at work within current rationalities, beliefs, and ideologies, whereby, once introduced, the technology provides a material validation of the social order that formed it.[1] On the other hand, by remaining mindful in a manner briefly described in Chapter 3 (i.e., in regards to *mètis* and its associated adaptive expertise), we avoid attending to only a limited set of available cues, and as such, circumvent being entrapped within explicitly defined categories.[2] Mindfulness, a basically phenomenological concept and process which we further examine in this chapter, allows us to both individually and collectively perceive and enact creative alternative organizational work practices. Mindfulness allows us to discern entrenched metaphors that have entrapped us within mindless behaviors. Through the use of "living" or creative metaphors, mindfulness allows designers, managers, and user-operators, to begin the process of enacting more creative and relevant human-centric socio-technical designs within the workplace. Such socio-technical systems bring forth, rather than repress, human adaptive expertise (*mètis*), and as such allow human users to maintain meaningful control.

8.2. Challenging Past and Current Enactments On and By Technology Across a Democratic Process

We have argued that AI technology reflect representational approaches (Chapters 1, 2, and 5), which have historical roots going as far back as Socrates, Plato, and Aristotle in their quest toward understanding reality in terms of representational categories (Chapter 4). These historical influences throughout the centuries on Western epistemological beliefs have been deep, long, and ubiquitous in nature, repressing any alternative perspective on the nature of human knowledge, skills, and expertise such as those proposed by the early Sophists regarding the uncategorizable (yet rich!) behaviour of *mètis*.[3] As such, we can understand Heidegger's substantivist (or "top-down") position, which not only describes technology as "revealing its essence" as representational mindsets which obsessively seek efficiency, but that this technology, in turn, has shaped (i.e. enacted) who and what we are in terms of reified and impoverished versions of humanity.[4] This one-way depiction of enactment is again taken up by Ellul, who argues the "technical phenomenon" as the defining characteristic of all modern societies which "has become autonomous."[5] However, this one-way phenomenon is re-questioned by both Marcuse and Foucault.[6] Marcuse's *One-Dimensional Man* argues that while technology, and the ruling elite that has used it to its benefit, attempts to evacuate all phenomenological aspects (such as "transcendence") out of society, such a trend can be reversed through democratic intervention.[7] Yet the details of what (and how) such democratic interventions would consist of remain vague. Foucault[8] proposes forms of local resistance, again "without any overall strategy."[9] While Feenberg acknowledges the enactive effects technology can have on society by way of its "materialized ideology," he reinforces Marcuse's idea of democratic intervention as a means of countering or "reversing" this one-way movement, but this time through a more explicit approach involving the "reassertion of the role of communication."[10] Moreover, "if one can loosen up the public vision of technology, introduce contingency into it, technical elites will have to be more responsive to a democratically informed public will."[11] As such, Feenberg proposes a social constructivist approach in which multiple points of views are considered, consistent with a social democratic process, to which we add, goes hand-in-hand with mindful states of being, mindful behavior, and mindful conversation.[12] Furthermore, once this democratic process is set in motion, technology itself no longer remains entrapped within Ellul's or Heidegger's description/diagnosis of "instrumental ideology." This, we argue, is because of the reciprocal enactive effect between society and technology. It is important to note that *enactment can just as much involve a reinforcing as well as a subversive response to what is being experienced.* In this sense, we once again rejoin Barad's sociomateriality in which the social and the material are mutually constitutive of one another.[13] We can better appreciate the fine-grained approach of Barad's agential realism and its "constitutive strands" of ongoing activity even within epochs of what appear like totalizing and monolithic technocratic dominations, in which reciprocal (yet, not necessarily symmetrical) responses occur, such as we see through Foucault's "subjugated knowledges" arising in opposition to such dominating rationalities.[14]

A socio-material, and more specifically, an agential realist view of reality entails activity or phenomena in which knowledge in the form of knowing as well as discrete possessions/outputs (or "cuts") are constantly emerging (i.e. as phenomena) from embedded practices and processes within and between agential bodies.[15] Here, power is inherently entangled with knowledge, in that it intra-acts with knowledge across judgments, inferences, and embodied practices to produce substantive consequences and actions in the form of adjustments (or adjusting to) and control (or controlling) of situations which enact other judgments, inferences, embodied practices, actions and consequences, and so on.[16] Power as discourse is shaped by discursive practice toward a state of continual becoming,[17] in that power as an entity/possession like all "entities … are abstractions … always 'becoming' rather than 'being' … always in formation, and never exist as entities in themselves."[18] Yet, from such material-discursive practices, enacted boundaries or agential "cuts" emerge as a result of intra-acting agencies.[19] As in Latour's temporary, imperfect, incomplete, and pragmatic "state of affairs,"[20] cuts allow for "certain phenomena to be momentarily distinguished" and become meaningful.[21] Here, we can speak of knowledge-as-interpretations and sensemaking. As such, cuts are transient, ephemeral abstractions constituted from ongoing movement and flux, which allow human agencies to examine something long enough to gain knowledge about it.[22] Cuts emerge through negotiated conversation, storytelling, and meaning.[23] In turn, power is bound to both sensemaking and sensegiving through material-discursive acts.[24] Of notable interest, sensegiving can normalize/shut down alternative interpretations to facilitate its implementation toward intended views of the world.[25] In a more general manner, material-discursive acts constrain/ enable what is said, creating bodies of knowledge as meanings, speech, and acts perceived as so-called entities corresponding to slower changing configurations of social relationships/exchanges.[26]

The above socio-material description is by no means a democratic process — all we are proposing is that it offers an enhanced perspective on what reality might entail.[27] For such a process to shift toward a social democratic one as argued by Feenberg,[28] we would add that human sensemaking must take a voluntary step toward mindfulness,[29] both as a state of being and doing, which we shall further discuss in the following section. As we argue throughout the following sections, it is through such mindfulness that the historically totalizing grip of technology's instrumental, categorical, and representational rationality can be counterenacted towards a socio-technico-economic environment that is open toward richer perspectives that are inclusive to both what can *and cannot* be reduced to mere technical/cognitive representations, explications, and modelizations.

8.3.   Mindfulness and its Role in Individual and Organizational Adaptive Expertise

Definitions on individual mindfulness differ, yet, as Sutcliffe *et al.* explain, "are more convergent than divergent."[30] Eastern approaches tend to emphasize and focus attention solely on present moment events in a non-judgmental fashion in which one refrains from making evaluations or interpretations.[31] While the Western approach pioneered by Ellen Langer does not preclude this perspective,[32] it also includes an "active" dimension across the drawing of novel distinctions as well as the enactment of creative actions and outcomes. As such, it is Langer's approach that we shall build upon throughout this chapter.

Langer, who was one of the first to research mindfulness, specifies "a mindful approach to any activity has three characteristics: the continuous creation of new categories, openness to new information, and an implicit awareness of more than one perspective."[33] According to Langer, mindfulness is both an act of learning and creativity[34]; it induces a meta-awareness of "now-ness," or more precisely, an "agency of the present" — in which the "pasts and the futures" are both "experienced" and "re-shaped," bringing forth a past solution creatively adapted for the future.[35] Of particular importance (and as previously mentioned in Chapter 3), is that "from a mindful perspective, one's response to a particular situation is not an attempt to make the best choice from among available options but to create options"[36]; more simply put, "if we are mindful, we can create the context."[37] In this sense, mindfulness is contradictory in nature in that it involves both a state of being and an act of "doing".[38]

We present individual mindfulness as involving three overlapping *non-sequential* stages. First, it involves present-centered consciousness, in which judgements and concepts are withheld or filtered.[39] It is primarily a state of being involving an expansive "attentional breadth" toward both external events and internal states,[40] open to new information,[41] whereby it attends to and accepts "the raw stream of experiences".[42] Here, we can also speak of the beginning stage of learning in which attention is paid to the unfolding experience of the present moment while withholding judgment.[43] Such mindfulness allows for the perception of dynamic complexity within the practice-at-hand without falling into pre-mature conceptualizations or "pre-interpretations" which risk being irrelevant in nature.[44] Second, in building upon the process of psychological detachment, mindfulness involves the conceptual, yet detached, interpretation of one's experience. Interpretations are not viewed as reality, but simply as possible alternative readings of a situation.[45] At this stage, mindful learning involves the co-mingling of being and acting (the latter, through the act of interpreting). Here, learning involves a divergent thinking approach that is always connected to context, thus allowing one to examine an idea by considering alternatives, thereby creating more possibilities rather than focusing on one outcome.[46] As one's experience grows, multiple solutions from multiple perspectives can eventually be drawn upon to fit multiple contexts. Finally, the third stage involves a "parsimonious intervention" benefitting from one's cumulative experience as well as openness to the situation-at-hand.[47] Here, a creative enactment occurs through the act of both *generating* a meaningful connection as well as the materialization or "doing" of a novel action or behavior based on the meaningful connection being made.[48]

As discussed previously in Chapter 3, *mètis'* adaptive nature and expertise is intimately linked to various aspects of individual mindfulness, involving "vigilance" or "keen attention,"[49] or more precisely a "mindful experience" through "mindful observation" that is called upon to achieve the required responsive anticipation and skill.[50] In the same spirit, both mindful observation and creative enactment is revealed through Adams and Ericsson's description of expert pilot's adaptive expertise as involving the ability to "perceive the necessity to alter (or not to alter) ingrained conceptual and procedural knowledge based upon the parameter and dynamics (cues and context) of the problem or situation encountered"[51] in which such alterations involve creative acts, i.e. "creatively respond to unique problems or novel task demands." Such acts of adaptive expertise are rapid and depend on the ability to deframe/reframe mental models, perceive relevant cues (situational awareness), rapidly *generate* meaningful relationships within the new situation at hand, and "do" the appropriate interventions.[52]

From an organizational point of view, seeking mindfulness is both an individual and collective endeavor. In contrast to the intrapsychic nature of individual mindfulness as related to individual expertise or *mètis*, collective mindfulness is a social process.[53] Similar to individual mindfulness, collective mindfulness counteracts the general tendency to simplify events into familiar categories by helping people detect previously unnoticed details (or cues) and strengthening the group's ability to creatively surface what is unique about events in question.[54] It also improves the group's capabilities to swiftly cope with what is seen,[55] thereby generating a group-like *mètis*.[56] Here, collective mindfulness as a social process involves interactions that occur in briefings, meetings, updates, and in ongoing work.[57] Most importantly, this involves a democratic discursive practice, i.e. bottom-up process that is relatively fragile and must be continuously reconstituted and reinforced through conversations.[58] In this sense, we complement and contribute to Feenberg's[59] concept of democratic social constructivism through the process of *mindful* conversations. Under mindful conversations, the content of conversations represent the principal means by which collective mindfulness enhances sensemaking, including co-production and co-completion of utterances,[60] reframing solutions,[61] re-questioning assumptions,[62] and portraying hazards in a manner which suspends final judgments in regards to them.[63] Mindful conversations are interactional processes that merge individual mindfulness with reflective, genuine, and adaptive exchanges.[64] Hence, we again find the co-mingling of mindful presence (i.e. state of non-judgmental being), mindful acts of reframing and re-interpreting information, and mindful creative interventions.[65] And, as in the case of individual mindfulness, collective mindfulness involves both the noticing of relevant cues as well as what the team does in relation to what they noticed.[66] As such, collective mindfulness involves enactment, but this time through a collective process.[67] Of particular importance are the management implications in maintaining successful mindful conversations within the work environment, in that it involves an equitable democratic approach toward every member.[68] It is the type of management that encourages the open expression of opinions as well as the shifting of conversations to where knowledge and expertise resides.[69] Such an approach is bottom-up and encourages plural leaderships.[70] Finally, it involves both a management and an organization that is open toward situations which require new or alternative ways of doing things in which best practices are no longer rules to be blindly obeyed, but can serve as starting points for crafting alternative practices and solutions.[71] This most certainly means managers willing to sacrifice illusory short-term gains in efficiency, which in fact are based on *ineffective* practices enacted through mindlessness — a mindlessness that, in turn, is continuously reinforced through the mesmerizing effect of automation's misleading reliability. Achieving coherent, yet creative, ideas and outputs through mindfulness require initial collective learning through adjustments, which in the longer term ensures we collectively avoid automation surprise when things go wrong.

In the next section, we examine how the "double-edged sword" of metaphors (which we briefly discussed in Chapter 7) can become a creative vehicle through the phenomenological state of mindfulness.

8.4. Alternative Futures Through Creative Metaphors

Metaphors are "pervasive in everyday life, not just in language, but in thought and action. Our ordinary conceptual system, in terms of which we both think and act, is fundamentally metaphorical in nature."[72] Metaphors bridge abstract constructs to concrete things.[73] In this manner, metaphors focus on "surface meaning of ideas or objects by providing an example of the point the speaker or writer is trying to make."[74] Here, we would critically add that when the correspondence between the abstract and concrete is explicated and becomes final, in other words "literalized," the metaphor becomes a "sign" (as opposed to a symbol) with a univocal meaning.[75] In Chapter 7, we discussed two ways in which metaphors as literal or "fixed" meanings can come about:

(1) either from personal self-imposed mindlessness in which we do not re-question the attributed meaning-as-category[76]; or

(2) by way of an imposed and accepted unequivocal image or imaginary[77] (such as our current socio-economic obsessions on efficiency, leading to the linear attribution of "tool" to efficiency as a "fixed" and unambiguous metaphor).

In both cases, our thoughts and actions become constrained within an existing paradigm or ideology.

Humans are averse to ambiguity and equivocality, and thus seek to reduce it.[78] As such, it is not surprising that organizational action has typically valorized goal-directed cognition, including "past and future focus; perception of reality filtered by concepts," interpreted through fixed metaphors and narratives "and automatic thoughts driving habitual actions."[79] Ironically, metaphors under such contexts become easy to manipulate signs, which can ultimately be algorithmically computed in a representative manner. Such metaphors become concepts that have "an unequivocal meaning and, in the exact sciences, a mathematical form, in the sense of course, of quantitative mathematics."[80] Under such conditions, metaphors have become reified.[81] Through their univocal meanings, they risk providing biased or ideological directions, thus slanting "our perceptions and reinforce a selective and partial view of organizational experience."[82] Finally, its repetitive and mindless usage "can lead to reinforce the status quo and inhibit active seeking of alternatives."[83]

Conversely, Ricoeur[84] refers to living metaphors able to liberate "the capacity to re-describe reality, generating new literal and symbolic meanings."[85] In this sense, living metaphors also challenge institutionally imposed categories by introducing "variations that prompt surprise, emotions and sensemaking."[86] Here, metaphors become vehicles of symbols as opposed to mere signs.[87] Symbols carry meanings that are equivocal, constantly emerging and are inherently phenomenological in character[88]:

"... a symbol can never be taken in a final and definite meaning ... a symbol itself possesses an endless number of aspects from which it can be examined and it demands from a man approaching it the ability to see it simultaneously from different points of views ... A symbol can never be fully interpreted. It can only be experienced."

As such, metaphors tap into the human capacity for symbolic transformation, which is "a veritable fountain of more or less spontaneous ideas."[89] As such, metaphors become alive[90]

"... as they produce a world, which is not limited to a rearrangement of the aspects or properties to be ascribed to a certain object, but rather of the conditions of perceptibility of phenomena. Thus, metaphors change reality by shattering language, so that 'with metaphor we experience the metamorphosis of both language and reality.'"

With this generative and creative quality, living metaphors "evoke new ways of doing things" through new meanings and interpretations to eventually break the existing order.[91] Such transformative metaphors involve lived embodied experiences, which cannot be reduced to mental cognitivist empiricism.[92] It is in relation to this type of living equivocal metaphor that Searle himself concluded could not be analyzed in a representational manner.[93]

Creative metaphors are brought to life or "energized" through mindfulness. Mindfulness both supports and enacts creativity.[94] Langer's conceptual integration of mindfulness and creativity are supported across Horan's "neuropsychological investigations into the nature of creativity and meditation, coupled with a theoretical framework describing transcendence and integration as key components common to both processes."[95] Such transcendence is inherently phenomenological, whereby "it is the experience as experienced" which counts,[96] and whose function makes transition from one attitude to another possible.[97] Transcendence involves a symbolic transformation process through which[98]:

"... thesis and antithesis, and in the shaping of which the opposite are united, is the living symbol...The symbol is always a product of an extremely complex nature since data from every psychic function have gone into its making. It is, therefore, neither rational nor irrational ... It certainly has a side that accords with reason, but it has another side that does not for it is composed not only of rational but also of irrational data supplied by pure inner and outer perception."

To which Von Franz adds[99]:

"... differentiated and primitive, conscious and unconscious are united in the symbol, as well as all other possible psychic opposites. Jung called the unknown activity of the unconscious which produces real, life-giving symbols the transcendent function because this process facilitates a transition from one attitude to another."

The living symbol as form provides different meanings and ideas in a never-ending process, which is the symbolic transformation process in itself.[100] In turn, living symbols "energize metaphors to life." Such metaphors provide "the potential to revive our creative capacities of seeing the world afresh, to stimulate the imaginative exploration of new possibilities."[101] This is in contrast to "dead" metaphors which are fixed and taken for granted assumptions which constrain our thinking and behaviors.[102]

A living metaphor we adhere to is that *humans are phenomenological beings*.[103] Contrary to images of mechanical, computational, and "modelizable" entities, which have been imposed upon us by computational theory of mind (CTM), we as humans, are irreducible and living. We are lived bodies. It is a metaphorical image that can never be completely explicated in a once-and-for-all-manner. It is an irreducible and therefore ambiguous metaphor, which becomes source of never-ending interpretations, never-ending inspirations, and infinite creativity. Keeping in mind that metaphors are pervasive in the language of both science and engineering,[104] this same living metaphor is what we would propose toward the design of human–technology systems.

8.5. Aiming for Meaningful Human Control Through the "Lived Body" Metaphor

Merleau-Ponty's phenomenology of perception has started to gain a wider acceptance in the design of certain technologies such as cellular phones, full-body computer games, technology-for-dance performance, and interactive art installations.[105] Yet, domains such as human–computer interaction (HCI) and computer-supported cooperative work (CSCW) have historically been (since the early 1980s), and, to a certain degree, continue to be influenced and shaped by the cognitive sciences based on the computer theory of mind (CTM). In this manner, human–computer interaction is viewed as information flowing from a separate artifact to a detached user, who "cognitively processes" this information, which in turn leads to actions such as "pushing a button."[106] By projecting a computer-like or "mechanical" metaphor onto humans, we technomorphize humans, and as such, force humans to bend and accommodate themselves toward technology. Such techno-centrism is implicitly detected across Bannon and Schmidt's early definition of CSCW, i.e. as "an endeavour to understand the nature and characteristics of cooperative work with the objective of designing adequate computer-based technologies."[107] Here, technologies as tools are disembodied or separated from the user, with the sole goal of being "objectively efficient."[108] Authors such as Ackerman, on the other hand, have warned against an overly technology-centric view emphasizing artifact creation and the generation of "cool toys," while ignoring how people really work and live in groups, organizations, communities, and other forms of collective life, thus leading to a gap between social requirements and technical feasibility, while "distorting collaboration and other social activity."[109] Schmidt's more recent critical examination of the concept of "work" attempts to provide a comprehensive description of what work actually constitutes, namely a description that goes far and beyond the prescriptive, so as to more fully understand what people actually do in terms of "real" work in regards to activities which managers typically ignore.[110] Heidegger's phenomenological perspective of the carpenter and his hammer as an example of tool-use provides a first early alternative across the work of Winograd and Flores on the use of computers.[111] Here, a computer remains transparent or in the "background" when used in a *ready-to-hand* mode. An example is when we use a 'Word' (or other) text editor, in which our focus is on the text, and not the text editor itself. When the text editor "crashes," our focus shifts toward the text editor itself. At this point, the computer ceases to be a "tool-in-use" and "emerges as an object in the world."[112] Yet, Heidegger's description of worldly involvement may be "unsatisfying,"[113] in that it appears "disembodied."[114] It is here that Merleau-Ponty builds upon Heidegger's account by stressing the body: "when you're skillfully coping ... without thinking, without rules, your body and its skills are drawing you to get this optimal grip on the situation."[115]

For Merleau-Ponty, the body is an undivided unity, using all of its senses toward a situation at hand, all of this by way of an embodied intentionality — thus providing the body the ability to adapt to a given situation[116]:

"A woman may, without any calculation, keep a safe distance between the feather in her hat and things which might break it off. She feels where the feather is just as we feel where our hand is. If I am in the habit of driving a car, I enter a narrow opening and see that I can 'get through' without comparing the width of the opening with that of the wings, just as I go through a doorway without checking the width of the doorway against that of my body. The hat and the car have ceased to be objects with a size and volume which is established by comparison with other objects. They have become potentialities of volume, the demand for a certain amount of free space."

More importantly, the "lived" body incorporates artifacts into its structure through changes in body schema. As Svaneas explains, our body schema consists of "non-conscious" knowledge of our lived body as well as "our potential for bodily actions in the world."[117] Such knowledge includes not only the position of our body at any given time, the embodied knowledge of our physical characteristics, such as length of arm, height of our shoulders, etc. Most importantly, it is our body's ability to update our body schema, which allows us to behave and act "in a skilful manner." Hence, when we use a tool, the body schema is changed to incorporate the "tool as part of our lived body." Svaneas provides the example of a blind man, who when he picks up his stick, the latter being an object in the external world, suddenly becomes part of his bodily structure.[118] Here we also add, that it is also how the stick, which has become part of the body, helps or enhances the blind man's ability to keep track of what is relevant around him and act upon it in a relevant manner — hence, help maintain meaningful control over the situation at hand.

As already presented previously in Chapter 6, meaningful control involves both the power to act upon as well as the ability to both detect and take relevant actions.

Meaningful Control → Actual decision-making authority or power + Ability (detect/enact relevant cues and take relevant actions)

The lived body metaphor helps designers ensure human users or operators maintain overall meaningful control of the socio-technical systems in question. To achieve meaningful human control, it is not sufficient to simply have a human presence or "being in the loop" within the human–technology system at hand.[119] Human operators must be able to influence all parts of the system in a relevant or meaningful manner. This includes having sufficient information and options over the system in question which goes beyond physico-cognitive reactions of "merely pushing a button as a reflex when a light goes on."[120] Human operators must be able to maintain an effective control that goes beyond relatively simple forms of causal control over events — i.e. they must be able to meet strict control conditions of knowledge, intention, and opportunity for action.[121]

This, we argue, is feasible through active engagement (i.e. direct bodily contact) with one's immediate environment in which relevant decisions and actions are carried out in a successfully adaptive manner through our "lived bodies," whereby body schemas are continually adjusted to the dynamic situation at hand. In this way, human experts at their highest level of mastery are able, through a holistic and phenomenological manner (i.e. through their senses), to gain a relevant picture (i.e. frame) of the problem or situation-at-hand, determine the relevant goals, and establish the relevant decisions and actions to achieve these goals — all of this, without recourse to analytical deliberations.[122] In other words, through their senses, human operators achieve an "optimal grip" of the situation at hand.[123]

Hence, meaningful human control for today's human users and operators who are part of a complex socio-technical system, becomes a matter of achieving a meaningful partnership between humans and technology.[124] As already discussed in Chapter 6, human operators are provided the leeway to creatively "enact their human agency in response to technology's material agency" through improvisation within a volatile and unpredictable work context on condition that they are (or can quickly become) knowledgeable and are provided the power/authority to do so.[125]

Designers, within a "lived body" perspective, must keep four aspects of perception in mind regarding the human user-operator in interaction with the technological artifact in question[126]:

(1) *Perception is shaped by the phenomenal field*: This is the horizon of the user, i.e. the phenomenal field that all his interactions take place within. Part of this phenomenal field is the habit of touching and trying things to learn more, which originates from our life with modern interactive artifacts.

(2) *Perception has directedness*: For a skilled operator, the artifact will give rise to a particular "directedness" — i.e. the artifact will present itself not primarily as a form to be viewed, but as something to be touched in order to learn more.

(3) *Perception is active*: Perception of the artifact's behavior requires action. The resulting user experience is the integrated sum of its visual appearance and its behavior. Without action, we are left simply with the visual appearance, thus missing out on the intended user experience of this artifact, which can only emerge through interaction.

Hence, the act of touching the artifact to learn more becomes part of the user's perceptual process of exploring its behavior.

(4) *Perception involves the whole body*: Experiencing the interactive artifact requires not only visual perception but also an arm and a hand. Arm, hand, and eye movements are integrated parts of the perceptual process that leads to perception of the artifact's behavior. The interactive experience is thus both created by and mediated through the body.

Through the "lived body" metaphor, human operators are kept actively engaged within the socio-technical system by way of actual and simulated manual actions and feedbacks.[127] Such an approach seeks to maintain human operator skills, by avoiding "operator hand-off" and subsequent "automation complacency" phenomena through haptic feedback support. This involves feedback to human senses through force vibrations, stiffness, etc. to stimulate and reinstate full-bodily engagement on the part of the human operator.[128] As such, meaningful human control is achieved and maintained. Recent research in haptic feedback within the spirit of the "lived body" appears to be promising in several human–machine applications. For example, specific variations in vibrations and force feedback have been investigated for aircraft pilots in order to help them overcome the current fly-by-wire "sensual gap" within automated cockpits and appear promising for immediate application in pilot training — and, importantly, "pilots expect aviation to be safer" through such haptic feedback systems.[129] Haptic feedback is also currently being used in numerous car vehicles with specific automated functions "to provide the traditional feel transmitted by pedals and steering," as well as "the vehicle's dynamics within a specific context" through "additional haptic elements — [such as] resistance, pulses, vibrations, physical guidance — used to guide and assist the human."[130]

While many challenges remain, there appears to be a process of honest and pertinent enquiry. Along such lines[131]:

"The role of the HMI (Human-Machine Interaction) is to make humans understand what is expected of them in terms of monitoring and active intervention. Such understanding is a pre-requisite for correctly calibrated trust and indeed for safe and comfortable operation in general. Misunderstanding between the vehicle and the human about what the other party will do has the potential to result in false expectations on the part of the system about what the human will notice, as well as over-reliance by the human on system capability and consequent disaster, as evidenced by the fatal crash of a Tesla in Florida in May 2016. At the opposite end of the spectrum, if users have too little trust in system capabilities, they may decide not to buy or use systems that could potentially be helpful and safety-enhancing."

The highest priority must always be to ensure the overall safety of the socio-technical system in question. This, in turn, requires that human operator are provided a "*sufficient* understanding of how the automation is operating and of what is expected of the human."[132] Designers of socio-technical systems must ensure that human operators are not only provided sufficient information through the phenomenological senses, but that their attention levels are also sufficient whereby mutual expectations between the human and the machine are correct. Automation surprise, specifically for car drivers, can be reduced by way of simple rules that can be indicated and are predictable.[133] The latter, for example, can be addressed through human visual sensing of displays (including look-ahead features commonly found in current navigation systems) showing what is about to happen (such as a lane change).

Finally, the "lived body" design metaphor is also being actively investigated for applications in teleoperation.[134] Teleoperation allows humans to operate within remote, hostile, or otherwise inaccessible environments. A literature survey examined the inclusion of both subjective presence and embodiment as phenomenological characteristics within applications of teleoperation.[135] Presence in itself, consistent with the Heideggerian concept of "being there," "describes the extent to which users feel they are actually in the remote environment, interacting with it."[136] Similarly, embodiment is understood in terms of "sense of one's own body" and is "intimately related to the sense of self."[137] The survey uncovered three interrelated guiding design principles toward embodiment and presence: self-identification, spatial bodily awareness, and mechanical fidelity.[138] Here, self-identification is related to presence of self or body "ownership," more specifically, an illusion of body ownership from a remote distance, which influences task execution in anthropomorphic settings, such as physical or psychological therapy, communication, or entertainment.[139] However, such body ownership can also influence performance in other remote physical tasks when "a user feels more involved and experiences flow."[140] In turn, spatial bodily awareness is attributed to the body schema as well as to spatial presence. Spatial bodily awareness as a design criteria helps ensure the facilitation of bodily navigation within a given mediated or virtual environment as well as to perceive possibilities for action.[141] Finally, mechanical fidelity is related to both the sense of agency and to body schema integration.[142] As a design criterion, mechanical fidelity also integrates the two previous principles (self-identification and spatial bodily awareness), to empower the user in regards to the physical tasks in question toward achieving meaningful human control.[143]

In the next chapter...

In the next chapter, we shall see that steering the design, management, and usage of socio-technical systems toward human-centric work environments, in which humans retain meaningful human control, requires (in itself) a meaningful and relevant conversation between human user-operators, management, and designers/manufacturers both as a process of inquiry and as a characteristic to be integrated within the implementation and usage of socio-technical systems. Such dialogue must be maintained in an ongoing fashion to prevent creative/"living" metaphors from transforming into "dead" or mindless metaphors.

Endnotes

[1] See Feenberg, A. (1999). *Questioning Technology* (London: Routledge).

[2] See Langer, E.J. (1989). *Mindfulness* (Cambridge, MA: Perseus Books).

[3] Starting with the variegated dimensions of human skills (as *mètis*) as described by both Detienne, M. and Vernant, J.P. (1978). *Les ruses de l'intélligence. La mètis des Grecs* (Paris: Flammarion) as well as De Certeau, M. (1984). *Practice of Everyday Life* (Berkeley: University of California Press); yet how these skills as first adhered to by the Sophists were never recognized in their own right by subsequent Western epistemologies whose first roots began with Socratic and Platonic principles of "pure" ideals (see Detienne and Vernant [1978] as well as Baumard, P. (1999). *Tacit Knowledge in Organizations* (London: Sage Publications), and finally Dreyfus, H.L. and Dreyfus, S.E. (2005). Peripheral vision expertise in real world contexts. *Organization Studies*, 26(5), 779–792.

[4] See Heidegger, M. (1977). *The Question Concerning Technology and Other Essays* (New York: Garland Publishing).

[5] Citing Ellul, J. (1964). *The Technological Society* (New York: Alfred A. Knopf Inc), p. 6.

[6] See Feenberg, A. (1999). *Questioning Technology* (London: Routledge)

⁷ See Marcuse, H. (1964). *One-dimensional Man: Studies in the Ideology of Advanced Industrial Society* (Boston: Beacon Press).

⁸ See Foucault, M. (1977). *Discipline and Punish: The Birth of the Prison* (New York: Vintage Books).

⁹ Citing Feenberg (1999, p. 8) (note 6).

¹⁰ Citing Feenberg (1999, pp. 7–8) (note 6).

¹¹ Citing Feenberg (1999, p. 8) (note 6).

¹² See Feenberg (1999) (note 6).

¹³ See both Barad, K. (2003). Posthumanist performativity: Toward an understanding of how matter comes to matter. *Signs*, **28**, 801–831; as well as Barad, K. (2007). *Meeting the Universe Halfway: Quantum Physics and the Entanglement of Matter and Meaning* (Durham, NC: Duke University Press).

¹⁴ Citing Foucault, M. (1980). *Power/Knowledge. Selected Interviews and Other Writings 1972-1977*. C. Gordon (ed.) (Suffolk: Harvester Press), pp. 81–82.

¹⁵ See Barad (2007) (note 13); also see Gherardi, S. (2009). Knowing and learning in practice-based studies: An introduction. *The Learning Organization*, **16**(5), pp. 352–359; as well as see Holford. W.D. (2020). *Managing Knowledge in Organizations: A Critical Pragmatic Perspective* (New York, NY: Palgrave MacMillan).

¹⁶ See both Wolfe, J. (2012). Does pragmatism have a theory of power? *European Journal of Pragmatism and American Philosophy*, **4**(1), 120–137; as well as Mukerji, C. (2014). The cultural power of tacit knowledge: Inarticulacy and Bourdieu's habitus. *American Journal of Cultural Sociology*, **3**(2), 348–375.

¹⁷ See both Fairhurst, G.T. and Putnam, L. (2005). Organizations as discursive constructions. *Communication Theory*, **14**(1), 5–26; as well as Tsoukas, H. and Chia, R. (2002). On organizational becoming: Rethinking organizational change. *Organization Science*, **13**(5), 567–582.

¹⁸ Citing Bakken, T. and Hernes, T. (2006). Organizing is both a verb and a noun: Weick meets Whitehead. *Organization Studies*, **27**(11), 1599–1616.

¹⁹ See Barad (2007) (note 13).

²⁰ See Latour, B. (2006). A Textbook Case Revisited: Knowledge As Mode of Existence. In *The Handbook of Science and Technology Studies*, Third Edition, E. Hackett, O. Amsterdamska, M. Lynch and J. Wacjman (eds.) (Cambridge, MA: MIT Press), pp. 83–112.

²¹ Citing Lynch, R. and Farrington, C. (2017). *Quantified Lives and Vital Data* (London, UK: Palgrave Macmillan), p. 117.

²² See Barad (2007) (note 13).

²³ See Weick, K.E. (1995). *Sensemaking in Organizations* (Thousand Oaks, CA: Sage Publications); also see Gephart, R.P. (1993). The textual approach: Risk and blame in disaster sensemaking. *The Academy of Management Journal*, **36**(6), 1465–1514; as well as see Maitlis, S. (2005). The social process of organizational sensemaking. *Academy of Management Journal*, **48**(1), 21–49.

24 See both Filstad, C. (2014). The politics of sensemaking and sensegiving at work. *Journal of Workplace Learning*, **26**(1), 3–21; as well as Weick, K.E., Sutcliffe, K.M. and Obstfeld, D. (2005). Organizing and the process of sensemaking. *Organization Science*, **16**(4), 409–421.

25 See Weick *et al.* (2005) (note 24); as well as Mills, J.H. (2003). *Making Sense of Organizational Change* (New York: Routledge); and finally, Maitlis, S. and Lawrence, T.B. (2007). Triggers and enablers of sensegiving in organizations. *Academy of Management Journal*, **50**(1), 57–84.

26 See Barad (2007) (note 13); as well as Nayak, A. and Chia, R. (2011). Thinking, becoming and emergence: Process philosophy and organization studies. In *Philosophy and Organization Theory. Research in the Sociology of Organization*, Tsoukas, H. and Chia. R. (eds.), pp. 281–309; and finally, Foucault, M. (1982). *The Archaeology of Knowledge and the Discourse on Language* (New York: Pantheon Books).

27 See both Barad (2007) (note 13) as well as Holford (2020, pp. 109–127) (note 15).

28 See Feenberg (1999) (note 6).

29 See Holford (2020, pp. 137–138) (note 15).

30 Citing Sutcliffe, K.M., Vogus, T.J. and Dane, E. (2016). Mindfulness in organizations: A cross-level review. *Annual Review of Organizational Psychology and Organizational Behavior*, **3**, 55–81.

31 See Kabat-Zinn, J. (1990). *Full Catastrophe Living* (New York, NY: Delta); as well as Hülsheger, U.R., Alberts, H.J., Feinholdt, A. and Lang, J.W. (2013). Benefits of mindfulness at work: The role of mindfulness in emotion regulation, emotional exhaustion, and job satisfaction. *Journal of Applied Psychology*, **98**, 310–325; and finally, see Sheldon, K.M., Prentice, M. and Halusic, M. (2015). The experiential incompatibility of mindfulness and flow absorption. *Social, Psychological and Personal Science*, **6**, 276–283.

32 See both Langer (1989) (note 2) as well as Langer, E.J. (2014). Mindfulness forward and back. In *The Wiley Blackwell Handbook of Mindfulness*, A. Ie, C.T. Ngoumen and E.J. Langer (eds.) (Chichester, UK: Wiley), pp. 7–20.

33 Citing Langer, E. (1997). *The Power of Mindful Learning* (Cambridge, MA: Da Capo Press), p. 4.

34 See Langer, E.J. (2000). Mindful learning. *Current Directions in Psychological Science*, **9**(2), 220–223.

35 Citing Hernes, T. (2014). *A Process Theory of Organization* (Oxford, UK: Oxford University Press), p. 4.

36 Citing Langer (1997, p. 113) (note 33).

37 Citing Langer, E. (2009). *Counter Clockwise. Mindful Health and the Power of Possibility* (London, UK: Hodder & Stoughton), p. 182.

38 See Lyddy, C.J. and Good, J.G. (2017). Being while doing: An inductive model of mindfulness at work. *Frontiers in Psychology*, 1–18. doi: 10.3389/fpsyg.2016.02060.

[39] See Kabat-Zinn (1990) (note 31); also see Brown, K.W. and Ryan, R.M. (2003). The benefits of being present: Mindfulness and its role in psychological well-being. *Journal of Personal and Social Psychology*, **84**, 822–848. doi: 10.1037/0022-3514.84.4.822; and finally, see Quaglia, J.T., Brown, K.W., Lindsay, E.K., Creswell, J.D. and Goodman, R.J. (2015). From Conception to Operationalization of Mindfulness. In *Handbook of Mindfulness: Theory, Research, and Practice*, K.W. Brown, J.D. Creswell and R.M. Ryan (eds.) (New York, NY: Guilford), pp. 151–170.

[40] See Dane, E. (2013). Things seen and unseen: Investigating experience-based qualities of attention in a dynamic work setting. *Organization Studies*, **34**, 45–78.

[41] See Langer (1997) (note 33).

[42] See both Brown and Ryan (2003) (note 39) as well as Good, D.J., Lyddy, C.J., Glomb, T.M., Bono, J.E., Brown, K.W., Duffy, M.K. *et al.* (2016). Contemplating mindfulness at work: An integrative review. *Journal of Management*, **42**, 114–142. doi: 10.1177/0149206315617003.

[43] See Guiette, A. and Vandenbempt, K. (2016). Learning in times of dynamic complexity through balancing phenomenal qualities of sensemaking. *Management Learning*, **47**(1), 83–99.

[44] *Ibid.*

[45] See Hülsheger *et al.* (2014) (note 31).

[46] See Langer (2000) (note 34).

[47] Citing Good *et al.* (2016, p. 134) (note 42).

[48] See Langer (2009) (note 37).

[49] Citing both Detienne, M. and Vernant, J.P. (1978). *Les ruses de l'intélligence. La mètis des Grecs.* (Paris: Flammarion), p. 4; as well as Raphals, L. (1992). *Knowing Words. Wisdom and Cunning in the Classical Tradition of China and Greece* (Ithaca, NY: Cornell University Press), p. xi.

[50] See Baumard (1999) (note 3) as well as Aftel, M. (2014). *Fragrant: The Secret Life of Scent* (New York: Penguin Books).

[51] Citing Adams, R.J. and Ericsson, A.E. (2000). Introduction to cognitive processes of expert pilots. *Journal of Human Performance in Extreme Environments*, **5**(1), 44–62. doi: 10.7771/2327-2937.1006.

[52] See Adams and Ericsson (2000, pp. 58–59) (note 51); as well as Ward, P., Gore, J., Hutton, R., Conway, G. and Hoffman, R. (2018). Adaptive skill as the condition sine qua non of expertise. *Journal of Applied Research in Memory and Cognition*, **7**(1), 35–50; and finally, see Wickens, C.D. and Dehais, F. (2019). Expertise in Aviation. In *The Oxford Handbook of Expertise* (Oxford, UK: Oxford University Press) in Ward, P, Schraagen, J.M., Gore, J. and Roth, E.M. (Eds), pp. 662–689.

[53] See both Cooren, F. (2004). The communicative achievement of collective minding analysis of board meeting excerpts. *Management Communication Quarterly*, **17**(4), 517–551; as well as Weick, K.E. and Sutcliffe, K.M. (2007). *Managing the Unexpected: Resilient Performance in an Age of Uncertainty*, Second Edition (San Francisco, CA: Jossey-Bass).

⁵⁴ See both Weick, K.E. and Sutcliffe, K.M. (2006). Mindfulness and the quality of organizational attention. *Organization Science*, **16**(4), 409–421; as well as Weick, K.E. (2011). Organizing for transient reliability: The production of dynamic non-events. *Journal of Contingencies and Crisis Management*, **19**(1), 21–27.

⁵⁵ See both Weick and Sutcliffe (2007) (note 53) as well as Weick, K.E., Sutcliffe, K.M. and Obstfeld, D. (1999). Organizing for high reliability: Processes of collective mindfulness. In *Research in Organizational Behavior*, Volume 21, B.M. Staw and L.L. Cummings (eds.) (Greenwich, CT: JAI Press, Inc), pp. 81–123.

⁵⁶ See Holford (2020, pp. 133–144) (note 15).

⁵⁷ See both Weick *et al.* (1999) (note 56) as well as Schulman, P.R. (1993). The negotiated order of organizational reliability. *Administration & Society*, **25**, 353–372.

⁵⁸ See both Barad (2007) (note 13) as well as Weick and Sutcliffe (2007) (note 53).

⁵⁹ See Feenberg (1999) (note 6).

⁶⁰ See Cooren (2004) (note 53).

⁶¹ See Hargadon, A.B. and Bechky, B.A. (2006). When collections of creatives become creative collectives: A field study of problem solving at work. *Organization Science*, **17**, 484–500.

⁶² See Madsen, P.M., Desai, V.M., Roberts, K.H. and Wong, D. (2006). Mitigating hazards through continuing design: The birth and evolution of a pediatric intensive care unit. *Organization Science*, **17**, 239–248.

⁶³ See Scott, C.W. and Trethewey, A. (2008). Organizational discourse and the appraisal of occupational hazards: Interpretive repertoires, heedful interrelating, and identity at work. *Journal of Applied Communication Research*, **36**(3), 298–317.

⁶⁴ See both Prince-Paul, M. and Kelley, C. (2017). Mindful communication: Being present. *Seminars in Oncology Nursing*, **33**(5), 475–482. doi: 10.1016/j.soncn.2017.09.004; as well as Burgoon, J.K., Berger, C.R. and Waldron, V.R. (2000). Mindfulness and interpersonal communication. *Journal of Social Issues*, **56**(1), 105–127.

⁶⁵ See Prince-Paul and Kelley (2017) (note 64).

⁶⁶ See Weick *et al.* (1999) (note 56).

⁶⁷ See Levinthal, D.A. and Rerup, C. (2006). Crossing an apparent chasm: Bridging mindful and less mindful perspectives on organizational learning. *Organizational Science*, **17**, 502–513.

⁶⁸ See Enriquez, E. (1992). *L'Organisation en analyse* (Paris: Presses Universitaires de France).

⁶⁹ *Ibid.*; also see both Weick and Sutcliffe (2007) (note 53) as well as Weick, K.E., Sutcliffe, K.M. and Obstfeld, D. (2008). Organizing for High Reliability: Processes of Collective Mindfulness. In *Crisis Management*, Volume III, Boin, A. (ed.) (Los Angeles: Sage), pp. 31–66.

[70] See both Weick and Sutcliffe (2007) (note 53) as well as Klein, J.K., Ziegert, J.C., Knight, A.P. and Xiao, Y. (2006). Dynamic delegation: Shared, hierarchical and deindividualized leadership in extreme action teams. *Administrative Science Quarterly*, **51**, 590–621.

[71] See Weick *et al.* (2008) (note 69).

[72] Citing Lakoff, G. and Johnson, M. (1980). *Metaphors We Live By* (Chicago, IL: University of Chicago Press), p. 3.

[73] See Ortony, A. (1979). *Metaphor and Thought* (Cambridge, UK: Cambridge University Press).

[74] Citing Krasovec, J. (2016). Metaphor, symbol and personification in presentations of life and values. *Bogoslovni vestnik*, **76**(3/4), 571–584.

[75] See Womack, M. (2005). *Symbols and Meaning* (New York: Altamira Press).

[76] See Langer (1989) (note 2).

[77] See Puschmann, C. and Burgess, J. (2014). Metaphors of big data. *International Journal of Communication*, **8**, 1690–1709)

[78] See Weick (1995) (note 23); as well as Chesley, J. and Wylson, A. (2016). Ambiguity: The emerging impact of mindfulness for change leaders. *Journal of Change Management*, **16**, 317–336. doi:10.1080/14697017.2016.1230334; and finally, see Carleton, R.N. (2016). Fear of the unknown: One fear to rule them all? *Journal of Anxiety Disorders*, **41**, 5–21. doi:10.1016/j.janxdis.2016.03.011.

[79] Citing Lyddy, C.J. and Good, J.G. (2017). Being while doing: An inductive model of mindfulness at work. *Frontiers in Psychology*, 1–18, doi: 10.3389/fpsyg.2016.02060; as well as see Walsh, J.P. (1995). Managerial and organizational cognition: Notes from a trip down memory lane. *Organizational Science*, **6**, 280–321; and finally, see Ashforth, B.E., Harrison, S.H. and Corley, K.G. (2008). Identification in organizations: An examination of four fundamental questions. *Journal of Management*, **34**, 325–374. doi: 10.1177/0149206308316059.

[80] Citing Needleman, J. and Baker, G. (2004). *Gurdjieff: Essays and Reflections on the Man and His Teachings* (New York: Continuum), p. 55.

[81] See Küpers, W. (2013). Embodied transformative metaphors and narratives in organizational life-worlds of change. *Journal of Organizational Change Management*, **26**(3), 494–528.

[82] Citing Barner, R. (2008). The dark tower: Using visual metaphors to facilitate emotional expression during organizational change. *Journal of Organizational Change Management*, **21**(1), 120–137.

[83] Citing Küpers (2013, p. 501) (note 81).

[84] See Ricoeur, P. (1978). *The Rule of Metaphor* (London, UK: Kegan Paul).

[85] Citing Küpers (2013, p. 500) (note 81).

[86] Citing Weber, K. and Glynn, M.A. (2006). Making sense with institutions: Context, thought and action in Karl Weick's theory. *Organization Studies*, **27**(11), 1639–1660.

[87] See Krasovec (2016) (note 74).

88 Citing Needleman and Baker (2004, p. 55) (note 80).

89 Citing Krasovec (2016, p. 577) (note 74).

90 Citing Küpers (2013, p. 501) (note 81), who in turn cites Ricoeur (1973). Creativity in language: Word, polysemy, metaphor. *Philosophy Today*, 17(Summer), 97–111.

91 Citing Küpers (2013, p. 501) (note 81); also see Cleary, C. and Packard, T. (1992). The use of metaphors in organizational assessment and change. *Group and Organization Management*, 17(3), 229–241.

92 See Küpers (2013) (note 81); as well as Zlatev, J. (2009). Phenomenology and cognitive linguistics. In *Handbook on Phenomenology and Cognitive Sciences*, Gallagher, S. and Schmicking, D. (eds.) (Oxford: Oxford University Press), pp. 415–444; and finally, see Depraz, N., Varela, F. and Vermersch, P. (2003). *On Becoming Aware. A Pragmatics of Experiencing* (Amsterdam: Benjamins Press) (French translation Depraz, N.,Varela, F. and Vermersch, P. (2010). *A l'épreuve de l'expérience. Pour une pratique phénoménologique* (Bucharest: Zeta Books).

93 Citing Searle, J.R. (1983). *Intentionality: An Essay in the Philosophy of Mind* (Cambridge, UK: Cambridge University Press), p. 149.

94 See both Langer (2000) (note 34) as well as Langer, E.J. (2006). *On Becoming an Artist: Reinventing Yourself Through Mindful Creativity* (New York, NY: Ballantine Books).

95 Citing Horan, R. (2009). The neuropsychological connection between creativity and meditation. *Creativity Research Journal*, 21(2–3), 199–222. doi: 10.1080/10400410902858691.

96 Citing Giorgi, A. (2009). *The Descriptive Phenomenological Method in Psychology: A Modified Husserlian Approach* (Pittsburgh, PA: Duquesne University Press); also see Morrissey, S.C. (2019). A Phenomenological Exploration of Mindfulness Meditation and the Creative Experience, Walden University, Ph.D. Dissertation.

97 See Jung, C.G. (1971). *Psychological Types (1921)* (Princeton: Princeton University Press).

98 *Ibid.*

99 Citing von Franz, M.-L. (1980). *Projection and Re-collection in Jungian Psychology: Reflections of the Soul* (Peru, IL.: Open Court), p. 83.

100 See Wagoner, B. (2015). Creativity as Symbolic Transformation. In *Rethinking Creativity: Contributions from Social and Cultural Psychology*, First Edition. V. Petre Glăveanu, A. Gillespie and J. Valsiner (eds.) (London: Routledge) pp. 16–30.

101 Citing Wagoner (2015, p. 22) (note 100), who in turn makes reference to Ricoeur (1978) (note 64).

102 See Wagoner (2015) (note 100).

103 As per Merleau-Ponty, M. (1962). *The Phenomenology of Perception*, C. Smith (trans.) (New York, NY: Routledge).

104 See Kuhn, T.S. (1993). Metaphor in Science. In *Metaphor and Thought* (Cambridge, MA: Cambridge University Press), pp. 409–419.
105 See Svanaes, D. (2013). Interaction design for and with the lived body: Some implications of Merleau-Ponty's phenomenology. *ACM Transactions in Computer-Human Interactions*, **20**(1), Article 8, 30 pp. doi: http://dx.doi.org/ 10.1145/2442106.2442114.
106 *Ibid.*
107 Citing Bannon, L.J. and Schmidt, K. (1992). Taking CSCW seriously. *Computer Supported Cooperative Work*, **1**(1–2), 7–40.
108 See Ackerman, M.S. (2000). The intellectual challenge of CSCW: The gap between social requirements and technical feasibility. *Human-Computer Interaction*, **15**(2), 179–203.
109 Citing Ackerman (2000, p. 199) (note 108).
110 See Schmidt, K. (2011). The concept of work in CSCW. *Computer Supported Cooperative Work*, **20**(4–5), 341–401.
111 See Winograd, T. and Flores, F. (1986). *Understanding Computers and Cognition: A New Foundation for Design* (Norwood, NJ: Ablex Publishing Corporation).
112 See Svanaes (2013) (note 105).
113 Citing Dreyfus, H.L. (1991). *Being-in-the-World: A Commentary on Heidegger's Being and Time* (Cambridge, MA: MIT Press), p. 137.
114 Citing Chanter, T. (2001). The Problematic Normative Assumptions of Heidegger's Ontology. In *Feminist Interpretations of Martin Heidegger*, N. Holland and P. Huntington (eds.) (New York: Routledge), p. 80.
115 Dreyfus conversation with Kreisler, H. (2005). Meaning, Relevance and the Limits of Technology — Conversation with H.L. Dreyfus. Conversations with History, Institute of International Studies, UC Berkeley; also see Dreyfus, H.L. (2014). *Skillful Coping: Essays on the Phenomenology of Everyday Perception and Action* (Oxford, UK: Oxford University Press).
116 Citing Merleau-Ponty, M. (1962). *The Phenomenology of Perception*, C. Smith (trans.) (New York, NY: Routledge), p. 143.
117 See Svanaes (2013) (note 15).
118 *Ibid.*
119 See Santonio de Sio, F. and van den Hoven, J. (2018). Meaningful human control over autonomous systems: A philosophical account. *Frontiers in Robotics and AI*, **5**(15), 1–14.
120 See both Horowitz, M.C. and Scharre, P. (2015). Meaningful human control in weapon systems: A primer. Available at: https://www.cnas.org/publications/ reports/meaningful-human-control-in-weapon-systems-a-primer; as well as Schultz, T.P. (2018). *The Problem with Pilots: How Physicians, Engineers and Airpower Enthusiasts Redefined Flight* (Baltimore, MA: John Hopkins University Press).

[121] See Santonio de Sio and van den Hoven (2018) (note 119).

[122] See both Dreyfus, H.L. (2007). Why Heideggerian AI failed and how fixing it would require making it more Heidegerrian. *Artificial Intelligence*, **171**(18), 1137–1160; as well as Flyvbjerg, B. (2001). *Making Social Science Matter: Why Social Enquiry Fails and How It Can Succeed Again* (Cambridge, UK: Cambridge University Press).

[123] See Dreyfus (2007) (note 122).

[124] See both Gaffary, Y. and Lécuyer, A. (2018). the use of haptic and tactile information in the car to improve driving safety: A review of current technologies. *Frontiers in ICT*, **5**(5), 1–11; as well as Abbink, D.A. and Mulder, M. (2009). Exploring the dimensions of haptic feedback support in manual control. *Journal of Computing and Information Science in Engineering*, **9**(1), 011006-1–011006-9.

[125] Citing Kallinikos, J., Leonardi, P.M. and Nardi, B.A. (2012). The Challenge of Materiality: Origins, Scope, and Prospects. In *Materiality and Organizing: Social Interaction in a Technological World*, P. Leonardi, B. Nardi and J. Kallinikos (eds.) (Oxford: Oxford University Press), pp. 1–22, p. 35; as well as Boudreau, M.-C. and Robey, D. (2005). Enacting integrated information technology: A human agency perspective. *Organization Science*, **16**(1), 3–18. doi:10.1287/orsc.1040.0103.

[126] Citing Svanaes (2013, p. 14) (note 105).

[127] See Gaffary and Lécuyer (2018) (note 123); also see Abbink, D.A., Mulder, M. and Boer, E.R. (2012). Haptic shared control: Smoothly shifting control authority? *Cognition Technology and Work*, **14**, 19–28; as well as Oguz, S.O., Kucukyilmaz, A., Sezgin, T.M. and Basdogan, C. (2010). Haptic negotiation and role exchange for collaboration in virtual environments. In *IEEE Haptics Symposium*, pp. 371–378. doi:10.1109/HAPTIC.2010.5444628; and finally, see Doherty, G. and Massink, M. (1999). Continuous interaction and human control. In *Proceedings of the XVIII European Annual Conference on Human Decision Making and Manual Control*, Alty, J. (ed.), pp. 80–96.

[128] See both Gaffary and Lécuyer (2018) (note 123) as well as Abbink and Mulder (2009) (note 124).

[129] Citing Van Baelen, D., Ellerbroek, J., van Paassen, M.M., Abbink, D. and Mulder, M. (2020). Using asymmetric vibrations for feedback on flight envelope protection. *AIAA Scitech 2020 Forum*, Orlando, FL, January 6–10, pp. 1–27. doi.org/10.2514/6.2020-0409.

[130] Citing Carsten, O. and Martens, M.H. (2019). How can humans understand their automated cars? HMI principles, problems and solutions. *Cognition, Technology & Work*, **21**, 3–20. https://doi.org/10.1007/s10111-018-0484-0.

[131] Citing Carsten and Martens (2019, p. 4) (note 130).

[132] *Ibid.*

[133] See Carsten and Martens (2019) (note 130).

[134] See Nostadt, N., Abbink, D.A., Christ, O. and Beckerle, P. (2020). Embodiment, presence, and their intersections: teleoperation and beyond. *Transactions on Human-Robot Interactions*, 9(4), Article 28, 19 pp. doi.org/10.1145/3389210.

[135] *Ibid.*

[136] Citing Nostadt *et al.* (2020, p. 2) (note 134), who in turn make reference to Hendrix, C. and Barfield, W. (1996). Presence within virtual environments as a function of visual display parameters. *Presence: Teleoperators and Virtual Environments*, 5(3), 274–289. doi.org/10.1162/pres.1996.5.3.274.

[137] See Longo, M.R., Schuur, F., Kammers, M.P.M., Tsakiris, M. and Haggard, P. (2008). What is embodiment? A psychometric approach. *Cognition*, 107(3) (2008), 978–998. doi: https://doi.org/10.1016/j.cognition.2007.12.004.

[138] See Nostadt *et al.* (2020) (note 84).

[139] See both Haans, A. and Ijsselsteijn, W.A. (2012). Embodiment and telepresence: Toward a comprehensive theoretical framework. *Interacting with Computers*, 24(4), 211–218. doi.org/10.1016/j.intcom.2012.04.010; as well as Kilteni, K., Groten, R. and Slater, M. (2012). The sense of embodiment in virtual reality. *Presence: Teleoperations and Virtual Environment*, 21, 4(2012), 373–387. doi: https://doi.org/10.1162/PRES.a.00124.

[140] Citing Nostadt *et al.* (2020, p. 13) (note 84).

[141] See Kilteni *et al.* (2012) (note 89).

[142] *Ibid.*; also see Haans and Ijsselsteijn (2012) (note 89).

[143] See both Nostadt *et al.* (2020) (note 84) as well as Holford, W.D. (2020). An ethical inquiry of the effect of cockpit automation on the responsibilities of airline pilots: Dissonance or meaningful control? *Journal of Business Ethics* [online] https://doi.org/10.1007/s10551-020-04640-z.

Chapter 9

Relevant Conversational Processes to Avoid "Success as the Seed of Future Mindlessness"

9.1. Introduction

Conversations are a natural part of organizational realities, and more specifically socio-technical systems.[1] When things go wrong, a first diagnostic involves examining the nature (or "health") of the conversations occurring within the systems' networks.[2] As such, this chapter examines the importance of attaining meaningful/relevant conversations both as a method of inquiry and as a key characteristic of socio-technical systems that allow meaningful human control to be both attained and maintained. Meaningful/relevant conversational processes provide mindful and democratic spaces for phenomenological, i.e. full-bodied human senses to be mobilized and expressed. Contrasting examples are presented in which meaningful conversations are either present or relatively absent, with the associated impacts and consequences which materialize. We then specifically examine how information systems (IS), as part of ongoing socio-technical systems, can better recognize and channel organizational knowledge as material-discursive practice. Finally, we remind readers and practitioners that such relevant conversations are enabled across specific conditions which management need to consider — especially within contexts in which organizational successes can easily transform themselves into organizational self-complacency.

9.2. Seeking Meaningful/Relevant Conversations as Both Inquiry and a Characteristic of Socio-Technical Systems

Conversations are a key part of individual and organizational sense-making,[3] in which sensemaking is "the process through which individuals work to understand novel, unexpected, or confusing events."[4] Sensemaking involves "conversational and social practices."[5] It occurs through both verbal and non-verbal means.[6] Individuals engage in gossip and negotiations; exchange stories, rumors, and past experiences; seek information; and take note of physical cues or non-verbal signs and signals, such as behaviors and actions, to infer and give meaning.[7] In a more general manner, material-discursive acts can both constrain and enable what is said, creating bodies of "knowledge claims" as meanings, speech, and acts.[8]

Conversation can enable creativity and knowledge sharing as well as enact new practices.[9] Conversation is an action whose negotiated utterances lead to the materialization of new or existing practices.[10] Conversations are more than just stating "facts" — its about interpretation and bringing these to life through utterances, thus creating new objects of debate and possible consensus for taking action toward existing or new practices.[11] Individuals in organizations often spend well over 50% of their time at work in various conversations.[12] The practice of managing centers on conversations — which managers engage in to create, take care of, and initiate commitments within an organization.[13] Organizational members participate in networks of conversations involving numerous topics, including but not limited to: requesting, determining, and committing toward actions to be carried out; examining policies to be explored, established, or navigated; keeping each other informed of activities, etc.[14] Hence, when there is a process breakdown, it most often means looking at the process of discursive practices within these networks.[15] Organizational socio-technical configurations involve integrated processes of practices-as-conversation. In this manner, conversations are key characteristics of socio-technical systems. Hence, such system configurations must be designed and implemented to enhance effective dialogue.[16]

We saw in Chapter 3 that being able to successfully address novel, unexpected, or confusing events and situations requires a proficient level of skill and expertise which Baumard referred to as *mètis*.[17]

Mètis is the adaptive expertise one acquires (Chapters 3 and 6) to be able to "creatively respond to novel situations" through *relevant* responses.[18] Determining relevant responses is also a mindful and creative enactment.[19] In Chapter 8, we further explained how mindfulness is both individual and social (collective) in nature, involving meaningful and open-minded conversations between individuals as well as with oneself consisting of narratives and reconstructed accounts.[20] Such mindful conversations merge individual mindfulness with reflective, genuine, and adaptive exchanges[21] to determine what is relevant to new and unexpected situations. This, as we discussed in Chapter 2, machines or AI cannot do. Such conversations are not just meaningful between participants but also seek relevancy and hence become *relevant* conversations. Such conversations allow tacit knowledge to be "shared" (or reconstructed), leading to specific and preferred material outcomes.[22] As previously argued in Chapter 6, conversation always carries a direct phenomenological dimension, whereby intersubjective communication is experiential in which "embodied communicating is intimately linked with implicit and tacit knowing and inter-knowing, and processes of organisational learning, respectively inter-learning."[23] Hence, in this sense, relevant conversations rejoin Dreyfus'[24] argument of achieving relevancy (Chapter 2) through irreducible phenomenological means as opposed to purely explicit representational means. Finally, we reiterate its democratic dimension, encouraging the open expression of opinions as well as the shifting of conversations to where knowledge and expertise resides.[25]

9.3. A Few Examples Showing the Importance of Meaningful/Relevant Conversations

In returning to a previous example presented in Chapter 7, management at the British Columbia (Canada) Children's Hospital had decided to implement the ETRIAGE digitized system at the emergency department (ED) without first sufficiently understanding the fundamental nature of the nurses' work regarding the actual triaging of patients.[26] Such work requires deep knowledge and expertise, as manifested across various workflows.[27] In turn, these workflows involve key conversational flows between colleagues as well as with the patients themselves.[28] The initial implementation strategy adopted was essentially top-down, whereby emphasis had been placed on enforcing general medical guidelines without taking into account local micro material-discursive practices at hand within the ED. Here, the ETRIAGE system's format of non-contextual categorizations of information prompts that had been imposed on nurses led to new interruptions in the multi-conversational flows normally occurring between nurses and patients in the typically hectic and chaotic environment.[29] Such workflow interruptions also cut or repressed self- (and partially tacit) narratives the nurses normally maintained during the handling and adjusting of their work within the emergent situations at hand.[30] Prior to ETRIAGE, triage nurses enacted what was known as "triage drift." In dealing with normal interruptions during periods of high volume, experienced nurses crafted mechanisms for stalling some of the patients while triaging new patients. However, with ETRIAGE, nurses were now required to justify (explicitize) such workarounds. Such time-consuming (and sometimes intimidating) information system prompts discouraged nurses from undertaking workarounds for non-medical reasons such as for smoothing workflow. Yet, as Dreyfus and Dreyfus argue, professional intuition is an aspect of work that is often intangible, making it very hard to apply rules and protocols against; and often impossible to rationally justify in its exercise.[31] The repression of tacit and embodied knowledge and skills across such technology-centric management controls led to the resulting interconnected consequences of mis-triage, increased patient line-ups, and dissatisfied nurses, whereby management eventually had to remove the poorly functioning system.[32] The cutting off of critical conversations led to the repression of embodied skills and knowledge on the part of the nurses, which in turn, resulted in material risks and consequences.

One lesson management learned from this exercise was to ensure that meaningful conversations be re-established between the designers of ETRIAGE and the end-users, i.e. between experienced nurses and management. This was to both better take into account the local practices carried out within the ED as well as to show an adequate level of human recognition toward the nurses themselves, the latter being a critical element in employee motivation and engagement.[33] In a subsequent system redesign, nurses and system designers collaborated together by conversing through multiple formal and informal meetings to identify aspects which could be "standardized without constraining important local flexibility and which aspects require[d] local reconfiguration to function in a particular work context."[34] From a power and knowledge perspective, the arrangement involved a more horizontal redistribution of decision-making with the nurses while also allowing the reconstruction (or "sharing") of issues with the designers, allowing them to better appreciate the more tacit work practices the nurses embodied. Interestingly, conversations were also used as a method of inquiry whereby existing processes (involving existing conversational flows) were openly discussed and renegotiated toward new proposed work practices.[35] The new work practices themselves required new types of conversational flows, which the nurses were able to reconfigure toward a satisfactory outcome.[36] Finally, through meaningful collaborative conversations, the designers had been able to better appreciate the nurses' *mètis*. As such, experienced nurses and designers were allowed to come out with new socio-material solutions (practices) that were subsequently embraced by the system end-users/ operators (i.e. nurses)[37] — and last but not least, reinstate meaningful control back into the hands of the human operator.

The next example deals with what could be considered more as a group endeavour in professional expertise in which conversational interactions play a vital role — namely, urological surgical interventions involving the introduction of new human-machine interaction (HMIs) within a specific surgical bloc of a regional hospital care unit in France.[38] Here, the introduction of a surgical robotic-assisting technology, as it was originally designed, has negative consequences on the conversational dynamics between members of the surgical team, or more precisely, amplifies communication barriers already in place across the spatial and temporal separation observed both within and outside of the operating theater.[39] The logic of the socio-technical design configuration in itself involves the physical separation of the surgeon with both the patient and the rest of the surgical team — i.e. the surgeon triggers the movement of the robotic instruments located near the patient from a separate IS console situated across the surgical room. Hence, both the anesthetist and nursing assistants who are also near the patient cannot directly see or necessarily clearly hear the surgeon working from a more remote distance.[40] As such, the pragmatic aspects of ongoing conversations (see Chapter 6) involving bodily, tacit, as well as intersubjective dimensions, in combination with key utterances and tonalities, are severely hampered.[41] Remembering that the entanglement of both the semantic and embodied aspects of language is inherent of the "dialogical meaning-making process," which transcends mere representational syntactics,[42] its absence or significant reduction can ultimately handicap the team toward being able to adaptively deal with unexpected occurrences.

Conversely, in previous Chapters 3 and 8, we saw that *mètis'* mindfulness involves a reluctance to simplify interpretations across the consideration of alternative mental frameworks.[43] Such mindfulness generates a variety of interpretations or "conceptual slack" offering divergent perspectives, which provide organizations with a broader set of assumptions to ultimately sensitize it to a greater variety of inputs.[44] As such High-Reliability Organizations (HROs), even within the most hierarchical organization (e.g. naval aircraft carriers, etc.), when facing emergencies, will temporarily move in a manner such that "hierarchical rank is subordinated to expertise and experience" — so as to increase the likelihood of successful outcomes, in which "expertise at the bottom of the pyramid ... rises temporarily to the top.[45] In this manner, HROs tap into a collective or group *mètis*, namely the collective resilience and improvisation, that is the "capacity to cope with unanticipated dangers after they have become manifest."[46] This involves the usage of both collective know-how and collective conceptual knowledge through the use of informal communication.[47] However, such collective know-how and knowledge can never become manifest if critical communication pragmatics are severely cut off or hampered, as is the case in the robot-assisted socio-technical surgical bloc configuration, as observed by Wannenmacher.[48] Furthermore, Wannenmacher pertinently points out that while certain technological design changes regarding the addition of more effective microphones within the robotic system could certainly improve the clarity of communications within the operating bloc, more basic communication barriers at the organizational level remained. Organizational assumptions regarding what the surgical team required as surgical expertise seemed to limit itself to purely technical competencies.[49] Consequently, general conversations and interactions amongst the surgical group's participants were very limited, both prior to and after surgeries, while communications between the surgeon and assistants and/or subordinates during surgeries were primarily directive or "top-down" in tone, thereby minimizing learning.[50] This stands in stark contrast to Weick *et al.*'s[51] mindful and horizontal HROs.

We now move on to an example involving a recent study in the field of computer supported cooperative work (CSCW), which examined the importance of ambiguity within human conversational interactions.[52] While some of the latest and growing organizational trends involves the use of what is known as conversational agents, or "chatbots," very often the very structures of these technologies are based on a techno-centric logic of attempting to completely explicate ("explicitize") the nature and purpose of conversation. Yet, as already shown in Chapter 6, flowing conversations cannot be reduced to such syntactic simplifications.[53] And this is without factoring in the emotional "charges" conversations carry.[54] This, of course, conversational agents are also unable to "master."[55] In this manner, conversational agents have failed to fully deliver.[56] We saw in a previous example how the initial ETRIAGE system attempted to force nurses to explicitize all conversations they had with patients in the emergency department (ED), which in the end, made them stop and stumble.[57] In attempting to transfer an embodied human action toward an external entity (non-human technology), we model and categorize in an attempt to approximate/theorize the embodied phenomenon in question.[58] However, when such attempts become endeavors to reduce approximations as "reality," we try to dissect the undissectible (i.e. the rich and unreducible embodied actions) out of humans to then transfer such dissections-as-impoverished-reductions into non-human agents (i.e. technologies). This critical realist attempt at attaining "Truth-objects," is what Winther,[59] in paraphrasing James[60] and Dewey,[61] refers to as the fallacious overselling of a model's capacity to depict epistemic "Truths." Two things can hypothetically happen along this potentially disastrous road when applied to chatbots: (1) conversational metaphors become literal, and therefore "die," and as such, (2) kill creativity by often driving users toward "forced" and meaningless conversations. Fortunately, another thing first happens — i.e. humans simply get turned off.[62] Dead clichés and slogans have a hard time sticking with people. This, however, still has consequences on organizations. Encouragingly, some have taken a more holistic, and therefore, less representational approach within CSCW — i.e. allowing the opportunity for individuals (or groups) who possess and act out embodied tacit knowledge to continue to do so in the presence of communication and information technology, which in turn, can act as enhancers of tacit knowledge creation and sharing within the groups and individuals in question.[63] Twenty years ago, O'Hara and Brown pertinently suggested that tacit knowledge within CSCW could only be maintained across technologies that could help initiate face-to-face conversations.[64] More recently, researchers such as Kytö and McGookin have continued along this more promising trajectory, in that rather than trying to replace face-to-face conversations with human/non-human conversational interfaces (e.g. chatbots), they investigated ways in which digital technologies can facilitate face-to-face conversations such as across remote distancing.[65] Specifically, rather than focusing on algorithmic matching approaches typically used in various types of representational language processing technologies, emphasis is placed on letting users choose or inventing their own ambiguous symbols and metaphors as a means of depicting themselves. These provided sources of ongoing interpretations, thereby supporting dynamic exchanges of information and "opening up rich topics of interaction that support conversation rather than concrete textual facts about someone. This is in contrast to less successful] algorithmic matching work which presented textual detailed and concrete topics to discuss."[66]

In the next section, we present a material-discursive approach to IS as an alternative to more mainstream critical realist systems.

9.4. Recognizing and Channeling Material-Discursive Practices Within IS

Critical realism is a stream of thinking that is attracting much attention within the study of IS. Within the IS literature, critical realism views materiality as distinct entities (e.g. computer hardware, software, belief systems, social structures) which may interact with one another but "have a separate and individual existence from the moment of their creation … [in which] their forms are elaborated and stabilized."[67] As such, it is argued that analytical procedures of various sorts can then be carried forward in time.[68] Underpinning this approach, is Roy Bhaskar's neo-platonic and essentialist belief that there exists an absolute and immanent reality that is "mind-independent" in nature and provides the fundamental "condition of possibility" for natural science in the form of an ultimate *episteme*.[69] Bhaskar's[70] critical realism is a post-positivist approach, which sees the possibility of attaining such *Truth* through a dialectical reasoning which "like Hegel, Bhaskar believes that the movement of our thoughts should follow the movements of 'reality' itself" to attain an eventual and ultimate 'illumination.'"[71] While we do not provide any opinion for or against Bhaskar's position of a possible accessibility to "ultimate truths," it is the misinterpretations of his approach within certain domains and spheres of IS which we question. Bhaskar's dialectical approach first analyzes the world into discrete structures, such as "human persons" or "social networks" — analogous to Hegel's *thesis*.[72] Here, many IS proponents of critical realism erroneously take this as a signal that once structures have been "identified," they become "more or less" permanently stabilized.[73] Yet, Bhaskar[74] clearly indicates that "we proceed by thinking through how interactions between these structures lead to changes in their properties or relationships or even to the *emergence of new structures*."[75] Hence, categories are subsequently modified or completely restructured into new entities as a result of interactions — hence, analogous to Hegel's *anti-thesis*. At the same time, Bhaskar[76] recognizes science to be "a human activity that is inevitably mediated (if not determined) by human language and social power."[77] In this regard, Bhaskar's[78] approach is not far off from Barad's agential realist approach involving material-discursive enactments into new or ongoing agential cuts as discussed in Chapter 8.

Hence, a major issue in current IS system approaches is that they do not go beyond the first step of Bhaskar's thesis, i.e. they considers all initial or incoming information categories as the first and final way information is categorized throughout any given organizational process.[79] Yet, "information is inward-forming. It is the change in a person from an encounter with data. It is a change in the knowledge, beliefs, values or behavior of the person."[80] In a similar vein, Checkland and Holwell view information as data that is selected and meaningful in a given context.[81] Kettinger and Li provide an additional tweak in that "information is the meaning produced from data based on a knowledge framework that is associated with the selection of the state of conditional readiness for goal-directed activities."[82] Furthermore, as Boel and Cecez-Kecmanovich pertinently point out, knowledge frameworks in themselves are subjective.[83] We also saw this through our examination of language in Chapters 3 and 6, in which "even if a common syntax is present, interpretations are often different."[84] Finally, one cannot forget information's time dependency, i.e. "what is considered information at some point in time may not be considered information at another point in time. Conversely, something that previously was not considered relevant or useful may suddenly become considered information."[85]

These new considerations to information can still be adequately covered under Bhaskar's[86] critical realism, in that like Barad's[87] agential realism, there exists a "reality" to which we are inseparable from. However, one feature which agential realism provides that is absent from Bhaskar's critical realism is the enactive effect, which ensues from interpretations. Bhaskar[88] provides a representative perspective, which, like the Computational Theory of Mind approaches discussed in Chapters 4 and 5, ignore human enactment. Barad's agential realism, on the other hand, views an agential cut as being interpretively acted out in a performative fashion. As such, "information can also bring about things into the world. When uttered or computed information can make the world or bring something into existence."[89] This is how knowledge is material-discursively produced.[90] More importantly, such agential "cuts" in the form of temporary categories can still be analyzed, contrary to arguments made by both Mutch and Leonardi,[91] but in a contingent rather than an absolute and "final" fashion. "Matter and meaning" are "mutually articulated" in an ongoing manner.[92] As such, agential realism allows for the analysis of organizations as a world of practice and actions, whereby long-established categories can be re-questioned and challenged "to recognize the difficulty of justifying any order beyond any given moment."[93] Hence, each category is tentative and temporary, that is to say, open to various interpretations and frameworks for a given occurrence, and temporary in regards to being applicable to the situation in question.[94] When critics point to agential realism's holistic and non-dichotomous approach as a reason for arguing that it (allegedly) lacks an explanatory power on reality,[95] this is to ignore the other half of agential realism's face, i.e. its pragmatic dimension by way of agential "cutting." For, in a manner similar to pragmatism's holistic yet also pragmatic view on reality,[96] i.e. despite our "transactions" or intra-actions with the surrounding environment, categories and abstractions (as models) are meant to be tools (albeit, temporary) that we must drop as the conditions warrant — and take on new tools (or categories) that better fit the reconfigured context in question.[97]

Finally, the discursive side of Barad's material-discursive practice does not preclude Carlile's[98] pragmatic aspect of language and conversation, which brings us back to the phenomenological dimension of direct realism, i.e. action as being both embodied and embedded within a given situation.[99] As such, information is also regarded (or felt) "as relevant and useful for solving problems, enabling taking action or making decisions."[100] Hence, all of these different and changing facets of information need to be taken into account in future IS approaches and socio-technical configurations going forward.[101] This argument is especially pertinent in face of the high failure rates IS development projects experience,[102] often suggested to be 70% or higher.[103]

However, if we were to stop our inquiry here, we would be as guilty as the CTM approaches which have sought to capture everything by way of representation. Information as a storable entity across all of its different facets and transient phases still *does not* cover everything in terms of ongoing phenomena. In fact, IS is part of a larger socio-technical system which needs to recognizes the "uncapturable" phenomenological aspect of tacit embodiment. Along these lines, Duguid describes how Suchman[104] showed that communication between a user and the machine was not, as Xerox "designers assumed, between two comparable intelligences. Ordinary conversation, ethnomethodologists had showed, with its efficient use of linguistic indexicals, its suggestive silences and gestures, its rituals of turn taking, its reliance on contextual resources, and its open-ended trajectory, was extraordinarily complex. In contrast, the idea of 'interaction' and 'intelligence' embedded (but not embodied) in the machines were remarkably impoverished."[105] Suchman drew a distinction between devices built to execute preordained plans with accuracy and efficiency, and humans who use plans in context and improvisation as one among many guides to action. As Duguid argues, "this reconceptualization of the plan presented a profound challenge to the assumptions of AI, Cognitive Science, and Human-Computer Interaction."[106] Of importance, Suchman's work argues that as preordained plans are rigid but context ever changing, intuition, improvisation, and interpretation in work are essential rather than unnecessary for deploying a plan. Also re-echoing Collin's[107] and Tsoukas'[108] incessant warnings on the limits and dangers of trying to completely explicitize and explicate tacit knowledge, Duguid adds, "implicit assumptions cannot all be made explicit ... Practical understanding is more fundamental than detached theoretical understanding ... We do not relate to things through having representations of them ... Meaning is fundamentally social, and cannot be reduced to the meaning-giving activity of individual subjects ... Suchman has provided central tools for the critique of AI and Cognitive Science and the general understanding of human-machine interaction and communication."[109]

In this sense, agential realism also offers the opportunity for individuals (or groups) who possess and act out embodied tacit knowledge to continue to do so in the presence of communication and information technologies. These technologies (as we saw, e.g. in the previous section of this chapter regarding a CSCW technology seeking to enhancing face-to-face conversation across remote distances) act as enhancers of tacit knowledge creation and sharing within the groups or individuals in question. Yet, tacit knowledge remains tacit without attempting to be fully articulated and thus avoids the perilous undertaking of disembodiment and subsequent knowledge impoverishment.[110] This clearly implies that humans must always be engaged with, and therefore not be dissociated (or dissected) from the socio-technical system in question.

9.5. A Few Words On How To Avoid "Success as the Seed of Future Failure"

Christensen's[111] Innovator's Dilemma (and its subsequent editions) highlights examples of historically successful (and initially innovative) corporations having progressively lost their creative edge through the self-imposition of inertia-setting organizational routines.[112] Here, Christensen argues this sort of organizational evolution as understandable, or even justifiable, in that such routines are meant to be fixed or "frozen" in place in order to maximize efficiencies.[113] In this manner, however, the imaginary of efficiency, as discussed in Chapter 7, comes back to haunt us[114] — in which the metaphor of "we must be efficient" becomes an obsessive and literal slogan viewing all creative behavior as deviating from this prime objective.[115] At best, innovation is limited to what Christensen refers to as "sustaining" — i.e. seeks to improve existing processes without "rocking established markets."[116] As such, all mindful behavior is evacuated or implodes in the face of mindless routinizations seeking efficiency in unequivocal, unidimensional manners.[117] Here, however, Christensen proposes a way out — namely that such organizations can reinvigorate creativity by either acquiring or creating a new organizational "arm." In this manner, the new inner organization, whose mandate is to seek new creative breakthroughs (in the form of "disruptive" innovations), is not hampered by the existing/incumbent organizational system. However, as Holford and Ebrahimi argue[118]:

> "What happens when this 'arm' eventually starts to routinize its own initially innovative successes? We are obliged to re-start the whole process of acquiring or creating another new 'creative' arm. Christensen's approach implies that any given locus within the overall organization is either creative or efficient, but not both."

Hence, initially mindful behavior and mindsets through the use of "living metaphors" toward seeking new ways of doing things, providing services or designing products must eventually atrophy toward "dead" or literal metaphors whose repetitive and mindless usage "reinforce the status quo and inhibit active seeking of alternatives."[119] In this manner, "once distinctions are created, they take a life of their own ... and are very hard to overthrow."[120] However, we do not adhere to Christensen's dichotomous view of efficiency vs creativity.[121] Holford and Ebrahimi showed

across the example of the Honda Corporation that creativity and efficiency are in fact complementary to one another, yet to remain conscious
of this requires continued individual and collective mindfulness.[122]

In a similar fashion, socio-technical system design, implementation, and
usage can avoid drifting toward mindlessness across a management which
provides an organizational vision that is sufficiently open to ambiguity such
that it provides conversational arenas open to creative (re-)interpretations —
i.e. through "living" metaphors.[123] In the previous chapter, we argued that
such metaphors must also mobilize ideas that lead toward embodied engagement on the part of human users to ultimately assure human meaningful
control within socio-technical systems at hand.[124] One such metaphor we
discussed is the "lived body" metaphor.[125] Yet, an infinite number of "living"
metaphors exist and can surely be found. But for this to happen, it is important that management maintain psychologically secure environments which
encourage open debate, openness to other's ideas, and last but not least,
mutual respect between all human stakeholders within the socio-technical
systems in question.[126] More specifically, such a psychological "safety net"
provides a shared belief among members that the group "is safe for interpersonal risk-taking,"[127] thereby encouraging relational engagements to occur
between interacting parties.[128] In turn, this leads toward what Tsoukas refers
to as a "productive dialogue," which is mindful in nature — i.e. where participants take a "distance from their customary and unreflective ways of
understanding and acting, and reconceptualize a situation at hand through
conceptual combination, expansion and/or reframing."[129]

In the next chapter...

In the next chapter, contrary to certain popular notions of redistributed
responsibility within "system-centered" perspectives, we examine why
and how socio-technical systems can successfully perform, on condition
that in a responsible fashion, responsibility is clearly attributed on the
human operator's shoulders.

Endnotes

[1] See Winograd, T. and Flores, F. (1986). *Understanding Computers and Cognition: A New Foundation For Design* (Reading, MA: Addison-Wesley); also see Latour, B. (2006). A textbook Case Revisited: Knowledge as Mode

of Existence. In *The Handbook of Science and Technology Studies*, Third Edition, E. Hackett, O. Amsterdamska, M. Lynch and J. Wacjman (eds.) (Cambridge, MA: MIT Press), pp. 83–112; as well as Barad, K. (2007). *Meeting the Universe Halfway: Quantum Physics and the Entanglement of Matter and Meaning* (Durham, NC: Duke University Press); and finally, see Orlikowski, W.J. (2007). Sociomaterial practices: Exploring technology at work. *Organization Studies*, **28**(9), 1435–1448.

2 See Winograd and Flores (1986) (note 1); as well as Brown, J. and Isaacs, D. (1996). Conversation as a core business process. *The Systems Thinker*, **7**(10), 1–6; and finally, see Orlikowski, W.J. and Scott, S. (2015). Exploring material-discursive practices. *Journal of Management Studies*, **52**(5), 696–705.

3 See Sonenshein, S. (2010). We're changing or are we? Untangling the role of progressive, regressive, and stability narratives during strategic change implementation. *Academy of Management Journal*, **53**(3), 477–512; as well as Rouleau, L. and Balogun, J. (2011). Middle managers, strategic sensemaking, and discursive competence. *Journal of Management Studies*, **48**(5), 953–983; and finally, see Cornelissen, J. (2012). Sensemaking under pressure: The influence of professional roles and social accountability on the creation of sense. *Organization Science*, **23**(1), 118–137.

4 Citing Maitlis, S. and Christianson, M. (2014). Sensemaking in organizations: Taking stock and moving forward. *The Academy of Management Annals*, **8**(1): 57–125.

5 Citing Gephart, R.P. (1993). The textual approach: Risk and blame in disaster sensemaking. *Academy of Management Journal*, **36**(6), 1465–1514.

6 See both Gioia, D.A. and Chittipeddi, K. (1991). Sensemaking and sensegiving in strategic change initiation. *Strategic Management Journal*, **12**(6), 433–448; as well as Gioia, D.A., Thomas, J.B., Clark, S.M. and Chittipeddi, K. (1994). Symbolism and strategic change in academia: The dynamics of sensemaking and influence. *Organization Science*, **5**(3), 363–383.

7 See both Gioia and Chittipeddi (1991) (note 6) as well as Gioia *et al.* (1994) (see note 6); also see Gioia, D.A., and Thomas, J.B. (1996). Institutional identity, image, and issue interpretation: Sensemaking during strategic change in academia. *Administrative Science Quarterly*, **41**(3), 370–403; as well as Isabella, L.A. (1990). Evolving interpretations as a change unfolds: How managers construe key organizational events. *Academy of Management Journal*, **33**(1), 7–41; and finally, see Labianca, G., Gray, B. and Brass, D.J. (2000). A grounded model of organizational schema change during empowerment. *Organization Science*, **11**(2), 235–257.

8 See Foucault, M. (1982). *The Archaeology of Knowledge and the Discourse on Language* (New York: Pantheon Books); as well as Barad (2007) (note 2); and finally, see Nayak, A. and Chia, R. (2011). Thinking Becoming and Emergence: Process Philosophy and Organization Studies. In *Philosophy and Organization Theory. Research in the Sociology of Organization*, Tsoukas, H. and Chia. R. (eds.), pp. 281–309.

9 See Latour (2006) (note 1); as well as Barad (2007) (note 1); and finally, see Rhodes, C. (2000). Doing Knowledge At Work: Dialogue, Monologue and Power in Organizational Learning. In *Research and Knowledge at Work: Perspectives, Case-studies and Innovative Strategies*, J. Garrick and C. Rhodes (eds.), pp. 217–231 (New York, NY: Basic Books).

10 See both Barad (2007) (note 1) as well as Maitlis, S. (2005). The social processes of organizational sensemaking. *Academy of Management Journal*, 48(1), 21–49.

11 See Flores, C.F. (1982). Management and Communication in the Office of the Future. Ph.D. Thesis, University of California, Berkeley.

12 See Hollingworth, M. (2007). Re-engineering today's core business process — strong and truthful conversation. Available at: https://iveybusinessjournal.com/ publication/re-engineering-todays-core-business-process-strong-and-truthful-conversation/

13 See Winograd and Flores (1986) (note 1); as well as Barad (2007) (note 1); and finally, see Orlikowski (2007) (note 1).

14 See Choo, C.W. (2002). *Information Management for the Intelligent Organization: The Art of Scanning the Environment* (Medford, NJ: Information Today Inc.).

15 See Winograd and Flores (1986) (note 1); as well as Brown and Isaacs (1996) (note 2); and finally, see Orlikowski and Scott (2015) (note 2).

16 See Brown and Isaacs (1996) (note 2); also see Barad (2007) (note 1); as well as Tsoukas, H. (2009). A dialogical approach to the creation of new knowledge in organizations. *Organization Science*, 20(6), 941–953; and finally, see Suchman, L.A. (2009). *Human-Machine Reconfigurations: Plans and Situated Actions*. Second Edition (Cambridge, UK: Cambridge University Press).

17 See Baumard, P. (1999). *Tacit Knowledge in Organizations* (London: Sage Publications).

18 Citing Adams, R.J. and Ericsson, A.E. (2000). Introduction to cognitive processes of expert pilots. *Journal of Human Performance in Extreme Environments*, 5(1), 44–62. doi: 10.7771/2327-2937.1006; also see Dreyfus, H.L. (2007). Why Heideggerian AI failed and how fixing it would require making it more Heidegerrian. *Artificial Intelligence*, 171(18), 1137–1160.

19 See Langer, E.J. (1989). *Mindfulness* (Cambridge, MA: Perseus Books); also see Boden, M.A. (2010). *Creativity and Art: Three Roads to Surprise* (Oxford, UK: Oxford University Press); as well as Boden, M.A. (2016). *AI: Its Nature and Future* (Oxford, UK: Oxford University Press); and finally, see Guiette, A. and Vandenbempt, K. (2016). Learning in times of dynamic complexity through balancing phenomenal qualities of sensemaking. *Management Learning*, 47(1), 83–99.

20 See both Maitlis (2005) (note 10) as well as Weick, K.E. and Sutcliffe, K.M. (2001). *Managing the Unexpected. Assuring High Performance in an Age of Complexity* (San Franscisco, CA: Jossey-Bass).

[21] See both Prince-Paul, M. and Kelley, C. (2017). Mindful communication: Being present. *Seminars in Oncology Nursing*, **33**(5), 475–482. doi: 10.1016/j. soncn.2017.09.004; as well as Burgoon, J.K., Berger, C.R. and Waldron, V.R. (2000). Mindfulness and interpersonal communication. *Journal of Social Issues*, **56**(1), 105–127.

[22] See Baumard (1999) (note 17); also see Orlikowski, W.J. (2002). Knowing in practice: Enacting a collective capability in distributed organizing. *Organization Science*, **13**(3), 249–273; and finally, see Collins, H. (2010). *Tacit and Explicit Knowledge* (Chicago: University of Chicago Press).

[23] Citing Küpers, W. (2012). "Inter-communicating": Phenomenological perspectives on embodied communication and contextuality. *Journal for Communication and Culture*, **2**(2), 114–138; also see Küpers, W. (2005). Embodied implicit and narrative knowing in organizations. *Journal of Knowledge Management*, **9**(6), 113–133; and finally, see Küpers, W. (2008). Embodied inter-learning' — an integral phenomenology of learning in and by organizations. *The Learning Organisation: An International Journal*, **15**(5), 388–408.

[24] See Dreyfus (2007) (note 18).

[25] See Enriquez, E. (1992). *L'Organisation en analyse* (Paris: Presses Universitaires de France); also see both Weick, K.E. and Sutcliffe, K.M. (2007). *Managing the Unexpected: Resilient Performance in and Age of Uncertainty*, Second edition (San Francisco, CA: Jossey-Bass); as well as Weick, K.E., Sutcliffe, K.M. and Obstfeld, D. (2008). Organizing for high reliability: Processes of collective mindfulness. In *Crisis Management*, Vol. III. A. Boin (ed.) (Los Angeles, CA: Sage), pp. 31–66.

[26] See Bjørn, P. and Balka, E. (2007). Health care categories have politics too: Unpacking the managerial agendas of electronic triage systems, *ECSCW'07: Proceedings of the Tenth European Conference on Computer Supported Cooperative*, pp. 371–390.

[27] See *Ibid.* as well as Dreyfus, H.L. and Dreyfus, S.E. (1986). *Mind Over Machine* (New York, NY: The Free Press).

[28] See Bjørn and Balka (2007) (note 26).

[29] *Ibid.*

[30] See Küpers (2008) (note 23); also see Tsoukas, H. (2003). Do we really understand tacit knowledge. In *The Blackwell Handbook of Organizational Learning and Knowledge Management*, M. Easterby-Smith and M. Lyles (eds.) (New York: Blackwell), pp. 410–427.

[31] See Dreyfus, H.L. and Dreyfus, S.E. (2005). Peripheral vision expertise in real world contexts. *Organization Studies*, **26**(5), 779–792; also see Dreyfus, H.L. (1986). *Mind Over Machine* (New York: The Free Press).

[32] See Bjørn, P. and Østerlund, C. (2014). *Sociomaterial-Design: Bounding Technologies in Practice* (New York, NY: Springer).

[33] See both Bjørn and Østerlund (2014) (note 32) as well as Nonaka, I., Von Krogh, G. and Ichijo, K. (2000). *Enabling Knowledge Creation* (New York: Oxford University Press).

[34] See Bjørn, P., Burgoyne,S., Crompton, V., MacDonald, T. and Pickering, B. (2009). Boundary factors and contextual contingencies: Configuring electronic templates for healthcare professionals. *European Journal of Information Systems*, **18**(5), 428–441.

[35] See Bjørn and Østerlund (2014, note 32).

[36] *Ibid.*

[37] *Ibid.*

[38] See Wannenmacher, D. (2020). Les impacts du robot chirurgical sur l'activité des blocs opératoires, L'Harmattan, *Marché et organisations*, **38**(2), 105–121 (in French).

[39] Citing Wannenmacher (2020, p. 133) (note 38).

[40] See Wannenmacher (2020, p. 133) (note 38).

[41] See Küpers (2005, 2008) (note 23); also see Tsoukas (2009) (note 16); and finally, see Carlile, P.R. (2002) A pragmatic view of knowledge and boundaries: Boundary objects in new product development. *Organization Science*, **13**(4), 442–455.

[42] Citing Lorino P., Tricard B. and Clot Y. (2011). Research methods for non-representational approaches to organizational complexity: The dialogical mediated inquiry. *Organization Studies*, **32**(6), 769–801.

[43] See Guiette and Vandenbempt (2016) (note 19).

[44] See Weick *et al.* (2008) (note 25); as well as Schulman, P.R. (1993). The negotiated order of organizational reliability. *Administration & Society*, **25**, 353–372.

[45] Citing Weick *et al.* (2008, p. 49) (note 25).

[46] Citing Wildavsky, A. (1991). *Searching for Safety* (New Brunswick: Transaction Books), p. 77; also see Baumard (1999) (note 17); and finally, see Weick *et al.* (2008) (note 25).

[47] See Rochlin, G.I. (1989). Informal organizational networking as a crisis — avoidance strategy: Us naval flight operations as a case study. *Industrial Crisis Quarterly*, **3**(2), 159–176.

[48] See Wannenmacher (2020) (note 38).

[49] See Wannenmacher (2020, p. 117) (note 38); also see Yule, S. and Paterson-Brown, S. (2012). Surgeons' non-technical skills. *Surgical Clinics of North America*, **92**, 37–50.

[50] See Wannenmacher (2020) (note 38).

[51] See Weick *et al.* (2008) (note 25).

[52] See Kytö, M. and McGookin, D. (2017). Augmenting multi-party face-to-face interactions amongst strangers with user generated content. *Computer Supported Cooperative Work*, **26**(4–6), 527–562.

[53] See Lorino *et al.* (2011) (note 42).

[54] See Küpers (2005, 2008) (note 23).

[55] See Belainine, B., Fatiha, S. and Lounis, H. (2020). Modelling a conversational agent with complex emotional intelligence. *Proceedings of the AAAI Conference on Artificial Intelligence*, **34**(10), 13710–13711. https://doi.org/10.1609/aaai.v34i10.7127.

[56] See Clark *et al.* (2019). What makes a good conversation? Challenges in designing truly conversational agents, *ACM CHI Conference on Human Factors in Computing Systems CHI 2019*, May 4–9, Glasgow, Scotland, UK.

[57] See Bjørn and Balka (2007) (note 26); also see Tsoukas (2003) (note 30).

[58] See both James, W. (1909). *A Pluralistic Universe: Hibbert Lectures at Manchester College on the Present Situation in Philosophy* (London: University of Nebraska Press) as well as Dewey, J. (1929). *The Quest for Certainty: A Study of the Relation of Knowledge and Action* (New York: Putnam); also see Winther, R.G. (2014). James and Dewey on abstractions. *The Pluralist*, **9**(2), 1–28.

[59] See Winther (2014) (note 58).

[60] See James (1909) (note 58).

[61] See Dewey (1929) (note 58).

[62] See Clark *et al.* (2019) (note 56).

[63] See both Kytö and McGookin (2017) (note 52) as well as O'Hara, K. and Brown, B. (2001). Designing CSCW technologies to support tacit knowledge sharing through conversation initiation. *ECSCW '01, European Conference on Computer Supported Cooperative Work*, Bonn, Germany.

[64] See O'Hara and Brown (2001) (note 62).

[65] See Kytö and McGookin (2017) (note 52).

[66] Citing Kytö and McGookin (2017, p. 540) (note 52), who in turn make reference to Nguyen, T.T., Nguyen, D.T., Iqbal, S.T. and Ofek, E. (2015). The known stranger: Supporting conversations between strangers with personalized topic suggestions. In *CHI '15. Proceedings of the 33rd Annual ACM Conference on Human Factors in Computing Systems*, B. Begole; J. Kim; K. Inkpen; and W. Woo (eds.), Seoul, Republic of Korea, 18–23 April (New York, NY: ACM Press) pp. 555–564.

[67] Citing Cuellar, M.J. (2016). Critical realism as a sociomaterial stream of research. *The DATA BASE for Advances in Information Systems*, **47**(4), 60–66.

[68] See *Ibid.*; as well as Mutch, A. (2013). Sociomateriality — taking the wrong turning? *Information and Organization*, **23**(1), 28–40; and finally, see Archer, M.S. (1995). *Realist Social Theory: The Morphogenetic Approach* (New York: Cambridge University Press).

[69] See both Bhaskar, R. (1994). *Plato, etc.: Problems of Philosophy and their Resolution* (London: Verso) as well as Bhaskar, R. (1997). *A Realist Theory of Science*, Second edition (London: Verso); also see Gorski, P.S. (2013). What is critical realism? And why should you care? *Contemporary Sociology: A Journal of Reviews*, **42**(5), 658–670.

[70] See Bhaskar, R. (1998). Critical realism and dialectic. In *Critical Realism: Essential Readings*, M. Archer, R. Bhaskar, A. Collier, C. Lawon and A. Norrie (eds.) (London: Routledge), pp. 589–640.

[71] Citing Gorski (2013, p. 667) (note 69).

[72] See Gorski (2013) (note 68).

[73] See both Cuellar (2016) (note 67) as well as Mutch (2013) (note 68).

[74] See Bhaskar (1998) (note 70).

[75] Citing Gorski (2013, p. 667) (note 69).

[76] See Bhaskar, R. (1997) (note 69).

[77] Citing Gorski (2013, p. 662) (note 69).

[78] See both Bhaskar (1997) (note 69) as well as Bhaskar (1998) (note 70).

[79] See both Cuellar (2016) (note 67) as well as Boell, S.J. and Cecez-Kecmanovic, D. (2015). What is 'information' beyond a definition? *36th International Conference on Information Systems ICIS 2015*, Association for Information Systems (AIS), Fort Worth, Texas, USA, pp 1–20.

[80] Citing Boland, R. (1987).The in-formation of information systems. In *Critical Issues in Information Systems Research*, R.J. Boland and R.A. Hirschheim (eds.) (New York, NY, USA: Wiley), pp. 363–379.

[81] See Checkland, P. and Holwell, S. (1998). *Information, Systems and Information Systems: Making Sense of the Field* (Chichester: Wiley).

[82] Citing Kettinger, W.J. and Li, Y. (2010). The infological equation extended: Towards conceptual clarity in the relationship between data, information and knowledge. *European Journal of Information Systems*, **19**(4), 409–421.

[83] See Boell and Cecez-Kecmanovic (2015) (note 79).

[84] Citing Carlile (2002, p. 444) (note 41).

[85] Citing Boell and Cecez-Kecmanovic (2015, p. 8) (note 79).

[86] See Bhaskar (1997) (note 69).

[87] See Barad (2007) (note 1).

[88] See both Bhaskar (1997) (note 69) and Bhaskar (1998) (note 70).

[89] Citing Boell and Cecez-Kecmanovic (2015, p. 8) (note 79).

[90] Citing Barad (2007, p. 91) (note 1).

[91] See both Mutch (2013) (note 68) as well as Leonardi, P. (2013). Theoretical foundations for the study of sociomateriality. *Information and Organization*, **23**(1), 59–76.

[92] Citing Barad (2007, p. 152) (note 1).

[93] Citing Nyberg, D. (2009). Computers, Customer service operatives and cyborgs: Intra-actions in call centres. *Organization Studies*, **30**(11), 1181–1199.

[94] See both Latour (2006) (note 1) as well as Weick, K.E. (2015). Ambiguity as grasp: The reworking of sense. *Journal of Contingencies and Crisis Management*, **23**(2), 117–123.

[95] See both Cuellar (2016) (note 67) as well as Mutch (2013) (note 68).

[96] See both Dewey (1929) (note 58) as well as James, W. (1955, orig. pub. 1907). *Pragmatism* (Cleveland, NY: Meridian Book).

[97] See Winther (2014) (note 58) as well as Barad (2007) (note 1); also see both Weick, K.E. (1993). The collapse of sensemaking in organisations: The Mann Gulch disaster. *Administrative Science Quarterly*, **38**(4), 628–652; as well as Weick, K.E. (2009). *Making Sense of the Organization (Volume 2): The Impermanent Organization* (West Sussex, UK: John Wiley and Sons).

[98] See Carlile (2002) (note 42).

[99] See Dreyfus (2007) (note 18).

[100] Citing Boell and Cecez-Kecmanovic (2015, p. 7) (note 79).

[101] See Boell and Cecez-Kecmanovic (2015) (note 78).

[102] See Doherty, N.F. and King, M. (2001). An investigation of the factors affecting the successful treatment of organizational issues in systems development projects. *European Journal of Information Systems*, **10**(3), 147–160); also see Vaidya, R., Myers, M. and Gardner, L. (2013). Major issues in the successful implementation of information systems in developing countries. In *International Working Conference on Transfer and Diffusion of IT (TDIT)*, IFIP Advances in Information and Communication Technology, AICT-402, Grand Successes and Failures in IT Public and Private Sectors, Y.K. Dwivedi, H.Z. Henriksen, D. Wastell *et al.* (eds.). Bangalore, India. Springer, pp. 151–163; and finally, see Lee, J.S., Cuellar, M.J., Keil, M. *et al.* (2014). The role of a bad news reporter in information technology project escalation: A deaf effect perspective. *ACM SIGMIS Database*, **45**(3), 8–29.

[103] See Doherty, N.F., Ashurst, C. and Peppard, J. (2012). Factors affecting the successful realization of benefits from system development projects: Findings from three case studies. *Journal of Information Technology*, **27**(1), 1–16; also see Keil, M. and Mähring, M. (2010). Is your project turning into a black hole? *California Management Review*, **53**(1), 6–31; and finally, see Drummond, H. (2005). What we never have, we never miss? Decision error and the risks of premature termination. *Journal of Information Technology*, **20**(3), 170–176.

[104] See Suchman, L.A. (2009) *Human-Machine Reconfigurations: Plans and Situated Actions*, Second Edition (Cambridge, UK: Cambridge University Press).

[105] Citing Duguid, P. (2012). On rereading. Suchman and situated action, *Le Libellio d' AEGIS*, **8**(2), 3–9.

[106] *Ibid.*

[107] See Collins (2010) (note 22).

[108] See Tsoukas (2003) (note 30).

[109] Citing Duguid, P. (2012, p. 5) (note 105).

[110] See Tsoukas (2003) (note 30).

[111] See Christensen, C.M. (1997). *The Innovator's Dilemma* (Boston: Harvard Business School Press).

[112] See Holford, W.D. and Ebrahimi, M. (2010). Honda's predisposition towards radical and disruptive innovation. In *Creating and Managing a Technology Economy*, Volume 3. F. Betz, T. Khalil, Y. Hosni and H.E. Mostafa (eds.) (New Jersey: World Scientific Publishing Co.), pp. 3–31.

[113] See Christensen (1997, pp. 200–202) (note 111)

[114] See both Alexander, J.K. (2008). *The Mantra of Efficiency: From Waterwheel to Social Control* (Baltimore: John Hopkins University Press); as well as Holford, W.D. (2019). The future of human creative knowledge work within the digital economy. *Futures*, **105**, 143–154.

[115] See Holford and Ebrahimi (2010) (note 112).

[116] See Christensen (1997) (note 111).

[117] See Holford and Ebrahimi (2010) (note 112).

[118] Citing Holford and Ebrahimi (2010, pp. 18–19) (note 112).

[119] Citing Küpers, W. (2013). Embodied transformative metaphors and narratives in organizational life-worlds of change. *Journal of Organizational Change Management*, **26**(3), 494–528.

[120] Citing Langer (1989, p. 11) (note 19).

[121] See Christensen (1997) (note 111).

[122] See Holford and Ebrahimi (2010) (note 112).

[123] See both Holford and Ebrahimi (2010) (note 112) as well as Nonaka, I. and Toyama, R. (2002). A firm as a dialectical being: Towards a dynamic theory of the firm. *Industrial and Corporate Change*, **11**(5), 995–1009.

[124] See both Nostadt, N., Abbink, D.A., Christ, O. and Beckerle, P. (2020). Embodiment, presence, and their intersections: Teleoperation and beyond. *Transactions on Human-Robot Interactions*, **9**(4), Article 28, 19 pp. doi. org/10.1145/3389210; as well as Holford, W.D. (2020). An ethical inquiry of the effect of cockpit automation on the responsibilities of airline pilots: Dissonance or meaningful control? *Journal of Business Ethics*, https://doi.org/10.1007/s10551-020-04640-z.

[125] See Svaneas, D. (2013). Interaction design for and with the lived body: Some implications of Merleau-Ponty's phenomenology. *ACM Transactions on Computer-Human Interaction*, **20**(1), Article 8, pp. 1–30. doi: http://dx.doi.org/10.1145/2442106.2442114.

[126] See both Holford, W.D. (2016). Boundary constructions as knowledge flows within and between work groups. *Knowledge Management Research and Practice*, **14**(1), 4–14; as well as Holford and Ebrahimi (2010) (note 112).

[127] Citing Edmonson, A. (1999). Psychological safety and learning behavior in work teams. *Administrative Quarterly*, **44**(2), 350–383.

[128] See Tsoukas (2009) (note 16).

[129] Citing Tsoukas (2009, p. 13) (note 16).

Chapter 10

Meaningful Human Control to Ensure Responsible Socio-Technical Systems

10.1. Introduction

In previous chapters, we introduced the concept of meaningful control.[1] It is both the capacity and the power to act in an adequate and successful fashion in the face of new or unexpected situations. Machines do not have this ability.[2] As such, socio-technical systems must be adequately designed to ensure human operators maintain such meaningful control. In this chapter, we revisit the notion of responsibility. We explain why and how socio-technical systems can only successfully act in a responsible fashion when responsibility is attributed clearly on the human operator's shoulders. Finally, for this to be ethically and morally acceptable, we reiterate our previous argument of socio-technical systems needing to be designed toward ensuring human operators both attain and maintain meaningful control over their systems. As such, we also critically examine certain popular notions of redistributed responsibility within "system-centered" perspectives.

10.2. A Short Recapitulation of Meaningful Human Control Through Mindful Organizational Enactments

As first discussed in Chapters 6 and 8, meaningful control involves the authority or power to take actions and/or make decisions *coupled* with the

175

ability to detect relevant cues and take relevant actions.[3] However, as also argued in Chapters 2 and 5, machines and Artificial Intelligence (AI) are unable to determine relevancy in new or unexpected situations due to the "frame regress" limitations inherent within the sole usage and processing of representational frames.[4] Conversely, as presented in Chapters 3, 5 and 6, humans have the potential capability of determining relevancy by way of the polymorphous adaptive expertise of *mètis*.[5] One of the principle reasons is that detecting relevant cues and taking relevant actions, especially within new or unexpected situations, is not just a matter of sifting through pre-existing options.[6] It is also a matter of creatively *enacting* relevant cues and relevant actions.[7] This, as presented in Chapters 8 and 9, requires the ambivalent nature of mindfulness involving both attentive non-judgmental presence[8] as well as creative actions/enactments.[9] Learning first occurs through detached alternative interpretation of one's experience.[10] As one's experience grows however, "parsimonious" and creative "interventions" regarding the situation-at-hand occur.[11] As such, both relevant cues and relevant actions are enacted across the generating of meaningful connections as well as the materializing or "doing" of novel actions or behaviors based on the meaningful connections that have been made.[12] Hence, when going from meaningful control to meaningful human control, the key process of *enactment* once again emerges to the forefront. As such, meaningful human control involves the authority or power to take actions and/or make decisions coupled with the ability to detect/*enact* relevant cues and take/*enact* relevant actions. Yet, as we discussed in Chapters 8 and 9, achieving such meaningful human control is not just a matter of a human operator becoming mindful within an existing socio-technical system. It involves the mindful participation of all stakeholders related to the socio-material system in question.[13] On the one hand, as we presented in Chapter 8, system designers must actively take into consideration the phenomenological or embodied aspects of the human operator.[14] However, this also requires management's mindful input as well as management's engagement toward avoiding or reducing top-heavy protocols, which may hinder both the designer's objectives as well as the human operator's needs.[15] Toward this end, a collective mindfulness as a social process is required, involving a democratic discursive practice that continuously reconstitutes and reinforces itself through conversations.[16] Such mindful conversations involve interactional processes, which merge individual mindfulness with reflective, genuine, and adaptive exchanges.[17] More specifically, new and emerging interpretations are enacted through the use of "living" metaphors, such as the "living body" metaphor, to ensure that the embodied phenomenological nature of the human operator is indeed fully considered (Chapter 8) — all this toward achieving and maintaining human meaningful control.[18]

In the next two sections, we look at how the ethical aspects of decision-making and actions within socio-technical systems must be actively taken into consideration, in that these are also entangled to (or constitutively part of) the pragmatic material functioning and consequences of the socio-technical system in question.[19]

10.3. Responsibility vs. Control

The term responsibility connotes numerous dimensions, including (but not limited to) a moral/deontological aspect, a legal aspect, as well as a causal dimension in relation to bringing about appropriate acts.[20] Flemisch *et al.* define it as "a moral obligation to behave correctly," "the state or fact of having a duty to deal with something," or "the state or fact of being accountable or to blame for something."[21] Dalcher examined the wide-ranging notions of responsibility in regards to airline pilots and proposed to include[22]:

- **Causal responsibility:** Associated with bringing something about either directly or indirectly (e.g. by ordering someone else).
- **Legal responsibility:** Associated with fulfilling the requirements for accountability under the law.
- **Moral responsibility:** Associated with having a moral obligation or with the fulfillment of the criteria for deserving blame or praise for a morally significant act, or omission, and the resulting consequences.
- **Role responsibility:** Associated with duties that are attached to particular professional, or societal, (or even biological) roles — failure to fulfil such duties can expose the role-holder to censure, which can be moral, legal, or constitutional.

These four dimensions of responsibility are, to various degrees, inter-related. For example, Dalcher argues that "moral responsibility normally assumes some degree of causal responsibility. Therefore a professional can be held morally responsible for failing to act."[23] Furthermore, as the above definition explicates, there is a moral aspect of responsibility to be found within role responsibility. As for legal responsibility, while the law is considered distinct from moral obligations, it integrates certain codified aspects of moral and ethical values meant to help regulate society.[24] Causal responsibility in itself is closely associated to authority, i.e. the "the power or right to give orders, make decisions, and enforce obedience."[25] All this is to say that, when responsibility is attributed, these four dimensions should be taken into consideration. This, for example, is the case for airline pilots across the International Civil Aviation Organization (ICAO), the International Air Transport Association (IATA), and US Federal Aviation Agency (FAA) rules and regulations.[26] For example the IATA in their first edition of the *Guidance Material and Best Practices for Command Training*[27] states the "Commander is the final authority as to the operation of the aeroplane. He is responsible for the safety of the aeroplane, its load and the persons on board from the moment he takes control of the aeroplane until the entire crew leaves the aeroplane," and "may delegate duties to qualified personnel but remains always responsible." In a similar and succinct fashion, the FAA stipulates that the PIC is "directly responsible for, and is the final authority as to, the operation of that aircraft."[28] Finally, the ICAO[29] states that "the pilot-in-command of an aircraft shall, whether manipulating the controls or not, be responsible for the operation of the aircraft in accordance with the rules of the air." In turn, these rules are based on the Civil Aviation Regulations of 1988[30] under the heading CAR224 Pilot-in-Command (PIC), more specifically, under the second sub-regulation, which states that the PIC is responsible for the start, continuation, diversion, and end of a flight by the aircraft; the operation and safety of the aircraft during flight; the safety of persons and cargo carried on the flight; and the conduct and safety of members of the crew on the aircraft.

Importantly, Matthias, who critically examined the relationship between autonomous systems and human operators in regards to control, reminds us that responsibility, for it to be "rightly" attributed implies that one must also have actual control over the scope of prescribed or attributed responsibility[31]:

Responsibility (Attributed) → Control (actual)

"[T]he agent can be considered responsible only if he knows the particular facts surrounding his action, and if he is able to freely form a decision to act, and to select one of a suitable set of available alternative actions based on these facts."

In turn, the term control in a real or actual sense implies not just the actual authority (or allowance) to act appropriately toward an aim established by the controller (agent) but also the actual ability to do so.[32] Authority allows or permits the agent to control the course of events, while ability enables (through skills and resources) the agent to control the course of events[33]:

$$\text{Control (Actual)} \rightarrow \text{Authority (Actual)} + \text{Ability (Actual)}$$

Hence, any agent that is attributed the responsibility of a given socio-technical system in question must be able to control it, i.e. have both the actual authority and the actual ability to meet its attributed responsibilities. In the next section, we examine how this simple but crucial "equation" can easily break down into both pragmatic and ethical incongruences when the agent(s) in question is (1) not in a position to ensure its ability to detect/enact relevant issues (or cues) nor take relevant decisions and actions in new or unexpected situations and/or (2) not given actual authority to take relevant decisions or actions in such situations. Such dissonances enact significant material consequences and outcomes and can only be avoided by ensuring a meaningful *human* control of the socio-technical systems in question.

10.4. Responsible Actions Require Meaningful Human Control

Human factor studies have shown through simulations involving full automation/control of cockpits that these were in fact unreliable in dealing with emergency situations.[34] This concurs with the frame "regress" problem already presented in previous chapters.[35] As such, we shall argue that machines alone should not be attributed responsibility of decisions and actions taken within *any* given socio-technical system. Yet, as already seen in Chapter 4, we have been historically hardwired to believe that all acquisition of new knowledge, skills, and expertise can be attained solely by way of representational means. Hence, from the pragmatic role aspect of responsibility, i.e. being able to meet one's physical objectives and requirements, such as maintaining the safety and security of all personnel on an aircraft during its entire mission, fully automated systems alone *cannot* be expected to successfully fulfil such a role within all possible situations.

This argument is further reinforced when we more closely examine the associated interrelated moral obligations. Ethical and moral decision-making and actions in themselves are more often matters of being "neither black nor white," i.e. requiring human judgement, varying interpretations, discernment, and debate on matters of *human relevance*. Hence, it becomes exceedingly difficult to simply relegate this to decisions carried out (or "suggested") by algorithmic/representational codes.[36] Yet, this is exactly what is now being envisaged.[37] Here, within clearly techno-centric approaches and perspectives, we hear words such as "the next generation technological era will be marked by the prevalence of highly automated decisionmaking systems (ADMS), which promote machine autonomy at the expense of human agency."[38] As such, research is now being aimed toward conceptualizing "what a responsible adoption process and a responsible adoption decision involves" within highly automated decision-making systems.[39] The ultimate aim would be to achieve an "integrative judgement model" based on a nomological framework to which "new or important insights" are kept in mind. These include the importance of "contextual factors,"[40] such as factors related to "integrative judgement," type of industry, decision-making contexts (culture, size, and subjective norms), degree of opacity of the algorithmic technology itself, and functional scrutiny, not to mention moral intensity[41] and embedded moral values.[42] These appear as "valiant" attempts at incorporating contextual, embedded, and embodied aspects of moral decision-making, across "a holistic effort in unifying insights and points of view in light of the norms and moral standards relevant to a specific societal context into which the ADMS [Automated Decision Making System] might be deployed."[43] Yet, as Coeckelbergh[44] argues, technology is not a moral being, but merely a representational reduction and approximation of one at best, and therefore should not be attributed full responsibility in the first place. Here, we add our own analogical argument based on Dreyfus'[45] objection to Wheeler's[46] proposed "Heideggerian AI," in that just as AI cannot phenomenologically attain a direct grasp of reality by way of representational frames, AI cannot attain a moral sensitivity of all situations through such attempts at codifying all manners of moral criteria and considerations through purely representational means. Numerous moral considerations transcend mere representational codifications and explications — for as Kristjánsson argues, independent of whether one adheres to a consequentialist or Kantian approach to ethical decision-making, direct skills in the form of human phenomenological (and thus, non-representational!) hands-on learning of being "directly involved" with the situation-at-hand is critical toward fully appreciating the ethical issues at stake.[47]

Unfortunately, within current techno-centric designs, human operators themselves often do not have full meaningful control of the socio-technical system in question. This, as previously discussed in Chapter 8, is typically because of "automation complacency" that sets in.[48] This typically involves "reduced visual attention to the primary information sources feeding automation which must be monitored to detect an abnormal event."[49] Wickens and Alexander refer to this as "cognitive tunneling" involving "the allocation of attention to a particular channel of information, diagnostic hypothesis, or task goal, for a duration that is longer than optimal, given the expected cost of neglecting events on other channels, failing to consider other hypotheses, or failing to perform other tasks."[50] Most importantly, however, is that automation complacency can also be associated toward a *shift in perceived responsibility* on the part of the human operator.[51]

> "Operators learn (and are instructed) that the automated aid is the 'best' cue for making a decision. If the system proves initially to be generally reliable, and reflective of the operators' own diagnostic processes, what may (and does) happen over time is that operators check automated output before anything else, and may not look further for traditional cues even when available, especially if time is short (e.g. Gigerenzer, Hoffrage and Kleinbölting, 1991). In some cases, automated cues may replace other information, making a cross-check with traditional cues impossible."

Research in social psychology has shown that as perceived responsibility is shared among more individuals and entities, people are less likely to intervene in emergencies.[52] Sometimes referred to as the "the problem of many-hands," the fact that one may perceive that he/she may not be called into individual account for a given act or decision may make it that he/she does not feel responsible beforehand.[53] Cummings argues that this has a propensity of manifesting itself across a "many things" version when considering human computer interface systems.[54] Here, he explains that such human–technology systems can create "moral buffers," a form of psychological distancing on the part of the human actor within the system, allowing people to ethically distance themselves from their actions.

This, in turn, reinforces decreased vigilance and eventual atrophy of human operator skills related to over-reliance on automation.[55] As such, socio-technological systems, when designed through techno-centric approaches, can create a new kind of computer-assisted error (both by long-term cognitive conditioning, as well as by faulty or erroneous actions and/or signaling on the part of the technology during the event in question), whereby a system designed to make a task safer is actually directly responsible for causing a disaster.[56] In the end, too many techno-centric design approaches have overemphasized short-term and well-defined machine efficiency and reliability in lieu of adaptability to unexpected situations and outcomes. Here, technology is designed to effectively replace human operator skills and decision-making based on well-defined reliability criteria and measured outputs — thus, leading to the paradox of high efficiency, yet low adaptability (as a result of human skills erosion).

Techno-centric design philosophies have attempted to circumvent the above issues across what is sometimes referred to as "system-centered approaches" toward the possible redistribution of responsibility.[57] For example, Flemisch *et al.*[58] argue that "human–machine systems must be designed for an appropriate relationship, allowing both parties to share responsibility, authority, and autonomy in a safe, efficient, and reliable fashion." Based on this reasoning, the argument provided is that to circumvent the issue that "technologies do not meet traditional criteria for full moral agency (and hence preconditions for responsibility) such as freedom and consciousness, and that therefore they also cannot be (held) responsible," human/social entities (i.e. designers and manufacturers) can be attributed responsibility for what technology does.[59]

Hence, the typical starting point for such system-centered (yet techno-centric) perspectives goes along the lines of "the humans behind the machines (e.g., the developers [and manufacturers]) are responsible for a correct behaviour within the state of the art described, e.g., in standards, while the human operator is responsible for a correct use of the machine, e.g., as described in the manual."[60] Within this spirit, it is reasoned that each entity's designation of responsibility should ensure that it has adequate control to fulfill the attributed responsibility in question.[61] So far so good. Furthermore, the very attribution of responsibility to the various entities within a given human–technology system inscribes the concept of "social accountability," which has been argued to address or mitigate the "many hands" and "many things" phenomena, leading to possible ethical (and related attention/performance) complacency on the part of human operators.[62] To help justify this position, many scholars such as German and Rhodes[63] have referred to Mosier *et al.*'s[64] study which "reported a higher internalized sense of accountability," leading to increased instances of human operators having verified that automation systems were indeed functioning correctly and committed fewer errors in automated environments. Yet, Mosier *et al.* have been careful to clarify that such results should not be generalized for all decision-making contexts, and that externally imposed accountability within the study had no positive effect on eliminating automation bias. Furthermore, others such as Parasuraman and Manzey[65] argue that Mosier *et al.*'s positive results were most likely due to higher levels of motivation and effort experienced among human operators as a result of the researchers having provided the participants with specific performance goals as well as performance feedbacks. Studies involving the establishment of performance goals and performance feedback by researchers have been linked to the well-known Hawthorne effect,[66] whereby at the conclusion of such studies, the beneficial behavioral effects among participants typically dwindle away.

More importantly, Parasuraman and Manzey,[67] through their own studies as well as an exhaustive review of prior research, argue that the overriding factor determining the onset (and maintenance) of automation bias (and loss of situational awareness), irrespective of training and accountability factors, is through a positive reinforcement loop of "learned carelessness," which builds upon the repetition of no abnormal issues or events arising from automated operations. Said another way, "higher reliability of automation and higher levels of automation have been associated with greater complacency, which can lead to worse error management."[68] Moreover, well-meaning intentions toward higher (imposed or internalized) accountability and ethics do not appear to significantly mitigate this troubling trend in any sustainable manner.[69]

So let us summarize what we have so far. Determining what is relevant and meaningful is key toward maintaining full control of a given socio-technical system in question. In turn, such relevant or meaningful control allows the human operator to adequately meet his/her responsibilities (moral, legal, and causal). Yet, paradoxically, human operators are losing both their ability and authority to do so because of current technocentric technological system applications and designs, which have overtly wrestled decision-making authority away from human operators, while also applying covert representational conditioning over human operators' cognitive processes.[70] Conversely, allowing technologies to take over responsibilities of the socio-technical system by way of so-called "instrumental control" is a risky avenue: for one, the frame problem points toward technology's limitations in determining what is relevant under situations of unexpected emergencies.[71] This concurs with human factor studies in which simulations involving full automation/control of cockpits were found to be unreliable in dealing with emergency situations.[72] Furthermore, there is the additional argument that a technology is not a moral being and therefore should not be attributed full responsibility in the first place.[73] Along these lines, our own phenomenological deconstruction of human adaptive expertise in contrast to AI's representational approach and limitations through both Chapters 2 and 5 allowed us to identify "the devil in the details." Contrary to what authors such as Elish[74] and Flemisch *et al.*[75] may suggest, our depiction of AI's frame problem strongly justifies the argument against the distribution of responsibility between human operators and technology. This logical, yet erroneous route of "risk sharing" is analogous to the fallacious use of a double inspection on an assembly line in which each inspector depends on the other to make the correct decision, with the end-result of neither doing an adequate inspection.[76]

This now brings us to this section's concluding argument: a socio-technical system can only meet its attributed responsibilities by attributing this directly onto the human operator's shoulders in terms of moral, legal, role, and causal responsibilities. However, prior to attributing such responsibilities, socio-technical design approaches must change toward allowing human operators to reappropriate full human meaningful control of the technical systems in question. This means adopting human-centric design approaches, as previously discussed and presented in both Chapters 6 and 8, which avoid "operator hand-off" and subsequent "automation complacency" phenomena by re-establishing the full-bodily engagement of the human operator.[77] As also discussed in Chapter 6, toward achieving such meaningful human control, it is not sufficient to simply "being in the loop" within the human-technology system at hand.[78] The operator must be able to influence all parts of the system in a relevant or meaningful manner in regards to moral, legal, role, and causal considerations. This includes having sufficient information and options over the system in question which goes beyond physico-cognitive reactions of "merely pushing a button as a reflex when a light goes on."[79] Furthermore, as discussed through Chapters 8 and 9, attaining such meaningful human control within future socio-technical system configurations requires meaningful and relevant conversations between human operators, management, and designers/manufacturers as stakeholders.[80] Toward this end, the material-discursive practices that materialize such mindful realities must also ensure that the responsibilities of each stakeholder toward achieving and ensuring meaningful human control is never deflected or sidestepped[81]:

> "Learning how to intra-act responsibly within and as part of the world means understanding that we are not the only active beings - though this is never justification for deflecting that responsibility onto other entities. The acknowledgement of 'nonhuman agency' does not lessen human accountability; on the contrary, it means that accountability requires that much more attentiveness to existing power asymmetries."

Hence, just as "designers shape decisions as actors in their own right, in others, they are part of the actor that was hired to solve a particular problem ... [but] tracing accountabilities does not end with designing it, but continues in use."[82] Furthermore, "ethical and moral deliberations in HCI should not only centre around the question what impact the technologies we create have on humans, but rather, what humans we become in the intra-actions with these technologies — and whether this is who we want to be."[83]

Finally, the human operator, now equipped with meaningful human control, can carry out his/her relevant actions and goals, which are both *pragmatic and ethical* in nature. Here, we draw upon Aristotle's concept of *phronesis* (practical wisdom) involving the capacity for moral actions toward good ends[84]; or more specifically, making relevant decisions and actions in the best possible manner toward good ends. Of importance is Heidegger's interpretation of Aristotle's *phronesis*, which renders it possible for an individual to provide an immediate pragmatic and ethical response to a "full concrete situation"[85]:

> "'[The phronimos] ... is determined by his situation in the largest sense ... The circumstances, the givens, the times and the people vary. The meaning of the action ... varies as well ... It is precisely the achievement of phronesis to disclose the [individual] as acting now in the full situation within which he acts' (citing Heidegger, 1997: 101). Of course, there will be problematic cases of conflicting goods where the phronimos does not see immediately what must be done. Thus, Aristotle says

the phronimos must be able to deliberate well (citing Aristotle, 1955: 180). But, according to Heidegger, most of our ethical life consists in simply seeing the appropriate thing to do and responding without deliberation, as when we help a blind person cross the street or when, after years of experience, we unreflectively balance, case by case, the demands of our professional and personal lives. As Aristotle says: 'Phronesis ... involves knowledge of the ultimate particular thing, which cannot be attained by systematic knowledge but only by 'perception' (citing Aristotle, 1955: 182)."

In the next chapter...

In the next chapter, we return to "live" metaphors and analogies regarding quantum theory. On the one hand, such analogies have provided added justification as to why the mind cannot be completely modeled as a computer. On the other hand, it is also currently being directed toward the field of narrow AI with the aim of exponentially enhancing the current processing power of conventional neural networks. Finally, we examine specific "live" metaphors inspired from quantum physics that help us further understand the nature of language and *mètis* — which in turn, once again, provide us additional insights as how to avoid certain pitfalls related to the categorization of knowledge.

References

Aristotle (1955). *The Ethics of Aristotle*, J.A.K. Thomson (trans.) (Harmondsworth: Penguin).

Gigerenzer, G., Hoffrage, U. and Kleinbölting, H. (1991). Probabilistic mental models: A Brunswickian theory of confidence. *Psychological Review*, **98**, 506–528.

Heidegger, M. (1997). *Plato's Sophist*, R. Rojcewicz and A. Schuwer (trans.) (Bloomington, IN, Indiana University Press).

Endnotes

[1] Also see Holford, W.D. (2020a). An ethical inquiry of the effect of cockpit automation on the responsibilities of airline pilots: dissonance or meaningful control? *Journal of Business Ethics*. doi: https://doi.org/10.1007/s10551-020-04640-z.

[2] See Dreyfus, H.L. (2007). Why Heideggerian AI failed and how fixing it would require making it more Heidegerrian. *Artificial Intelligence*, **171**(18), 1137–1160.

[3] See Holford (2020a) (note 1).
[4] See Dreyfus (2007) (note 2).
[5] See both Holford, W.D. (2020b). The repression of mètis within digital organizations. *Prometheus: Critical Studies in Innovation*, **36**(3), 253–276; as well as Holford. W.D. (2020c). *Managing Knowledge in Organizations: A Critical Pragmatic Perspective* (New York, NY: Palgrave MacMillan); also see Baumard, P. (1999). *Tacit Knowledge in Organizations* (London: Sage Publications).
[6] See Dreyfus (2007) (note 2); also see both Dreyfus, H.L. (1992). *What Computers Still Can't Do: A Critique of Artificial Reason* (London, UK: MIT Press) as well as Dreyfus, H.L. and Dreyfus, S.E. (2005). Peripheral vision expertise in real world contexts. *Organization Studies*, **26**(5), 779–792.
[7] See both Dreyfus and Dreyfus (2005) (note 6) as well as Dreyfus, H.L. and Dreyfus, S.E. (1986). *Mind Over Machine* (New York: The Free Press); also see Boden, M.A. (2010). *Creativity and Art: Three Roads to Surprise* (Oxford, UK: Oxford University Press); as well as Boden, M.A. (2015). *Artificial Intelligence* (Boston: MIT Technology Review) and also Boden, M.A. (2016). *AI: Its Nature and Future* (Oxford, UK: Oxford University Press); and finally, see Holford (2020c) (note 5).
[8] See both Kabat-Zinn, J. (1990). *Full Catastrophe Living* (New York, NY: Delta) as well as Dane, E. (2013). Things seen and unseen: Investigating experience-based qualities of attention in a dynamic work setting. *Organization Studies*, **34**, 45–78.
[9] See Langer, E. (2009). *Counter Clockwise. Mindful Health and the Power of Possibility* (London, UK: Hodder & Stoughton).
[10] See both Langer, E.J. (2000). Mindful learning. *Current Directions in Psychological Science*, **9**(2), 220–223; as well as Hülsheger, U.R., Lang, J.W., Depenbrock, F., Fehrmann, C., Zijlstra, F.R.H., Alberts, H.J. *et al.* (2014). The power of presence: The role of mindfulness at work for daily levels and change trajectories of psychological detachment and sleep quality. *Journal of Applied Psychology*, **99**, 1113–1128. doi: 10.1037/a0037702.
[11] Citing Good, D.J., Lyddy, C.J., Glomb, T.M., Bono, J.E., Brown, K.W., Duffy, M.K. *et al.* (2016). Contemplating mindfulness at work: An integrative review. Journal of Management, **42**, 114–142. doi: 10.1177/0149206315617003; also see Langer (2009) (note 9).
[12] See Langer (2009) (note 9).
[13] See Holford (2020a) (note 1).
[14] See both Nostadt, N., Abbink, D.A., Christ, O. and Beckerle, P. (2020). Embodiment, presence, and their intersections: Teleoperation and beyond. *Transactions on Human-Robot Interactions*, **9**(4), Article 28, 19 pp. doi. org/10.1145/3389210; as well as Svanaes, D. (2013). Interaction design for and with the lived body: Some implications of Merleau-Ponty's phenomenology. *ACM Transactions on Computer Human Interaction*, **20**(1), Article 8, 30 pp. doi: http://dx.doi.org/10.1145/2442106.2442114.

[15] See Holford (2020a) (note 1) as well as Holford (2020b) (note 5); and finally, see Weick, K.E., Sutcliffe, K.M. and Obstfeld, D. (2008). Organizing for high reliability: Processes of collective mindfulness. In *Crisis Management*, Vol. III, Boin, A. (ed.) (Los Angeles: Sage), pp. 31–66.

[16] See Weick, Sutcliffe and Obstfeld (2008) (note 15) as well as Barad K. (2007). *Meeting the Universe Halfway: Quantum Physics and the Entanglement of Matter and Meaning* (Durham, NC: Duke University Press); and finally, see Enriquez, E. (1992). *L'Organisation en analyse* (Paris: Presses Universitaires de France).

[17] See both Prince-Paul, M. and Kelley, C. (2017). Mindful communication: Being present. *Seminars on Oncology Nursing*, **33**(5), 475–482. doi: 10.1016/j. soncn.2017.09.004; as well as Burgoon, J.K., Berger, C.R. and Waldron, V.R. (2000). Mindfulness and interpersonal communication. *Journal of Social Issues*, **56**(1), 105–127.

[18] See both Svanaes (2013) (note 4) as well as Küpers, W. (2013). Embodied transformative metaphors and narratives in organizational life-worlds of change. *Journal of Organizational Change Management*, **26**(3), 494–528.

[19] See both Barad (2007) (note 16) as well as Holford (2020a) (note 1).

[20] See both Flemisch, F. *et al.* (2012). Towards a dynamic balance between humans and automation: Authority, ability, responsibility and control in shared and cooperative control situations. *Cognition, Technology & Work*, **14**, 3–18; as well as Dalcher, D. (2007). Why the pilot cannot be blamed: A cautionary note about excessive reliance on technology. *International Journal of Risk Assessment and Management*, **7**(3), 350–366.

[21] Citing Flemisch *et al.* (2012, p. 7) (note 20).

[22] Citing Dalcher (2007, p. 359) (note 20).

[23] *Ibid.*

[24] See Bilz, K. and Nadler, J. (2009). Law, psychology, and morality. In *The Psychology of Learning and Motivation*, D.M. Bartels, C. W. Bauman, L. J. Skitka and D. L. Medin (eds.), Vol. 50. *Moral Judgment and Decision Making* (San Diego: Elsevier Academic Press), pp. 101–131. doi: https://doi.org/10.1016/S0079-7421(08)00403-9.

[25] Citing Flemisch *et al.* (2012, p. 6) (note 20).

[26] See Holford (2020a) (note 1).

[27] See IATA (2020). Clause 3.1.1 from *Command Training, Guidance Material and Best Practices*, First Edition (Montreal: International Air Transport Association).

[28] Citing FAA FAR (2021). Clause 91.3: "Responsibility and Authority of Pilot in Command", US Federal Aviation Authority. Available at: https://www.ecfr. gov/cgi-bin/text-idx?node=14:2.0.1.3.10#se14.2.91_13 (accessed March 29th, 2021).

[29] See IACO (2005). Rules of the Air, Annex 2, International Civil Aviation Organisation. Available at: https://www.icao.int/Meetings/anconf12/Document%20Archive/an02_cons%5B1%5D.pdf (accessed March 29th, 2021).

[30] See CAR (1988). Civil Aviation Regulation. Available at: https://lawlex.com. au/tempstore/consolidated/7460.pdf (accessed March 29th, 2021).

[31] Citing Matthias, A. (2004). The responsibility gap: Ascribing responsibility for the actions of learning automata. *Ethics and Information Technology*, **6**, 175–183.

[32] See Flemisch *et al.* (2012) (note 20).

[33] *Ibid.*

[34] See both McBride, S.E., Rogers, W.E. and Fisk, A.D. (2014). Understanding human management of automation errors. *Theoretical Issues Ergonomic Sciences*, **15**(6), 545–577; as well as Mosier, K.L. and Skitka, L.J. (1996). Human decision makers and automated decision aids: Made for each other? In *Automation and Human Performance: Theory and Applications*, R. Parasuraman and M. Mouloua (eds.), pp. 201–220 (Boca Raton, FL: CRC Press).

[35] See both Dreyfus (2007) (note 2) as well as Schultz, T.P. (2018). *The Problem with Pilots: How Physicians, Engineers and Airpower Enthusiasts Redefined Flight* (Baltimore, MA: John Hopkins University Press).

[36] See both Coeckelbergh, M. (2009 — Virtual moral agency, virtual moral responsibility. AI & Society 24(2), 181–189) as well as Coeckelbergh, M. (2019 — Artificial Intelligence, Responsibility Attribution, and a Relational Justification of Explainability, Science and Engineering Ethics, https://doi.org/10.1007/s11948-019-00146-8).

[37] See Grange, C. and Pinsonneault, A. (2021 — The Responsible Adoption of (Highly) Automated Decision-Making Systems, 54th Hawaii International Conference on System Sciences (HICSS-54), January 5–8, pp. 1–10).

[38] Citing Grange and Pinsonneault (2021, p. 1) (note 37).

[39] *Ibid.*

[40] See Hong, W., Chan, F.K.Y., Thong, J.Y.L., Chasalow, L.C. and Dhillon, G. (2013). A framework and guidelines for context-specific theorizing in information systems research. *Information Systems Research*, **25**(1), pp. 111–136.

[41] See Jones, T.M. (1991). Ethical decision making by individuals in organizations: An issue-contingent model. *Academy of Management Review*, **16**(2), 366–395.

[42] See both Newell, S. and Marabelli, M. (2015). Strategic opportunities (and challenges) of algorithmic decision-making: A call for action on the long-term societal effects of 'datification.' *The Journal of Strategic Information Systems*, **24**(1), 3–14; as well as Mittelstadt, B.D., Allo, P., Taddeo, M., Wachter, S. and Floridi, L. (2016). The ethics of algorithms: Mapping the debate. *Big Data & Society*, **3**(2), pp. 1–21.

[43] Citing Grange and Pinsonneault (2021, p. 6) (note 37).

[44] See Coeckelbergh (2009, 2019) (note 36).

[45] See Dreyfus (2007) (note 2).

[46] See Wheeler, M. (2005). *Reconstructing the Cognitive World: The Next Step* (Cambridge, MA: MIT Press).

⁴⁷ See Kristjánsson, K. (2014). Phronesis and moral education: Treading beyond the truisms. *Theory and Research in Education*, **12**(2), 151–171.

⁴⁸ See both Dao, A.-Q. *et al.* (2009). The impact of automation assisted aircraft separation on situation awareness. In *Human Interface*, Part II, HCII 2009, LNCS 5618, M.J. Smith and G. Salvendy (eds.) (Berlin, Heidelberg: Springer-Verlag), pp. 738–747, as well as German, E.S. and Rhodes, D.H. (2016). Human-model interactivity: What can be learned from the experience of pilots with the glass cockpit? *Conference on Systems Engineering Research*, p. 10.

⁴⁹ Citing Parasuraman, R. and Manzey, D.H. (2010). Complacency and bias in human use of automation: An attentional integration. *Human Factors*, **52**(3), 381–410; also see Wickens, C.D. and Alexander, A.L. (2009). Attentional tunneling and task management in synthetic vision displays. *The International Journal of Aviation Psychology*, **19**(2), 182–199. https://doi.org/10.1080/10508410902766549.

⁵⁰ Citing Wickens and Alexander (2009, p. 182) (note 49).

⁵¹ Citing Mosier and Skitka (1996, p. 218) (note 34).

⁵² See Billings, C.E., Grayson, R., Hecht, W. and Curry, R. (1980). A study of midair collisions in US terminal airspace. NASA Aviation Safety Reporting System: Quarterly Report No. 11 (NASA TM81225).

⁵³ See Bovens, M. (1998). *The Quest for Responsibility. Accountability and Citizenship in Complex Organisations* (Cambridge, UK: Cambridge University Press).

⁵⁴ See Cummings, M.L. (2006). Automation and accountability in decision support system interface design. *The Journal of Technology Studies*, **32**(1), 23–31.

⁵⁵ See Foushee, H.C. (1982). The role of communications, socio-psychological and personality factors in the maintenance of crew coordination. *Aviation, Space and Environmental Medicine*, **53**(11), 1062–1066; as well as see Sarter, N.B. and Woods, D.D. (1994). Decomposing automation: Autonomy, authority, observability and perceived animacy. In *Human Performance in Automated Systems: Current Research and Trends*, M. Mouloua and R. Parasuraman (eds.) (Hilldale, NJ: Lawrence Erlbaum Associates), pp. 22–27; also see Mosier and Skitka (1996) (note 34); and finally, see Skitka, L.J., Mosier, K.L. and Burdick, M.D. (2000). Accountability and automation bias. *International Journal of Human-Computer Studies*, **2000**, 701–717.

⁵⁶ See Dalcher (2007) (note 20).

⁵⁷ See both Dalcher (2007) (note 20) as well as Flemisch *et al.* (2012) (note 20); also see Holden, R.J. (2009). People or systems? To blame is human. The fix is to engineer. *Professional Safety*, **54**(12), 34–41; and finally, see Elish, M.C. (2019). Moral crumple zones: Cautionary tales in human-robot interaction. *Engaging Science, Technology, and Society*, **5**, 40–60.

⁵⁸ Citing Flemisch *et al.* (2012, p. 10) (note 20), who in turn, reference Miller, C. and Parasuraman, R. (2007). Designing for flexible interaction between humans

and automation: Delegation interfaces for supervisory control. *Human Factors*, **49**, 57–75.

[59] Citing Coeckelbergh (2019, p. 4) (note 36); also see Flemisch *et al.* (2012) (note 20).

[60] Citing Flemisch *et al.* (2012, p. 10) (note 20); also see Elish (2019) (note 57).

[61] See both Dalcher (2007) (note 20) as well as Flemisch *et al.* (2012) (note 20); also see Elish (2019) (note 57); and finally, see McKenna, M. (2008). Putting the lie on the control condition for moral responsibility. *Philosophical Studies*, **139**(1), 29–37.

[62] See Skitka, Mosier and Burdick (2000) (note 55).

[63] See German and Rhodes (2016) (note 48).

[64] See Mosier, K.L, Skitka, L.J., Heers, S. and Burdick M.D. (1998). Automation bias: Decision making and performance in high-tech cockpits. *The International Journal of Aviation Psychology*, 47–63.

[65] See Parasuraman and Manzey (2010) (note 49).

[66] See both Schwartz, D., Fischhoff, B., Krishnamurti, T. and Sowell, F. (2013). The Hawthorne effect and energy awareness. *Proceedings of the National Academy of Science USA*, **110**, 15242–15246 as well as Schwartzman, H.B. (1993). *Ethnography in Organizations* (Newbury Park, CA: Sage Publications).

[67] See Parasuraman and Manzey (2010) (note 49).

[68] Citing McBride *et al.* (2014, p. 15) (note 34).

[69] See Parasuraman and Manzey (2010) (note 49).

[70] See Dalcher (2007) (note 20); as well as Parasuraman and Manzey (2010) (note 49); also see Elish (2019) (note 57); as well as Schultz (2018) (note 34); and finally, see Carr, N. (2015). *The Glass Cage — How Our Computers Are Changing Us* (New York: W.W. Norton and Company).

[71] See both Dreyfus (2007) (note 2) as well as Schultz (2018) (note 34).

[72] See both McBride *et al.* (2014) (note 34) as well as Mosier and Skitka (1996) (note 34).

[73] See Coeckelbergh (2009, 2019) (note 36).

[74] See Elish (2019) (note 57).

[75] See Flemisch *et al.* (2012) (note 20).

[76] See Deming, W.E. (1986) *Out of the Crisis* (Cambridge, MA: MIT/CAES).

[77] See both Gaffary, Y. and Lécuyer, A. (2018). The use of haptic and tactile information in the car to improve driving safety: A review of current technologies. *Frontiers in ICT*, **5**(5), 1–11; as well as Abbink, D.A. and Mulder, M. (2009). Exploring the dimensions of haptic feedback support in manual control. *Journal of Computing and Information Science in Engineering*, **9**(1), 011006-1–011006-9.

[78] See Santonio de Sio, F. and van den Hoven, J. (2018). Meaningful human control over autonomous systems: A philosophical account. *Frontiers in Robotics and AI*, **5**(15), 1–14.

79 See both Schultz (2018) (note 35) as well as Horowitz, M.C. and Scharre, P. (2015). Meaningful Human Control in Weapon Systems: A Primer. Available at: https://www.cnas.org/publications/reports/meaningful-human-control-in-weapon-systems-a-primer.

80 See Elish (2019) (note 57).

81 Citing Barad (2017, p. 218) (note 16).

82 Citing Frauenberger, C. (2019). Entanglement HCI the next wave? *ACM Transactions on Computer-Human Interaction*, **27**(1), Article 2, pp. 1–27.

83 Citing Frauenberger (2019, p. 18) (note 82).

84 See Bourdieu, P. (1994). Practical Reason (Cambridge, UK: Polity); as well as Angier, T. (2010). *Techné in Aristotle's Ethics: Crafting the Moral Life* (New York, NY: Continuum International); and finally, see Sayer, A. (2011). *Why Things Matter To People: Social Science, Values and Ethical Life* (Cambridge, UK: Cambridge University Press).

85 Citing Dreyfus, H.L. (2014). *Skillful Coping: Essays on the Phenomenology of Everyday Perception and Action* (Oxford, UK: Oxford University Press), pp. 109–110.

Chapter 11

A Few Analogies and Metaphors on Quantum Physics as Related to Mind, Artificial Intelligence, Language, and *Mètis*

11.1. Introduction

Analogical thinking across the use of "live" metaphors transcends "similarities at hand" to become creative acts.[1] One family of analogies and metaphors currently being voiced is in regards to quantum theory. In recent years, quantum physics has fueled added debate on AI and human capabilities. While this chapter does not pretend to go into rigorous detail on all fronts, we examine how, on the one hand, analogies regarding quantum physics has provided added justification as to why the mind cannot be completely modeled as a computer.[2] On the other hand, we also examine how quantum physics has been directly investigated within the field of narrow AI with the aim of exponentially enhancing the current processing power of conventional neural networks.[3] Finally, we look at specific "live" metaphors inspired by quantum physics to help understand the nature of language and *mètis*, once again providing us insights as to how to avoid certain pitfalls related to the categorization of knowledge.

11.2. A Few More Words on Metaphorical Thinking and Analogical Reasoning

In Chapters 7–9, we discussed how metaphors play a role in how we make sense of events and situations — whether in a mindful or mindless fashion. According to Lakoff and Johnson,[4] metaphors are used in a pervasive fashion through most, if not all, of our experiences. Here, the authors first refer to an "embodied realism" involving all of our thought, symbolic expressions, and interactions, which in turn are intimately tied to our embodiment as well as the aesthetic nature of all our experiences. As such[5]:

> "[M]etaphors and reasoning with them are both constitutive of the structure of bodily experience, as well as emerge from this experience. As one of their functions, embodied metaphor(ising) translates an experienced reality into a perceptible object that has emotive import as well as discursive content, and both are inseparable from the creative imagination that poetically co-creates the 'object'. In this way metaphors have and mediate meanings that transcend, and are not reducible to either emotive utterance or rational discourse."

As we saw in Chapter 8, "live" metaphors have the potential to become part of a creative symbolic understanding of phenomena and therefore can provide a vehicle for meaningful understanding and communication.[6] "Live" metaphors are only "partial truths,"[7] in that they are open toward the development of new meanings and insights.[8] In turn, such metaphorical thinking as a basic mode of symbolism plays a key part analogical reasoning.[9] "Analogy-making pervades human thinking … imagining, speaking and understanding at all levels, as well as it is guiding in unfamiliar or decision-making situations and helps finding order out of the chaos of the world."[10] In this manner, according to Hofstadter and Sander,[11] making analogies lies at the very core of human thought.

Analogical thinking involves the abstracting of details from a particular context and comparing this with another context to identify and extract structural similarities and commonalities. In this manner, it can be used for problem-solving based on previous examples and also to provide counter-arguments in critical debates and thinking.[12] Importantly, analogical thinking through the use of "live" metaphors becomes an inference-making process which can transcend "similarities at hand," thus becoming a creative act in which features of importance emerge through enactment rather than simply being transferred from one context to another.[13]

In this sense, the next section examines an open-ended analogy in the form the "quantum mind analogy."[14]

11.3. The Quantum Mind Analogy as an Open-Ended Non-Modelable Approach

The puzzle of consciousness has led certain researchers to use quantum physics to explain it — yet, not without strong skepticism and criticism that it consists of mystical rubbish.

Niels Bohr first drew attention between quantum processes at the subatomic level and inner experiences and thought processes of the mind.[15] In similar fashion, Pylkkänen[16] explains how physicist David Bohm compared the uncertainty principle of quantum theory and specific aspects of thought, whereby just as one cannot measure position and momentum simultaneously with arbitrarily high accuracy[17]:

> "If a person tries to observe what he is thinking about at the very moment that he is reflecting on a particular subject, it is generally agreed that he introduces unpredictable and uncontrollable changes in the way his thoughts proceed thereafter. Why this happens is not definitely known at present ... If we compare (1) the instantaneous state of a thought with the position of a particle and (2) the general direction of change of that thought with the particle's momentum, we have a strong analogy."

Contrary to quantum physics, in classical physics, one can measure both the momentum and position of a particle accurately at the same time.[18] At the quantum level, this is not possible and is referred to as the Uncertainty Principle established by Heisenberg — i.e. one cannot measure both position and momentum at the same time with a very high level of accuracy. As such, with the Uncertainty Principle being such a fundamental part of quantum physics, one cannot help but inquire if it indeed applies to human thought processes.[19] In this manner, Bohm considered this a "strong analogy"[20]:

> "[A] person can always describe approximately what he is thinking about without introducing significant disturbances in his train of thought.

But as he tries to make the description precise, he discovers that either the subject of his thoughts or trend or sometimes both become very different from what they were before or sometimes both become very different from what they were before he tried to observe them."

Bohm[21] also drew attention to the holistic features of thought in comparison with quantum processes in regards to the nature of meaning[22]:

"[I]f a person attempts to apply his thinking more and more precisely defined elements, he eventually reaches a stage where further analysis cannot even be given a meaning."

Furthermore, Bohm explained that just as the mind carries out specific logical processes, so we find classical properties of physics, and alternatively the overall holistic processes of the mind, including the process of creativity, can be compared to quantum physics[23]:

"[T]he laws of quantum physics must be so chosen that in the classical limit, where many quantas are involved, the quantum laws lead to the classical equations as an average."

"Without the development of logical thinking, we would have no clear way to express the results of our thinking, and no way to check its validity. Thus just as life as we know it would be impossible if quantum theory did not have its present classical limit, thought as we know it would be impossible unless we could express its results in logical terms ... Yet the basic thinking process probably cannot be described as logical. For instance, many people have noted that a new idea often comes suddenly, after a long and unsuccessful search and without any apparent direct cause."[24]

Beyond the above analogies, Bohm believed (although was never able to prove) that there were indeed quantum processes at work in human brain.[25] To this day, it is a hypothesis that has been relentlessly pursued by subsequent researchers, with one of the most promising proposed by Hameroff and Penrose[26] consisting of microtubules in neurons which vibrate in such a way as to display quantum effects. While the microtubule theory has not been clearly proven, more recent studies conducted by Fischer[27] seem to reinforce Hameroff and Penrose's[28] theory by arguing that phosphate ions in the brain, which have different nuclear spins, attain entangled states, thus explaining the non-local or more holistic properties of thought. This too, however, remains to be clearly proven.

The idea of describing the mind using both classical and quantum processes (such as quantum super-positioning and quantum uncertainty), albeit controversial, if proven right, would confirm the impossibility of modeling by way of a programmatic algorithmic language.[29] As such, a second strong analogy also can be found between Hameroff's[30] and Penrose's[31] argument that the mind, being quantum in nature, cannot be modeled due to its inherent indeterminacy, and hence irreducibility vs Dreyfus'[32] own epistemological and phenomenological critique of Artificial Intelligence (AI) — i.e. contrary to the representational and computational perspective of Computational Theory of Mind (CTM), we as humans grasp our realities in a "direct" manner through irreducible, transcendent qualities and experiences of the senses as whole-body inter-actions with one's environment, which can never be fully modeled in a representational manner.[33]

11.4. Quantum Effects as Part of Narrow AI's Ongoing Developments

Quantum physics has been investigated within the field of narrow AI with the aim of exponentially enhancing the current processing power of con-ventional neural networks.[34] In this manner, machine learning techniques have started to integrate the quantum "many-body" phenomena to speed up current machine learning approaches toward what is commonly referred to as "quantum computing."[35] Here, all symbolic and connection-ist representational approaches previously discussed in Chapters 1, 2, and 5 still apply, but orders of magnitude more "efficiently." In this sense, "a plausible goal for the near term is the development of models that com-bine quantum many-body (entanglement) physics with machine learning that delivers the necessary accuracy required for the prediction of novel phenomena at the speed of modern machine learning."[36] However, beyond current neural network approaches, the aim is to considerably improve overall processing speeds across "quantum machine learning algorithms such as the quantum Boltzmann machine, quantum Helmholtz machine, and the Born machine."[37] Quantum machine learning integrates quantum algorithms within conventional machine learning programs.[38] Typically, this involves machine learning algorithms for the analysis of classical data executed on a quantum computer — otherwise referred to as "quantum-enhanced machine learning."[39] While conventional machine learning algorithms use data, quantum machine learning utilizes qubits to improve computational speeds.[40] Such machines include hybrid methods involving both classical and quantum processing, whereby computationally long or difficult subroutines can be "outsourced" to a quantum module.[41]

In effect, these types of approaches are analogous to the application of Heidegerian principles of embodiment to classical representational computational approaches discussed in Chapter 5, resulting in so-called Heideggerian AI. While these approaches, i.e. both classical and quantum computing, have certainly provide impressive inroads as tools and aids to human users regarding various tasks and uses, once again we should not take this as proof that the human mind is indeed computational and modelable. Beyond Dreyfus'[42] arguments against the computational theory of mind (CTM) presented throughout this book, others such as Turing, Gödel, and Penrose also provide complementary arguments in this sense. For example, Turing showed that there were tasks that even the most powerful computing machine could not perform, more specifically, known as the halting problem.[43] The halting problem is the problem of determining, from a description of an arbitrary computer program and an input, whether the program will finish running, or continue to run forever. As such, Turing argued that a general algorithm to solve the halting problem, which is in the form of a "halt tester," for all possible program-input pairs cannot exist. To this, one can also add Gödel's incompleteness theorem, which essentially says there are true statements of mathematics (in the form of theorems) which can never be proven as true.[44] In this sense, both Turing and Gödel showed that it is impossible to acquire all human knowledge by way of computations "alone given the method's inherent limits."[45] Finally, along the same spirit, Penrose argued there exists a class of problems that defy classical mathematical descriptions.[46] This includes consciousness and awareness, intuition, feeling, and various cognitive "biases" in human judgment.

In the next section, we return to the quantum analogy as "live" metaphors, first as inspiration on how to regard words and discursive practice, and second toward how we can regard *mètis*.

11.5. The Quantum Metaphors — From Language to *Mètis*

Quantum phenomena as source of inspirational metaphors is not new to the social sciences and humanities. In fact, as Hunt[47] and Smith[48] explain, it is not an accident that such metaphors can be easily transferred, for example, toward ecological psychology. Neils Bohr was quite familiar with the works of William James, whereby it can be argued that he used James' work regarding "stream[s] of consciousness in his understanding of the quantum world."[49] In this manner[50]:

> "The unavoidable influence on atomic phenomena caused by observing them corresponds to the well-known change of the tinge of the psychological experiences which accompanies any direction of the attention to one of their various elements."

Within this spirit, Libben proposes the notions of wave/particle duality and superposition as a way of understanding language lexicons in an alternative way from the sole cognitivist assumption that the mind/brain contains representations for words.[51] More precisely, Libben postulates that words "exist as superstates that have specific realizations only when they are observed."[52] Here,

> "The notion of lexical superstates builds metaphorically on the claim within the quantum physics community that particles are in superposition until they are actually measured at one location or another. The notion of superposition is related to the claim of wave-particle duality in quantum physics. An, electron, for example, can be both particle and wave, despite the fact that these states seem intuitively to be mutually exclusive. When observed, an electron will show itself to have wave or particle properties, depending on which of these is measured. Up to the point of measurement, however, it can be said to be in superposition, being neither (and both) a wave or particle. According to what has come to be known as The Copenhagen Interpretation (citing Heisenberg, 1958), it is only at the point of observation that there is a resolution of the state of superposition (also referred to as the 'collapse of the wave function')."[53]

According to Libben, depending on the context, a word goes into a particular state as a result of reflection or of an act of language use.

This can be as a noun, a verb, a morphological structure, etc. Libben goes further by explaining that much of the knowledge claims we have established in regards to language usage is in the form of accounts of what is externally observed. Yet, we often mistake this as knowledge of how our internal states indeed behave. For example, it may "be the case that the idea that I possess the word wallpaper in my mind/brain at all, is illusory. Rather, it may be the case that the notion of a word as a particle-like entity only occurs as a result of observation in the acts of language production or comprehension and, in particular, conscious reflection on such acts."[54] In this sense, we rejoin Baumard[55] and Scott's[56] argument that behind many modern approaches to knowledge acquisition lies a cognitive gap between knowledge that we think we have used, and knowledge that we have really used. Libben's[57] other corollary argument, as inspired by Bohr himself as well as rejoining Weick[58] in regards to enactive sensemaking, is that the methods of knowledge acquisition we use are not neutral, but rather bias the results toward how we see or envision the world in the first place. As such[59]:

"The fact that we can use words in the world, even the fact that words may be extremely prominent in the world, does not mean that we need to postulate them existing as inherently particle-like entities in the mind. Indeed, in the case of the question of the underlying nature of lexical knowledge and ability, there is good reason to suspect that going from things in the world (especially if those things are artifacts of human creation) and then "placing" them in the mind, will lead us further away from, rather than closer to, a better approximation of the truth."

Across the phenomenological-like words of "it is experience that is at the core of our cognitive ability" as inspired by William James,[60] Libben adds[61]:

"It may be the case that, until they are actually used in productions, what we call words in the mind exist only as potentials for realization as specific items with semantic and formal characteristics. Thus, the fact that words may have specific properties at the time of observation, does not require that they have single or specific representations in the mind."

However, Libben's position is more constructivist than phenomenological — in that, he clarifies how personal experiences lead to different ways of representing a given lexical term or phrase.

A major issue with the quantum analogy used by Libben is the inherent duality between particle and wave as viewed by the Copenhagen Interpretation of quantum theory. Whilst, both aspects (particle and wave) are present in the world of potentials, and by metaphorical extension according to Libben,[62] the lexical act versus the lexical entity as representation is present within individuals as potential expression until an event-context occurs, the final observation (or event-context) when it occurs remains dualistic as an either or result — i.e. either we observe a particle or a wave, in other words, either we observe a lexical representation as entity or a lexical process. This would at best appear naïve not only when considering human behavior and actions ultimately leading to *mètis*, but also when we go back towards applying this to human conversations. In Chapter 6, we argued that within language usage there exists an overlapping and hybridization of phenomenological (or pragmatic/direct realist), constructionist (or semantic ambiguous/non-representational), and cognitivist (or representational) dimensions — and not just as potential, but in its actual usage. Similarly for general human behavior and actions leading toward *mètis* (in the actualized sense and not just as a potential for), we proposed that cognitivists can still offer insights, albeit incomplete ones.[63] In this sense, human behavior can be partially explained through both representational and non-representational theories, whereby the aggregate summation of both offers us at best only a partial insight as to what constitutes daily human activities. The rest remains unfathomable transcendence and indeterminacy to which phenomenology's *mètis* embraces without needing to provide a cognitive, epistemological, or philosophical account.[64] To capture these overlapping dimensions (as language or general *mètis*), we argue that an alternative (and preferable) quantum metaphor avoiding the dualistic pitfalls discussed above can be found across what is known as Bohmian quantum mechanics.

Bohmian mechanics avoids the wave-particle duality involving Schrödinger's instantaneous wave function collapsing into either a wave or particle once an event occurs. However, the wave function in its fullest potential (i.e. fullest expression) still applies, but only now, in terms of *actual* events and observations. This observed description is completed by the pilot wave equation, i.e. a description of a particle displacing itself in a wave-like motion. Thus, by analogy we have representational vs non-representational behaviors melding together. Finally, just as in the Bohmian mechanics metaphor, we still cannot determine both position and velocity of particles at the same time, in human behavior there still remains an irreducible or unexplainable dimension in terms of phenomenology.

Reference

Heisenberg, W. (1958). *Physics and Philosophy: The Revolution in Modern Science* (New York: Prometheus Books).

Endnotes

[1] Citing Küpers W. (2011). Analogical reasoning. In *Encyclopedia of the Sciences of Learning*, Seel N.M. (ed.) (Boston, MA: Springer). doi: https://doi.org/10.1007/978-1-4419-1428-6_788.

[2] See both Penrose, R. (1994). *Shadows of the Mind: An Approach to the Missing Science of Consciousness* (Oxford, UK: Oxford University Press) as well as Penrose, R. (1997). *The Large, the Small and the Human Mind* (New York: Cambridge University Press); also see both Hameroff, S.R. (2006). Conscious neurobiology and quantum mechanics. In *The Emerging Physics of Consciousness*, Tuszynski, J.A. (ed.) (Berlin: Springer; New York: Heidelberg), pp. 193–254; as well as Hameroff, S.R. and Penrose, R. (1996). Conscious events as orchestrated spacetime selections. *Journal of Consciousness Studies*, **3**, 36–53; and finally, see Bohm, D. and Hiley, B.J. (1993). *The Undivided Universe: An Ontological Interpretation of Quantum Theory* (London: Routledge).

[3] See both Behrman, E.C. and Steck, J.E. (2013). Multiqubit entanglement of a general input state. *Quantum Information and Computation*, **13**, 36–53; as well as Behrman, E.C., Steck, J.E., Kumar, P. and Walsh, K.A. (2008). Quantum algorithm design using dynamic learning. *Quantum Information and Computation*, **8**(1–2), 12–29.

[4] See both Lakoff, G. and Johnson, M. (1980). *Metaphors We Live By* (Chicago: Chicago University Press) as well as Lakoff, G. and Johnson, M. (1999). *Philosophy in the Flesh: The Embodied Mind and its Challenge to Western Thought* (Berkeley, CA: Basic Books).

[5] Citing Küpers W. (2011, p. 3) (note 1).

[6] See Cassirer, E. (1955). *The Philosophy of Symbolic Forms. Vol II: Mythical Thought* R. Manheim (trans.) (New Haven: Yale University Press).

[7] Citing Morgan, G. (1996). An Afterword: Is There Anything More To Be Said About Metaphor? In *Metaphor and Organizations*, Grant and C. Oswick (eds.) (London: Sage), pp. 227–240.

[8] See both Cornelissen, J.P., Kafouros, M. and Lock, A.R. (2005). Metaphorical images of organization: How organizational researchers develop and select organizational metaphors. *Human Relations*, **58**(12), 1545–1578; as well as Enriquez, E. (1992). *L'Organisation en analyse* (Paris : Presses Universitaires de France)

[9] See Küpers W. (2011) (note 1).

[10] Citing Küpers W. (2011, p. 1) (note 1).

[11] See Hofstader, D. and Sander, E. (2010). *The Essence of Thought* (New York: Basic Books).

[12] See both Küpers W. (2011) (note 1) as well as Shelley, C. (2004). Analogy counterarguments: A taxonomy for critical thinking. *Argumentation*, **18**, 223–238. doi: https://doi.org/10.1023/B:ARGU.0000024025.45062.24.

[13] Citing Küpers W. (2011, p. 4) (note 1).

[14] See Pylkkanen, P. (2014). Can quantum analogies help us understand the process of thought? *Mind and Matter*, **12**(1), 61–91.

[15] See Bohr, N. (1934). *Atomic Theory and the Description of Nature* (London: Cambridge University Press).

[16] See Pylkkanen (2014) (note 14).

[17] Citing Bohm, D. (1951). *Quantum Theory* (Englewood Cliffs: Prentice-Hall), p. 169.

[18] See Pylkkanen (2014) (note 14).

[19] Citing Pylkkanen (2014, p. 67) (note 14).

[20] Citing Bohm, D. (1951, p. 169) (note 17).

[21] *Ibid.*

[22] See Pylkkanen (2014, p. 67) (note 14).

[23] Citing Bohm, D. (1951, p. 31) (note 17).

[24] Citing Bohm, D. (1951, p. 171) (note 17).

[25] See Pylkkanen (2014) (note 14).

[26] See Hameroff and Penrose (2014) (note 2).

[27] See Fisher M.P.A. (2015). Quantum cognition: The possibility of processing with nuclear spins in the brain. *Annals of Physics*, **362**, 593–602.

[28] See Hameroff and Penrose (2014) (note 2).

[29] See Zizzi, P. and Pregnolato, M. (2012). The non-algorithmic side of the mind. *Quantum Biosystems*, **4**(1), 1–8.

[30] See Hameroff (2006) (note 2).

[31] See Penrose (1994) (note 2).

[32] See Dreyfus, H.L. (1987). Misrepresenting human knowledge. In *Artificial Intelligence: The Case Against, Rainer Born* (London: Croom Helem Ltd). In Born, R. (Ed), pp. 41–54.

[33] See Küpers, W. (2012). "Inter-communicating": Phenomenological perspectives on embodied communication and contextuality. *Journal for Communication and Culture*, **2**(2), 114–138.

[34] See both Behrman, E.C. and Steck, J.E. (2013). Multiqubit entanglement of a general input state. *Quantum Information and Computation*, **13**, 36–53; as well as Behrman, E.C., Steck, J.E., Kumar, P. and Walsh, K.A. (2008). Quantum algorithm design using dynamic learning. *Quantum Information and Computation*, **8**(1–2), 12–29.

[35] See Carrasquilla J. (2020). Machine learning for quantum matter. *Advances in Physics: X*, **5**(1). doi: 10.1080/23746149.2020.1797528.

[36] Citing Carrasquilla J. (2020, p. 29) (note 35).

[37] Citing Carrasquilla J. (2020, p. 30) (note 35), who in turn references Bahri, Y., Kadmon, J., Pennington, J. *et al.* (2020). Statistical mechanics of deep learning. *Annual Review of Condensed Matter Physics*, **11**, 501–528; also see both Benedetti, M., Realpe-Gómez, J. and Perdomo-Ortiz, A. (2018). Quantum-assisted Helmholtz machines: A quantum–classical deep learning framework for industrial datasets in near-term devices. *Quantum Science Technology*, **3**, 034007; as well as Amin, M.H., Andriyash, E., Rolfe, J. *et al.* (2018). Quantum Boltzmann machine. *Physics Review X*, **8**, 021050. doi: 10.1103/PhysRevX.8.021050.

[38] See Schuld, M. and Petruccione, F. (2018). Supervised learning with quantum computers. *Quantum Science and Technology*. doi:10.1007/978-3-319-96424-9.

[39] See Lee, J.-S., Bang, J., Hong, S., Lee, C., Seol, K.H., Lee, J. and Lee, K.-G. (2019). Experimental demonstration of quantum learning speedup with classical input data. *Physical Review A*, **99**(1), 012313.

[40] See Schuld, M., Sinayskiy, I. and Petruccione, F. (2014). An introduction to quantum machine learning. *Contemporary Physics*, **56**(2), 172–185.

[41] See Benedetti *et al.* (2018) (note 37).

[42] See Dreyfus, H.L. (2007). Why Heideggerian AI failed and how fixing it would require making it more Heidegerrian. *Artificial Intelligence*, **171**(18), 1137–1160.

[43] See Turing, A.M. (1937). On computable numbers, with an application to the Entscheidungsproblem. *Proceedings of the London Mathematical Society*, **42**, 230–265.

[44] See Gödel, K. (1931). Über formal unentscheidbare Sätze der Principia Mathematica und verwandter Systeme I. *Monatshefte für Mathematik Physik*, **38**, 173–198. English translation in van Heijenoort (1967, 596–616) and in Gödel (1986, 144–195).

[45] Citing Wang, H. Smith, J.W. and Sun, Y. (2013). Simulating cognition with quantum computers. *Neurons and Cognition*, p. 2. Corpus ID: 168169722.

[46] See Penrose (1997) (note 2).

[47] See Hunt, H. T. (2001). Some perils of quantum consciousness — Epistemological pan-experientialism and the emergence–submergence of consciousness. *Journal of Consciousness Studies*, **8**, 35–45.

[48] See Smith, C.U. (2006). The 'hard problem' and the quantum physicists. Part 1: The first generation. Brain *and Cognition*, **61**(2), 181–188.

[49] Citing Libben, G (2017). The quantum metaphor and the organization of words in the mind. *Journal of Cultural Cognitive Science*, **1**, 49–55. doi: https://doi.org/10.1007/s41809-017-0003-5.

[50] Citing Bohr (1934, p. 100) (note 15).

[51] See Libben (2017) (note 49).

[52] Citing Libben (2017, p. 51) (note 49).

[53] *Ibid.*

[54] Citing Libben (2017, p. 52) (note 49).

[55] See Baumard, P. (1999). *Tacit Knowledge in Organizations* (London: Sage Publications).

[56] See Scott, J.C. (1998). *Seeing like a State: How Certain Schemes to Improve the Human State have Failed* (Binghamton, NY: Vail-Ballou Press).

[57] See Libben (2017) (note 49).

[58] See Weick, K.E. (1995). *Sensemaking in Organizations* (Thousand Oaks, CA: Sage Publications).

[59] Citing Libben (2017, p. 52) (note 49).

[60] See James, W. (1890). *The Principles of Psychology* (New York: Dover)

[61] Citing Libben (2017, pp. 54–55) (note 49).

[62] See Libben (2017, p. 52) (note 49).

[63] See Massis, J. (2014). Naturalizing dasein. Aporias of the neo-Heideggerian approach in cognitive science. *Cosmos and History: The Journal of Natural and Social Philosophy*, **10**(2), 158–181.

[64] See Massis (2014, p. 177) (note 63); also see Dreyfus (2007) (note 42); as well as Scott (1998) (note 56).

Chapter 12

Conclusion: More Than Just "Connecting the Dots"

Certain pundits argue that the very notion of machines and/or Artificial Intelligence (AI) replacing humans is alarmist or over-exaggerated. David H. Autor, Professor of Economics at MIT, for example, argued that "given that these technologies demonstrably succeed in their labor saving objective and, moreover, that we invent many more labor-saving technologies all the time, should we not be somewhat surprised that technological change hasn't already wiped out employment for the vast majority of workers?"[1] To this he added, "these questions underline an economic reality that is as fundamental as it is overlooked: tasks that cannot be substituted by automation are generally complemented by it." Finally, he concluded that while "some of the tasks in many current middle-skill jobs are susceptible to automation, many middle-skill jobs will continue to demand a mixture of tasks from across the [human] skill spectrum."[2] A subsequent 2017 McKinsey and Co. report appeared to support Autor's claim in predicting that close to half the activities carried out by workers "today" would have the potential to be automated, but that "for most occupations, partial automation is more likely than full automation in the medium term, and the technologies will provide new opportunities for job creation." Other big consulting firms such as PwC have joined this growing chorus where machines and humans are seen as working together, and job creation as a result of AI and automation (in terms of specialized expertise to oversee these machines) will more than offset job losses in the more traditional areas of competencies. Conversely, a working paper by Acemoglu and Restrepo presented an opposite view arguing that significant jobs losses would not be offset by jobs created whereby "we estimate large and robust negative effects of robots on employment and wages across commuting zones."[3] Others such as Kim *et al.*[4] have also rallied toward this more sober analysis — arguing that even though in the longer run, human workers will be in demand for more creative work, the current workforce will undoubtedly face higher unemployment, and that it is imperative governments provide various forms of intervention to ease the transition. However, a more recent 2020 report, again by Acemoglu and Restrepo,[5] partially reverses their more dire 2017 predictions in that "different industries have different robot footprints in different places in the U.S."[6] In certain commuting zones each robot added to the workplace "replaced about 6.6 jobs locally," while in other areas of the US "adding robots in manufacturing benefited people in other industries and other areas of the country — by lowering the cost of goods, among other things. These national economic benefits are the reason the researchers calculated that adding one robot replaces 3.3 jobs for the country as a whole."[7] In an interview with MIT News' Peter Dizikes,[8] Acemoglu stated that such numbers "certainly won't give any support to those who think robots are going to take all of our jobs … But it does imply that automation is a real force to be grappled with."

These competing-then-converging economic studies serve as a preamble to our own conclusion: machines and AI replacing humans is a *false debate*. It acts as a decoy to remove our attention from something else at work for over 100 years to which we have become anesthetized. However, before unpacking this family of phenomena which has been unfolding in front of our mesmerized eyes, let us assure you that today's captains of industry would certainly not allow humans to be completely replaced by machines in any "physical" sense of the term. They have learned a lot from Marx's warnings that in eliminating the human means of production, they would essentially "cut their own throats" — for, as long as money and capital exists, it could not continue to grow indefinitely without continued consumption and demand, and therefore, the accompanying wages to fuel this. Of course, one of the most notorious captains, Elon Musk, would want to prove us wrong in "predicting" that robots and AI will effectively render human "jobs irrelevant"[9] — to which he added at the World Artificial Intelligence Conference at Shanghai "probably the last job that will remain will be writing AI software, and then eventually the AI will just write its own software."

As such, he encourages people to study things like engineering and physics.[10] Considering the industries Musk now controls, the crowding effect on such knowledge-intensive jobs in terms of lowering the economic value of work is, of course, farthest from his mind.

On this somewhat ironic note, let us return to the previous economic reports published by both Autor[11] and Acemoglu and Restrepo[12] to which we highlight similarly nuanced elements at work. First, Autor makes reference to machines outdoing humans both in terms of speed and performance in a variety of tasks. As such, the overall quest for continued cost reductions — in not only monotonous tasks but also in more complex professional tasks requiring elaborate analysis, calculations, and certain levels of tacit knowledge — is not only being pursued through reduced labor costs but also across productivity improvements via increased speeds and efficiencies.[13] Within this spirit, Autor[14] makes reference to the contemporary mantra of "doing more with less" as the general marching orders for all industries to *mindlessly* follow. Acemoglu and Restrepo[15] confirm this trend as they show that between 1990 and 2007, the introduction of robots led to a decrease in wages of 0.4% — while adding, "we find negative wage effects, that workers are losing in terms of real wages in more affected areas, because robots are pretty good at competing against them."[16] Indeed, Gere sees such disturbing tendencies as confirming Babbage's reduction in the economic value of work.[17] This is now present through various forms of digital Taylorism even amongst knowledge workers.[18] As workers experience intensified precarity, intense competition and anxiety for jobs, they internalize the imperative to perform using their "mind to subordinate their body to the ego-ideal and hence to the economic system … a process increasingly supplemented by machines that expand processes of workplace discipline" through the use of wearable monitoring devices.[19] More specifically, it is argued that autonomous workers are expected to incarnate a dialectic of self-observation and self-exploitation.[20] Along these lines, the phenomena appears to be evermore exploited by management to control and extract value from mobile yet increasingly precarious creative knowledge work[21] — leading to widespread deception as knowledge workers compare their actual achievements with the myth of what they are able to achieve without concrete social transformation across valorization and real monetary gains.[22] Airline pilots, for example, argue that pilot salary reductions combined with less manual training is leading airlines toward hiring less skilled pilots, whose profession is progressively being reduced to the status of technicians.[23] According to Bailey and Scerbo,[24] pilots have been forced to become system monitors more than pilots, resulting in decreased job satisfaction, as well as making it harder to remain engaged during routine flights. Gawron also raises the psychosocial aspect of cockpit automation in terms of job satisfaction, prestige, and self-valorization.[25] Close to 60% of airline pilots felt their employer did not care about their wellbeing; over 50% were worried about losing their job; and 40% were concerned that autonomous technologies could render the role of the pilot redundant.[26] Similarly, for medical physicians in the US, Robert M. Wachter from the University of California (San Francisco) explains how digital technology was first introduced into the practice of medicine across massive pressures for cost reductions in general healthcare by insurers and hospital administrations.[27] In this manner, *Forbes*[28] describes AI as a "massive opportunity" for healthcare potentially resulting in annual cost savings of US$150 billion by 2026. Such pressures have been especially acute in regards to radiologists, in which AI/IT companies have "convinced" both purse string managers and society-at-large that radiology can be completely reduced to the representational capture and processing of images for pattern detections. Of course, the discourse provided is that a human will always be required to supervise all of this, but once again, as a system monitor rather than as a hands-on radiologist.[29] As such, we are witnessing a profession being reduced to mere execution of tasks, rather than using and practicing its deep smarts in the face of contradictory weak signals, which require meaningful interpretations going outside of AI's representational envelope.[30] Electronic health records in the US, is another example brought up by Wachter,[31] which had a difficult start, with many of the medical staff complaining that it is time-consuming due to poor user interfaces and connectivity. This, in turn, has led to both patients and physicians complaining that key face-to-face interactions between patients and physicians is lacking, thus leading to numerous misdiagnosis, due to the fact that once again medical practitioners are becoming more like system monitors as they increasingly spend more time on their computers. Yet, Wachter is not a Luditte and most certainly believes, as in this book, AI can bring many benefits to the medical community. However, the manner in which we have techno-centrically designed and implemented such technologies with an obsessive-myopic regard toward cost "efficiencies" is indeed enacting Elon Musk's prediction that we shall all "become like cats." Yet, what Musk fails to state is that when humanity does become like "cats," AI will not solve all of our problems — it will only *enact upon us the mindless impression that it does.*

So how did we get to this state of affairs? More importantly, how can we change it? And, to what do we want to change it to? While this book does not pretend to offer "complete" explanations and answers to any of these question, it does attempt to enact a few "ecological disturbances" with the aim of provoking further sensemakings on our part.[32] First, toward answering how we got to this state of affairs, in Chapter 4 we highlighted certain historic underpinnings to "our" continued quest for knowledge representations. Socrates, Plato, and Aristotle played important roles toward our Western rational and empirical abstractionisms across both the idea of the universal (as positivistic generalizations) and categories.[33] This ranges from "a series of footnotes to Plato"[34] to how cognitive sciences were greatly influenced by both Socrates and Plato's assumptions that "intelligence is based on principles and ... that these principles must be strict rules, not based on taken-for-granted background understanding."[35] In turn, Western science's interpretation of Aristotle's Categories played a fundamental role in its quest for classifications and certainty.[36] As such, establishing explicit rules and representations on the nature of "things" and processes has become our predominant method of "intelligent" inquiry.[37] At the same time, efficiency is one of the major themes emerging from past and current theorists on technology, starting with Heidegger's The Question Concerning Technology, which was concerned with ontology and being.[38] For Heidegger, the essence of technology was anything but technological, in that it is a kind of thinking that reveals to us only one way of existing whose essence is to seek more and more efficiency for its own sake, i.e. producing the most with the least energy and expense possible.[39] In a similar, yet complementary vein, Ellul's[40] technological society is a society of techniques requiring that we always choose the most rationally efficient techniques for every endeavor. Technique is a mindset or ideology which values efficiency over all other things.[41] This "certain frame of mind ... of looking at situations," which seeks maximum yield with least amount of effort, involves a rationality consisting of mathematical calculations, systematizations, and the creation of standards.[42] Finally, Marcuse, who took inspiration from Heidegger, sees technology as consisting of a *Gestell* or enframing in which human agents and the natural environment are treated as resources: "technics becomes the universal form of material production, [in which] it circumscribes an entire culture; it projects a historical totality — a 'world.'"[43] More recent authors such as Son[44] and Alexander[45] have argued along these lines by describing how efficiency is prominent in contemporary society due to the force of technology. To this we add, *such quests for efficiency are being achieved through purely representational means.* Hence, it is no accident that neo-liberal thought and engineering's obsession for efficiency through purely representational means became a "marriage made in heaven." Marx referred to this as machinism. Captains of industry had found their "efficient tool" or means toward achieving their very goals of profit maximization.[46] As such, F.W. Taylor's ideas[47] became responsible for creating the employee as a consciously designed utilitarian project by stressing (in his Preface) the need for national efficiency, whereby "efficiency means achieving desired effects or results with minimum waste of time and effort; through minimizing the ratio between effective or useful output to the total input in any system."[48] Despite critiques of its deleterious effects on worker morale and wellbeing by other notable researchers and practitioners, Taylorism remained the predominant method adopted by the majority of companies across all industries.[49] Interestingly, Kakar addresses such critics with the following words[50]:

> "These arguments with Taylorism have to do with matters of means; with Taylor's ends there is no quarrel. All who reject Taylor's system for its ignorance or depreciation of the social and psychological dimensions of work gear their arguments and justify their cases with reference to a common goal — increased productivity."

The doctrine of scientific management stressed the "rationalization of production across the rationalization of the body."[51] "This process ... separates skill and knowledge even in their narrower relationship. When it is completed, the worker is no longer a craftsman in any sense, but is an animated tool of the management."[52]

Today, our quest for both representational knowledge and representational means for establishing methods of efficiency has materialized itself into techno-centric AI and information technology/information systems (IT/IS) expert system approaches.[53] In parallel, Taylorism has morphed into what Brown *et al.* specifically refer to "Digital Taylorism," a system based on the global organization of both routine as well as "knowledge work," whereby the latter involves creative and intellectual tasks being subject to the same process as chain work.[54] Their argument is that, once codified and digitalized, such tasks can be conducted by automatic programs with computerized decision protocols, thereby replacing human decisions and judgments. Behind this state of affairs lie three intercoupled dominant socio-technical imaginaries:

(1) Knowledge is only knowledge when it can be reduced into a representational form.
(2) Representational knowledge quests must be directed toward attaining the most efficient methods.
(3) Such efficient methods must be directed toward attaining maximum profits.

In turn, these social imaginaries hold the majority of people in mindless captivity across Weick's now-famous dictum: "sense may be in the eye of the beholder, but beholders vote and the majority rules."[55] In turn, social imaginaries influence the way people make decisions — or as the Thomas theorem states: "If men define situations as real, they are real in their consequences." One of these consequences is clearly presented through Chapters 2, 5, and 6, namely our *increasing inability* to determine what is relevant in changing or new circumstances. Starting from the representational "frame regress" problem to our mindless dependency (or "automation complacency") on purely techno-centric technologies, we are gradually losing our adaptive abilities or expertise (as presented in both Chapters 3 and 6) in dealing with sudden or unexpected change. In a similar spirit, Wachter[56] clearly warns us about the medical practice depending too much on various automated diagnostic tools now being used or developed. The precious human quality at stake is what Detienne and Vernant[57] referred to as *mètis*, first repressed by Plato in his quest to "control sophistry" (Chapter 4), to which we ourselves would add[58]:

"Like humans, mètis can't be pinned down to any one thing or process. It involves actions, yet also involves retained rules-of-thumb. It involves the whole body as well as the brain. It is both individual and collective. It can't be permanently categorized into one neat box. That's because it is human. It makes no pretention at being the Truth. It's always changing and hopefully, always learning. Like sensemaking, it tries to 'wrestle' or appropriate on-going flows of events across bracketing or 'snapshots'. Yet, mètis continues to learn, that is remains mètis, when it doesn't settle down on its newly created categories. Armed with mindfulness, mètis dismantles and rebuilds categories and models as the situation warrants. Mètis, embodied within humans, is the seat of innovation, both incremental and disruptive — whether in saving lives, like Captain Sullenberger did that wintery morning on New York's Hudson River in a situation he was never trained for; or in keeping the workflow moving, as nurses skillfully do in chaotic emergency wards."

So how do we change this state of affairs? Part of the answer lies in the nature of *mètis* itself, i.e. its punctual mindfulness. Only mindfulness, both individually and collectively,[59] can offset mindlessness,[60] often in the form of techno-centric mindsets through entrenched metaphors. This, we argued through both Chapters 7 and 8. Mindfulness, in itself means being in tune with our phenomenological nature, starting from the transcendental and non-representational aspect of language as mobilized or "energized" through "live" metaphors, as described in both Chapters 6 and 8. It is a rule-breaking creative process that cannot be reduced to mere knowledge representations.[61] It involves our whole and sensual phenomenological bodies.[62] Radical embodied cognitivists recognized this,[63] yet in attempting to capture it all, still partially missed the point (Chapter 6).

So with mindfulness what do we want to change? A simple-minded and perhaps humble starting point would be "getting back to *mètis*." *This*, as we discussed in Chapters 8 and 9, requires reconfiguring our sociotechnical systems so that they enable our *mètis* to shine through. In turn, this requires our re-appreciation of our irreducible phenomenological selves[64] through mindful and relevant conversations — between system designers, system operator/users, and last, but not least, managers. Within this perspective, designs are reconfigured through living metaphors which stimulate and trigger our creativity. The "live body" metaphor is just one example.[65] As such, socio-technical systems bestow meaningful control to humans, which is also a morally ethical approach as *phronimos* (Chapter 10). In the end, across our humble emphasis on *mètis*, we hope to have provided a metaphorical inspiration toward more democratic processes and engagements within the workplace which prioritize human creativity (and its emergence) in regards to human–technology interactions. That is, a human creativity (including our more recent explorations in quantum physics) directed toward human-centric interactions in which technology is subservient to society's wellbeing — and *not* the other way around.

Endnotes

[1] Citing Autor, D.H. (2015). Why are there still so many jobs? The history and future of workplace automation, *Journal of Economic Perspectives*, **29**(3), 3–30.

[2] *Ibid.*

[3] See Acemoglu, D. and Restrepo, P. (2017). Robots and jobs: Evidence from the US Labor Market. The National Bureau of Economic Research, NBER Working Paper no. 23285.

[4] See Kim, Y.J., Kim, K. and Lee, S. (2017). The rise of technological unemployment and its landscape on the future macroeconomic landscape. *Futures*, **87**, 1–9.

[5] See Acemoglu, D. and Restrepo, P. (2020). Robots and jobs: Evidence from US labor markets [in press], *Journal of Political Economy*, **128**(6), 2188–2244.

[6] See Dizikes, P. (2020). How many jobs do robots really replace? MIT economist Daron Acemoglu's new research puts a number on the job costs of automation. May 4, MIT News Office. Available at: https://news.mit.edu/2020/how-many-jobs-robots-replace-0504.

[7] *Ibid.*

[8] *Ibid.*

[9] See Al-Heeti, A. (2019). Elon Musk says AI will make jobs irrelevant: Get a job writing AI software, he recommends. Until AI takes that over, too. *CNET*, August 29. Available at: https://www.cnet.com/news/elon-musk-says-ai-will-make-jobs-irrelevant/.

[10] *Ibid.*

[11] See Autor (2015) (note 1).

[12] See Acemoglu and Restrepo (2020) (note 5).

[13] See Autor (2015) (note 1).

[14] *Ibid.*

[15] See Acemoglu and Restrepo (2020) (note 5).

[16] See Dizikes (2020) (note 6).

[17] See Gere, C. (2008). *Digital Culture* (London: Reaktion Books).

[18] See Brown, P., Lauder, H., and Ashton, D. (2011). *The Global Auction: The Broken Promise of Education, Jobs and Incomes* (New York: Oxford University Press, Inc); also see both Moore P. and Robinson A. (2016). The quantified self: What counts in the neoliberal workplace. *New Media & Society*, **18**(11), 2774–2792. doi:10.1177/1461444815604328; as well as Holford, W.D. (2019). The future of human creative knowledge work within the digital economy. *Futures*, **105**, 143–154.

[19] Citing Moore and Robinson (2016, p. 2) (note 18).

[20] See Schmiz, A. (2013). Migrant self-employment between precariousness and self-exploitation. *Ephemera*, **13**(1), 53–74.

[21] See both Brophy, E. and de Peuter, G. (2007). Immaterial labor, precarity and recomposition. In *Knowledge Workers in the Information Society*, C. McKercher and V. Mosco (eds.) (Lanham, MD: Lexington), pp. 177–192; as well as Kapur, J. (2007). New economy/old labour: Creativity, flatness, and other neoliberal myths. In *Knowledge Workers in the Information Society*, C. McKercher and V. Mosco (eds.) (Lanham, MD: Lexington), pp. 163–176.

[22] See Moore and Robinson (2016) (note 18)

[23] See both Couric, K. (2009). Capt. Sully worried about airline industry. *CBS Evening News*, Feb. 10. Available at: https://www.cbsnews.com/news/capt-sully-worried-about-airline-industry/; as well as Vartabedian, R. and Masunaga, S. (2019). Lion Air crash shows cockpit computers are no substitute for pilot skills. *Los Angeles Times*, February 4. Available at: https://www.latimes.com/business/la-fi-lion-air-crash-20190204-story.html.

[24] See Bailey, N. and Scerbo, M. (2008). Automation induced complacency for monitoring highly reliable systems; the role of task complexity, system experience, and operator trust. *Theoretical Issues in Ergonomics Science*, **8**(4), 321–348.

[25] See Gawron, V. (2019). Automation in aviation accident analyses. Center for Advanced Aviation System Development — MITRE Technical Report MTR190013. The MITRE Corporation. 20 pp.

[26] See FlightGlobal (2020). Pilot survey reveals high levels of stress and job insecurity. Available at: https://www.aviationpros.com/airlines/press-release/21125772/flightglobal-pilot-survey-reveals-high-levels-of-stress-and-job-insecurity.

[27] See Wachter, R.H. (2015). *The Digital Doctor: Hope, Hype, and Harm at the Dawn of Medicine's Computer Age* (New York: McGraw-Hill Education).

[28] See *Forbes* (2019). AI And healthcare: A giant opportunity. Feb. 11. Available at: https://www.forbes.com/sites/insights-intelai/2019/02/11/ai-and-healthcare-a-giant-opportunity/?sh=66f0fc174c68.

[29] See Wachter (2015) (note 27).

[30] See both Faraj, S., Pachidi, S. and Sayegh, K. (2018). Working and organizing in the age of the learning algorithm. *Information and Organization*, **28**, 62–70; as well as Holford, W.D. (2020a). The repression of mètis within digital organizations. *Prometheus*, **36**(3), 253–276. www.jstor.org/stable/10.13169/prometheus.36.3.0253.

[31] See Wachter (2015) (note 27).

[32] See Weick, K.E. (1995). *Sensemaking in Organizations* (Thousand Oaks, CA: Sage Publications).

[33] See both Dewey, J. (1929). *The Quest for Certainty: A Study of the Relation of Knowledge and Action* (New York: Putnam) as well as Whitehead, A.N. (1929). *Process and Reality, An Essay in Cosmology* (New York: Ma); also see Baumard, P. (1999). *Tacit Knowledge in Organizations* (London: Sage Publications).

[34] Citing Whitehead (1929, part 2, Chapter 1) (note 33).

[35] Citing Dreyfus, H.L. (1988). The Socratic and Platonic basis of cognitivism. *AI & Society*, **2**, 99–112. https://doi.org/10.1007/BF01891374.

[36] See both Dewey (1929) (note 33) as well as Kuntz, M.L. and Kuntz, P.G. (1988). Naming the categories: Back to Aristotle by way of Whitehead. *The Journal of Speculative Philosophy, New Series*, **2**(1), 30–47.

[37] See Dreyfus (1988) (note 35).

[38] See Heidegger, M. (1977). *The Question Concerning Technology and Other Essays* (New York: Garland Publishing).

[39] See Hanks, C. (2010). *Technology and Values: Essential Readings* (Oxford: John Wiley/Blackwell Publishing); also see Van Vleet, J.E. (2014). *Dialectical Theology and Jacques Ellul: An Introductory Exposition* (Minneapolis, MN: Fortress Press); and finally, see Dreyfus, H. (2009). Heidegger on Gaining a Free Relation to Technology. In *Readings in the Philosophy of Technology*, D.M. Kaplan (ed.) (Lanham, MA: Rowman and Littlefield Publishers), pp. 25–33.

[40] See Ellul, J. (1990). *La technique: ou L'enjeu du siècle*, Édition Économica, Paris.

[41] See Ellul, J. (1980). *The Technological System* (New York: Continuum), pp. 1–20.

[42] Citing Ellul (1980, pp. 23–33, 48) (note 40).

[43] Citing Marcuse, H. (1964). *One-dimensional Man: Studies in the Ideology of Advanced Industrial Society* (Boston: Beacon Press), p. 158.

[44] See Son, W.-C. (2013). Are we still pursuing efficiency? Interpreting Jacques Ellul's efficiency principle, In *Jacques Ellul and the Technological Society in the 21st Century*, M. Jerónimo, J.L. Garcia and C. Mitcham (eds.) (Springer), Heidelberg, Germany, pp. 49–62.

[45] See Alexander, J.K. (2008). *The Mantra of Efficiency: From Waterwheel to Social Control* (Baltimore: John Hopkins University Press).

[46] See Clegg, S., Courpasson, D. and Phillips. N. (2006). *Power and Organizations* (London: Sage Publications); as well as Clair, M. (2016). The limits of neoliberalism: How writers and editors use digital technologies in the literary field. *Communication and Information Technologies Annual*, **11**, 169–201; and finally, see Marcuse, H. (1941). Some Social Implications of Modern Technology in Technology, War, and Fascism. In *The Collected Papers of Herbert Marcuse: 1*, D. Kellner (vol. ed.) (New York: Routledge), pp. 41–65.

[47] See Taylor, F. W. (1911). *The Principles of Scientific Management* (New York: Harper and Brothers).

[48] Citing Clegg *et al.* (2006, p. 48) (note 45).

[49] See Kakar, S. (1970). *Fredrick Taylor: A Study in Personality and Innovation* (Cambridge, MA: MIT Press).

[50] Citing Kakar (1970, p. 190) (note 47).

[51] See Rabinbach, A. (1990). *The Human Motor: Energy, Fatigue, and the Origins of Modernity* (Los Angeles, California: University of California Press).

52 Citing Hoxie, R.F. (1921). *Scientific Management and Labor* (New York: D. Appleton), pp. 131–132.

53 See both Dreyfus, H.L. and Dreyfus, S.E. (2005). Peripheral vision expertise in real world contexts. *Organization Studies*, **26**(5), 779–792; as well as Gorski, P.S. (2013). What is critical realism? And why should you care? *Contemporary Sociology: A Journal of Reviews*, **42**(5), 658–670.

54 Citing Brown *et al.* (2011, pp. 7–9) (note 18).

55 Citing Weick (1995, p. 6) (note 32).

56 See Wachter (2015) (note 27).

57 See Detienne, M. and Vernant, J.P. (1978). *Les ruses de L'intélligence: La mètis des Grecs* (Flammarion, Paris).

58 Citing Holford, W.D. (2020b). *Managing Knowledge in Organizations: A Critical Pragmatic Perspective* (New York, NY: Palgrave MacMillan), p. 177.

59 See Brown, A.D., Colville, I. and Pye, A. (2015). Making sense of sensemaking in organization studies. *Organization Studies*, **36**(2), 265–277. doi:10.1177/0170840614559259; also see both Weick, K.E., Sutcliffe, K.M. and Obstfeld, D. (2005). Organizing and the process of sensemaking. *Organization Science*, **16**(4), 409–421; as well as Weick, K.E., Sutcliffe, K.M. and Obstfeld, D. (2008). Organizing for High Reliability: Processes of Collective Mindfulness. In *Crisis Management, Vol. III*, A. Boin (ed.) (Los Angeles: Sage), pp. 31–66.

60 See Langer, E.J. (1989). *Mindfulness* (Cambridge, MA: Perseus Books).

61 See Lorino, P., Tricard, B. and Clot, Y. (2011). Research methods for non-representational approaches to organizational complexity: The dialogical mediated inquiry. *Organization Studies*, **32**(6), 769–801.

62 See Küpers, W. (2005). Embodied implicit and narrative knowing in organizations, *Journal of Knowledge Management*, **9**(6), 113–133; as well as Küpers, W. (2008). Embodied inter-learning — an integral phenomenology of learning in and by organizations. *The Learning Organisation: An International Journal*, **15**(5), 388–408; and finally, see Küpers, W. (2013). Embodied transformative metaphors and narratives in organizational life-worlds of change. *Journal of Organizational Change Management*, **26**(3), 494–528.

63 See Chemero, A. (2013). Radical embodied cognitive science. *Review of General Psychology*, **17**(2), 145–150.

64 See Dreyfus, H.L. (2014). *Skillful Coping: Essays on the Phenomenology of Everyday Perception and Action* (Oxford, UK: Oxford University Press).

65 See Svanaes, D. (2013). Interaction design for and with the lived body: Some implications of Merleau-Ponty's phenomenology. *ACM Transactions on Computer-Human Interactions*, **20**(1), Article 8, p. 30. doi: http://dx.doi.org/10.1145/2442106.2442114.

Index

Printed in the United States
by Baker & Taylor Publisher Services